W9-COY-164

JAN - - 2006

INDIAN TRAILS
PUBLIC LIBRARY DISTRICT
WHEELING, ILLINOIS 60090
847-459-4100

Praise for *God Without Religion* . . .

"As never before, the world needs serious and bold reflection on religious belief and practice. *God Without Religion* asks some difficult questions and advocates a more intelligent and thoughtful approach to the spiritual life. At the same time, it offers positive ways to develop a spiritual viewpoint. Take it on a retreat. Read it slowly, in sections, and become a positive influence toward religious understanding in the world."

—Thomas Moore, author of *Care of the Soul* and *Dark Nights of the Soul*

"It is clear that one of the darkest forces menacing the future of humanity is old-style religion with its outmoded dogma and exclusivist practices. This fine, fierce, wise, and deeply helpful book challenges everyone to find a direct relationship with the divine beyond the confines of the past, and offers rich advice and a bevy of powerful practices that can sustain such a relationship and continue to expand it."

—Andrew Harvey, author of *The Direct Path* and *Sun at Midnight*

"In this day when religions seem to be caught in stages of mind-numbing dogma, justification of violence, and meaningless ritual that do no more than sanctify greed and secular superiority, Śaṅkara Śaranam's book offers hope and relief. You don't have to be Jewish, Christian, or Muslim to see the real message here— God is part of us all and Western religions may be getting in the way of that realization if they continue on their present paths."

—Fred Alan Wolf, PhD
Theoretical physicist, author of *The Yoga of Time Travel*,
and a National Book Award winner

"All religions, it seems, inevitably give way to the excesses of religious zeal and exclusivity. That is why the 'contributions' of religion have so often been horrific and disastrous, and why every major religion has dirty hands. Currently our world is aflame with religious hatred that shows no sign of abating, and the narrow religious fundamentalisms within our own society are a major part of the problem. Our civilization is at a crossroads. The hour is late and there is no time to tippy-toe around the obvious: we urgently need an alternative link with the divine that bypasses the pitfalls of traditional religion. That is the significance of *God Without Religion*. This book's bold message is vital. It is a path straight up the mountain that avoids the swamps of religious dithering, divisiveness, and destructiveness. It is a way out of darkness. It affirms the unity of all humans not only with one another, but with all of life and the Absolute. If we are to survive on the earth, heeding this message is not merely optional but required."

—Larry Dossey, MD
Author of *Healing Beyond the Body* and *Reinventing Medicine*

"In *God Without Religion,* Śaṇkara Śaranam charts a brave course for spiritual seekers no longer served by religious doctrine (if indeed they ever were) and eager to create deep, authentic, meaningful relationship with the sacred by methods Śaranam clearly describes as a 'direct path to God.' This is a courageous, stand-out book for readers ready to part the veil of illusion and see the truth that every religious tradition must periodically and systematically reexamine itself and account for its teachings."

—Meredith Jordan, author of *Embracing the Mystery*

"Twenty-first-century humanity has inherited the historical struggle between Dark Age religious fundamentalism, which proclaims the world to be the kingdom of a remote, transcendent, authoritarian God, in opposition to the spiritually awakened views of the secular humanists, who perceive an accessible, immanent, egalitarian God existing within all of creation. In exploring this ideological conflict, Śaṇkara Śaranam has created one of the most extraordinary books of our time—a time in which misguided religious zealots have the capacity to decide that the world will be their God's Kingdom . . . or nothing. *God Without Religion* is Śaranam's response, presenting us with a historical perspective on the political underbelly of our organized religions, then drawing science and spirituality together to offer us a new profile of divinity—one that casts light on the relationship between human existence and the cosmos, one that extends salvation to us all."

—Hank Wesselman, PhD, anthropologist and author of
The Spiritwalker Trilogy and _The Journey to the Sacred Garden_

"*God Without Religion* is a rare book, combining spiritual insight and practice with social criticism and an appreciation of the many contradictions of modern life. I highly recommend this book for anyone seeking to maintain intellectual integrity while simultaneously retaining reverence for the unity of all things."

—Jeffrey Mishlove, PhD
President, Intuition Network; author of _The PK Man; and_
former host of _Thinking Allowed,_ a national public television series

"The full body-count may not be in, but we can certainly imagine the numbers: the millions upon millions of our species who have been killed in war, hanged, burned at the stake, tortured to death, and otherwise silenced in the name of religion over the centuries. Śaṅkara Śaranam's *God Without Religion* makes the point that we can have a profound and rewarding personal spiritual life without religion, which has been so terribly destructive and which we may have actually outgrown. Unlike other books that tear religion down without offering anything in its place, *God Without Religion* sets out helpful alternative approaches to personal spirituality. This is an inspiring, positive, wonderful book that emphasizes the truth that we are spiritual beings making a human journey. Reading it will greatly enhance your personal relationship with the creator-energy."

—Joseph Dispenza
Author of _The Way of the Traveler_ and _Live Better Longer_

"The pursuit of a personal connection with God has been the ultimate challenge of seekers throughout the millennia. The Buddha's and Jesus's examples teach that we must sometimes turn our backs on the social organizations that at one time may have offered us support in our quest. Nevertheless, leaving the path forged by others before us can be both bewildering and frightening. Like a guide in the wilderness, Śaṇkara Śaranam helps us bridge the gap between organized religion and progressive spirituality, encouraging us to ask our own questions about the nature of God, so that our experience of our own divinity might expand. This work is a breath of fresh air at a time when seekers everywhere are questioning the limits of organized religion."

—**Hal Zina Bennett, PhD, author of *Writing Spiritual Books***

"Avoiding all kinds of extremism and exclusiveness of the so-called institutionalized religions, Śaṇkara's *God Without Religion* enlightens us with an unusual approach toward understanding religion as a form of life with special emphasis on its human face. Spirituality instead of religiosity has been initiated as the central point of this form of life, and this is a significant departure from the oft-trodden track of understanding religion. Śaṇkara's book inspires us with a proper perception of our present concerns, a clear understanding of the significance of the past, and commitments to and vision of the future. It seems to be an inspiring source and hope for the survival of peace-loving people in the world."

—**Dilipkumar Mohanta**
Professor of Philosophy, University of Calcutta, India, and editor of
The Journal of the Indian Academy of Philosophy

"Śaṇkara Śaranam has written a powerful book, and one that, if it were taken seriously and allowed to reform global attitudes, could liberate the world of religious strife and lay a sound foundation for a global ethic. Śaranam suggests we stop relying on revelation, tradition, prejudices, dogma, and authority. Instead, we should trust our human critical and intuitive faculties and become 'spiritual investigators' who learn through open-ended dialogue in which all participants are free to doubt, challenge, and explore. . . . While Śaranam smashes the idols of institutional religion, he clearly believes in a meaningful cosmos and the spiritual potential of humanity. . . . It is to be hoped that followers of the religions Śaranam attacks will not dismiss him as an enemy calling believers to apostasy but rather as one who challenges believers to break through the hard shells of fundamentalism and become change agents within their respective faiths. Religious followers can take Saranam's challenge and show the world that their religions need not be rigid and that there is no reason why people of all faiths cannot learn to be critical, thoughtful, proactive weavers of their traditions."

—Ingrid Shafer, PhD
Professor of Philosophy and Religion
University of Science and Arts of Oklahoma

"God Without Religion. Those words grabbed my attention and spoke to my spirit before I even opened the pages. This book is timely, for we live in an age of so much religion without God. Śaṇkara Śaranam presents us with the opportunity to declare our independence from dusty, petrified religious structures and forge vibrant, meaningful relationships with our brothers and sisters, as well as the Creator. I love the way Śaṇkara writes. His style is both scholarly and approachable, a rare accomplishment indeed. When I read the section "Celebrating Apostasy," I knew this book would become an old friend, to be read and reread throughout the years. *God Without Religion* is a treasure, a pearl of great price. Sankara's gift of literary prasada enriches us all and is a worthy companion on anyone's path."

—Robert Ransom Odom
Internationally published author, columnist, and spiritual teacher

"The number one predictor of a person's religion is not just their parents (the usual sociological explanation) but their epoch and place of birth on the planet. How anyone can observe this simple fact of history and come to the conclusion that theirs is the One True Religion or God and the other 9,999 are False Religions or Gods is almost incomprehensible. . . . There are many ways to be spiritual. For me, the awe provoked by nature, the cosmos, and the scientific worldview is transcendently spiritual. There are so many other paths to spiritual enlightenment as well, and Śaṇkara Śaranam has beautifully articulated some of these through his book *God Without Religion,* a work appropriate for anyone in search of spiritual meaning, regardless of their official 'faith.' A truly inspiring work."

—Michael Shermer, publisher of *Skeptic* magazine,
columnist with *Scientific American,* and author of
Why People Believe Weird Things* and *The Science of Good and Evil

"*God Without Religion* by Śaṇkara Śaranam is a courageous attempt to present a serious, nonreductive spirituality that avoids the divisive impact of institutionalized religions. Drawing on the wisdom of ancient mystical traditions, the author passionately argues for the need to transcend those very traditions. Combining various disciplinary approaches, *God Without Religion* offers a sensitive alternative to organized religion, an alternative that seeks to overcome the prejudices and biases of the different traditions. What is most impressive is that the way to God without religion is a deepening of the very paths that must be abandoned. There is no question that this is a timely work inspired by eternal truths."

—Elliot R. Wolfson
Abraham Lieberman Professor of
Hebrew and Judaic Studies
New York University

"Religions are dangerous. No matter what good they produce, one must admit that these cultural institutions bring with them great risks to humanity at large. All of the great spiritual leaders taught criticism of tradition as a way toward revitalizing the sacred. Śaṇkara Śaranam rekindles this vital flame in his book *God Without*

Religion. For the critic, Śaranam offers fine insights into the dangers and errors that religious intolerance provokes, and for the mystic his book teaches practical techniques for spiritual development. The genuine seeker must utilize both the critical mind and the generous heart. *God Without Religion* honors both."

—John J. McGraw
Author of *Brain & Belief*

"*God Without Religion* is a provocative challenge to the smug assertions of those who would claim to know the truth."

—Robert S. Alley
Professor of Humanities, Emeritus, University of Richmond

"Śaṇkara Śaranam argues for an 'expansive sense of self' which can get rid of narrow, sectarian divisions that characterize most of human society today. His approach has strong resonances to the Vedic/Upanishadic concept of 'an expansive sense of the self,' and many yogic practices like pranayama are advocated to gradually realize this 'expanded self.' Regardless of one's personal views on religion, changing the outlook of societies that identify themselves within a paradigm of narrow, ethnic boundaries is an imperative that needs to be taken seriously."

—T. S. Rukmani
Concordia University, Montreal, Canada

"Religious fundamentalism is the biggest spiritual threat to society. This practical as well as theoretical volume encourages people to have direct, firsthand experience of the divine, unmediated by the trappings of organized religion. Śaṇkara Śaranam promotes the spiritual discipline of "active wondering" and the triumph of reason over revelation. There is much to question about all religious writing, and the author hopes readers question his book as well."

—Mary E. Hunt, PhD, codirector of WATER
(Women's Alliance for Theology, Ethics and Ritual)

"*God Without Religion* leads the reader to true spirituality. It is extraordinary, elegant, beautiful, informed, practical. It is good medicine in a troubled world."

—**David Carson, coauthor of** *Medicine Cards*

"At a time when suicide bombers kill in the name of God, when religious teachings are distorted to spread hatred, and when the clergy peddle theological doctrines for personal gain, here is a book that restores God's place in the human heart. *God Without Religion* offers, through exquisite prose and profound substance, a way out of religious shackles and abuse—a direct path to God. This path of self-discovery reveals humanity's capacity to reach unparalleled new heights guided by a force that resides within the soul of every human being."

—**Alon Ben-Meir, PhD, professor of International Relations The Center for Global Affairs, New York University, and Middle East Project Director at the World Policy Institute**

"*God Without Religion* is a genuine contribution to the religion and spirituality debate raging today. . . . This thoughtful and insightful book will help increase the spiritual literacy that is a necessary part of our true higher education if we are going to individually and collectively find the peace and freedom, harmony and love that we seek. I heartily recommend it to anyone striving to further refine and develop both inner spiritual life and social activism in today's volatile world."

—**Lama Surya Das Author of** *Awakening the Buddha Within* **and founder of the Dzogchen Meditation Center**

"*God Without Religion* transcends dogma, with a commonsense approach that leads the way to inner peace, spiritual solidarity, and the clear understanding that we are all one."

—**Melissa Etheridge, musician**

GOD WITHOUT RELIGION

THE COSMIC BODY OF GOD

GOD
WITHOUT
RELIGION

Questioning
Centuries of
Accepted Truths

Śaṇkara Śaranam
FOREWORD BY ARUN GANDHI

THE PRANAYAMA INSTITUTE
INCORPORATED

East Ellijay, Georgia

Published by:

THE PRANAYAMA INSTITUTE, INC.
PO BOX 1360
EAST ELLIJAY, GA 30539-1360

The Pranayama Institute, Inc. is a nonsectarian, nonprofit educational
organization dedicated to offering pranayama teachings worldwide at no
cost. All proceeds from the sales of its books directly benefit the aims and
ideals of the Institute.

Editor: Ellen Kleiner
Book design and typography: Angela Werneke
Frontispiece art: Cheri Freund
Diagram art: Angela Werneke
Medical art: Todd Buck

Copyright © 2005 by Śaṅkara Śaranam

All rights reserved. No part of this publication may be reproduced in any
form whatsoever without written permission from the publisher, except
for brief quotations embodied in literary articles or reviews.

Printed in the United States of America on recycled paper

PUBLISHER'S CATALOGING-IN-PUBLICATION DATA

Śaranam, Śaṅkara.
    God without religion / by Śaṅkara Śaranam.
    p. cm.
    Includes index.
    LCCN 2002094411
    ISBN 0-9724450-1-3
    0-9724450-0-5 (softcover)

    1. Spiritual life. 2. Religion. 3. God.
  I. Title.

BL624.S27 2002   291.4

                           QBI02-2--676

10 9 8 7 6 5 4 3 2 1

For Ekkaia

In Gratitude . . .

My deepest gratitude first goes to my mother, Dina, without whose unconditional support and reliable sponsorship this book would largely have remained in my head.

I would like to thank my father, Alon, and my brothers, David, Jason, and Sam, for their enthusiasm and encouragement.

I must also thank the great minds and hearts of the past who did not complain when I climbed on their shoulders and greedily borrowed from their ideas. Their names are too numerous to mention, but without them there would be no *God Without Religion*.

Neither would there be a book without Ellen Kleiner's editorial expertise, Ann Mason's photographic memory, Angela Werneke's gift for design, Hillary Welles's publicity efforts and enthusiasm, Peggy Keller's insights and knack for subtitles, and Lynda Kenny's ability to get things in gear.

I would also like to thank my students and friends around the world. Coming from every imaginable background, we all sought the truth. Your eagerness to be challenged, willingness to challenge me, encouragement, and generosity are inestimable. If *God Without Religion* is one day widely regarded as more than just another book on spirituality, it will be because of you.

Thanks, too, to Ginger, for keeping things light and warming my feet on cold nights at the computer.

Finally, I am grateful to my wife, Wendy, for her patience, support, and love through it all.

Contents

The greatest enemy of truth is very often
not the lie—deliberate, contrived, and dishonest—
but the myth—persistent, persuasive, and realistic.
Too often we hold fast to the clichés of our forebears.

—John F. Kennedy

Foreword

The question "What is God?" has baffled humankind for eons and will continue to defy logical understanding as long as we live with the concept that there is a heaven up above, where God sits judging all of humanity and punishing those who misbehave. Eminent thinkers throughout history have tried to find a logical answer to this vexing question, with little success. On the other hand His Holiness Gautama, the Buddha, did *tapasya* (Sanskrit for asceticism) under a banyan tree and, like some others, found that God exists within every human heart in the form of love, compassion, understanding, and other positive attributes humankind is capable of but often chooses to suppress. It seems that instead of trying to assert strict logic or put a solid image to our concept of God, we ought to follow their example and devote greater energy to intuitively understanding the meaning of God.

This book, *God Without Religion: Questioning Centuries of Accepted Truths* by Śaṅkara Śaranam, helps us do just that. It offers a refreshing attempt to provide humankind with a modernized spiritual road-map for use in our eternal quest to comprehend God.

Since the identity of God is so inscrutable (if not the best-kept secret in the world) and the philosophy surrounding this power so impenetrable, religious leaders of various faiths have defined God in ways that raise more questions than they answer. The easiest and most accepted explanation is to see God in the shape of those who are considered God's messengers—among Jews, Moses and the Hebrew Prophets; among Christians, Jesus; among Muslims, Muhammad; among Hindus, Krishna; and among Buddhists, Gautama.

The common thread running through the lives of God's many messengers is love, compassion, understanding, commitment, and respect for all living creatures. It might therefore be assumed that by exhibiting these qualities they were demonstrating to the rest of humanity the way our Creator expects us to live. Although I do not attribute saintly qualities to my grandfather, Mohandas Karamchand Gandhi, what he said about a week before his assassination on January 30, 1948, is pertinent in this regard: "They [the Indian people] will follow me in life, worship me in death, but not make my cause their cause." These prophetic words could have been said by Moses, Jesus, Muhammad, Krishna, or the Buddha—beings whose life stories and lessons were enshrined into scriptures we generally read with little intention of making them a part of our lives. Bypassing divine go-betweens, Śaṇkara Śaranam's book attempts to give us a more direct and immediate perspective of God. Like Śaṇkara, I hesitate to say its perspective is absolutely right, because as mere mortals, irrespective of our profound scholarship, experience, knowledge, training, or vision, we cannot fathom the depths of spirituality enough to presume we have the right way.

I recall the wisdom my grandfather imparted to our family when I was living with him as a young teenager. He said human beings can only hope to understand God and aspire to reach "salvation," which he defined as living a life of service, sacrifice, and satisfaction. He believed the greatest religion was to ensure that we wipe the tears from every eye and bring hope and decency to every life. If performed with utmost humility, he said, this service would grant us the magnanimity to recognize and accept the many ways we are called to see God in humanity.

I am convinced that at the root of the spiritual problem we face today is the intense competitiveness we have injected into religion. Each of us believes our religion is the best and it is incumbent upon us to save the world by converting everyone else to our mode of worship.

I recall a painfully sad episode that took place a few years ago when I was invited to explain the Hindu way of life to Christian students of comparative religion. Also invited were Muslim and Jewish clergymen. After my talk one of the clergymen prefaced his presentation with remarks that were obviously addressed to me, stating: "We Christians, Muslims, and Jews have a few things in common. We not only have a common source but we are a 'book religion,' unlike you who are pagan." The implication was clear. He believed that the Christian, Muslim, and Jewish word of God came in the form of a book whereas the Hindu scriptures were transmitted orally and therefore inferior. He concluded that Hindus believe in fifty thousand Gods while followers of the Western family of religions believe in only one.

The perceived superiority of book-based religions, I explained, is a common misconception in the West. In fact, an ancient philosopher once said the easiest way to kill a philosophy is by writing a book, for then it becomes a dogma and ceases to be a vibrant, living philosophy. As for believing in fifty thousand or more Gods, I added, the Hindu belief is not that there are so many Gods (or, according to some, as many Gods as human beings) but that there are many possible images of God.

The admission that no one really knows the true God behind all these images leads to an understanding that human beings can only pursue the truth and not "possess" it, as many religious zealots claim to do. Pursuit implies humility, acceptance, openness, and appreciation, while possession suggests arrogance, close mindedness, and lack of appreciation. Herein lies the rub: if we persist in competing to possess the truth instead of working in unity to pursue it, we are going to face untold grief—and worse, violence.

When asked what he thought of the meaning of God, Grandfather said: "There is an indefinable mysterious power that pervades everything. I feel it, though I do not see it. It is this unseen power which makes itself felt and yet defies all proof, because it is so unlike all that I perceive through my senses. It transcends the senses. But it is possible to reason out the existence of God to a limited extent.

"I do dimly perceive that whilst everything around me is ever-changing, ever-dying, there is underlying all that change a living power that is changeless, that holds all together, that creates, dissolves, and re-creates. That informing power or spirit is God. . . . For I can see that in the midst of death, life persists; in the midst of untruth, truth persists; in the midst of darkness, light persists. Hence I gather that God is life, truth, light."

Sometimes Grandfather referred to God as love, or the supreme good, or other attributes reflecting his belief that God lives within us as well as outside of us. He also implied we have a hotline to God, an instant connection enabling us to invoke God when necessary. In humankind's eternal quest for a tangible answer to the elusive meaning of God, *God Without Religion* adds an ancient dimension—the idea of self—in a radically new way that I hope will bring the reader a few steps closer to unraveling this divine mystery.

—Arun Gandhi
Cofounder of The M. K. Gandhi Institute for Nonviolence
Memphis, Tennessee

Preface

*R*eligion never satisfied me, and often infuriated me. Though I was raised to be a Jew, I thought of myself first and foremost as a human being and never viewed myself as wiser, luckier, or happier because my parents were Jewish or I adhered to the accepted truths of their religious tradition. To my mind, I would be progressing intellectually and spiritually only by understanding what was universally right and natural in life, why these things were right and natural, and how to live accordingly.

After years of attending Hebrew school, I rebelled against the dogma I had been taught there. In college I focused instead on subjects requiring the use of logic that appealed to my scientific mind—physics, mathematics, engineering. However, I eventually found that while the material sciences could answer some questions concerning how the world worked, they could not explain why, nor could they offer spiritual direction or prescribe an ethical way to live.

Searching further, I investigated mystical techniques. I began practicing concentration exercises, breath regulation, and more sophisticated methods of pranayama (sense introversion), eventually entering a monastic order. There, I implemented an *inner* science to address the concerns unresolved by my earlier scientific studies. While practicing pranayama over the next decade, I came to realize God as a spiritually expansive substance extending throughout the cosmos—a much more universal presence than that proposed by many organized religions. God, I found, was everything, and being godlike meant identifying with, and not merely tolerating, more and more people. Understanding that the idea of God signified absolute unity, I concluded that anyone advocating unquestioning loyalty to a restrictive group such as a faith, ethnicity, or nation was in fact promoting the fall of humanity by advancing its division.

Following these realizations, I knew I could play a part in introducing the expansive idea of God to people who had given up on God out of either disillusionment with organized religion or lack of spiritual direction. I knew, too, that before sharing my discoveries with others I had to learn more: I needed to comprehend why people cling to their religions; to assess various religions from a historical perspective; and to understand them in the contexts of psychology, sociology, physiology, mythology, cosmology, theology, and ontology. Consequently, in addition to earning my bachelor's and master's degrees in religion, philosophy, Hebrew, and Sanskrit, I spent six years studying the larger implications of organized religion's accepted truths.

In the process, I learned that religions were never intended to support the search for an expansive God and are actually antithetical to it. Probing further, I discovered that human beings aspired to know God long before religions were established, suggesting that the real worship of God could outlive the forms of worship currently in existence. Simultaneously, I found an unholy trinity of political, economic, and religious forces fostering and perpetuating massive greed, poverty, and ignorance. I then began to work with people seeking a more unifying understanding of God.

God Without Religion: Questioning Centuries of Accepted

Truths was written to encourage a redefinition of the idea of God; to reveal how organized religion has been destructive to individual societies and humanity as a whole; and to inspire a more inclusive embrace of spirituality. This book questions the goals and divisive beliefs that religion espouses, religious interpretations of historical events, the perilous rift between scientific and spiritual inquiry, and the intellectual honesty of many New Age spiritual movements. It is aimed at the countless scientists, philosophers, academicians, and other professionals who, while signing off on institutionalized forms of worship, threw out the baby of God along with the bathwater of organized religion. It is also for Hindus, Buddhists, Muslims, Jews, Christians, Mormons, Jains, and Taoists who realize violence is provoked by ideologies that, in championing exclusivity, promote contentiousness and bigotry. Ultimately this book is for people who want to see an end to the destructive influence of organized religion and New Age movements alike, and who seek a more fulfilling understanding of God through approaches that place their awareness of God in their own hands, making them more self-reliant. It is my hope that by encouraging an inner search for God based on timeless techniques beneficial to spiritual freedom, this book contributes to a broadening of perspectives around the world, culminating in the eventual unification of humanity.

Introduction

Not to engage in this pursuit of ideas is to live like ants instead of like men.

—Mortimer J. Adler

*I*n today's complex world, many people are beginning to examine their religious beliefs in light of their longing for a more meaningful sense of God. Some individuals, while asking challenging questions about the religious beliefs handed down to them in childhood, are uncovering seedbeds of prejudice and divisiveness. Others, exploring New Age spiritual movements, are finding many to be as dogmatic as organized religions. People dissatisfied with dogma and prejudice change radically when they turn inward for direct knowledge of God.

Two steps are involved in preparing to seek direct knowledge of God. The seeker's first step is to assess his reliance on beliefs instilled in him by spiritual leaders, teachers, self-appointed gurus, or well-intentioned parents or friends. It is important to realize that the truth of an idea cannot be established based on the authority of its proponents. In fact, because of their positions some religious leaders no longer engage in actively seeking the truth. Ultimately, only when individuals are free to challenge authority does spiritual growth become possible.

The seeker's second step in preparing for a more meaningful understanding of God is to use his own intellectual faculties to evaluate his beliefs. A critical investigation of beliefs increases the willingness to take responsibility for them and also nurtures self-reliance. My work with students in recent years demonstrates that by holding beliefs up to the mirror of reason it is possible not only to have a profound understanding of God but to identify with a more expansive God.

While evaluating an organized religion handed down to them, many people stop short upon discovering the goodness of an entrenched belief system that teaches such principles as loving thy neighbor and doing God's work. However, just as machines that squeeze oranges are rated not by the health value of orange juice but by their effectiveness in producing juice, organized religions need to be evaluated in terms of their practical influence in the world rather than the ideals they preach, which existed long before the advent of religion. When viewed through this lens, it becomes clear that any good accomplished by an organized religion could have come about without the artifice of a belief system, while the faith's violent outcomes could not be mitigated by attributing them to God's will. Compared with religionists, secularists are just as worthy of emulation when they serve others, and no more culpable when they commit crimes against humanity.

Pressing beyond the positive biases of an inherited religion proves to be extremely beneficial. It unveils negative biases rooted in the seeker's religious background. It also furnishes training in individual and collective psychology, providing tools for penetrating the mysteries of the mind, including the extremes of human behavior, the need for spirituality, and the paradox of our existence as thinking creatures aware of our mortality yet aspiring to overcome it. Many great thinkers who rejected religious beliefs in an afterlife still pursued quests for immortality by striving to improve the human condition through their deeds.

But the study of only one organized religion, as helpful as it is, affords little insight into the overall impact of religion on humanity. For this, we must turn to the study of religious history—a horror story of immense proportions. An examination of religious history reveals that adherents of all faiths have consistently sought immortality at the cost of their earthly existence. Religions fostering a desire to be in a sectarian heaven do not inspire peace in their followers but instead tend to provoke injustices. Even religions that consider suicide a sinful act indoctrinate their followers with beliefs that breed inner turmoil, leading to a slow death. And sadly, the lives of "infidels" and "heretics" have historically been even more disposable in the adherents' bids for immortality.

Another awareness gleaned from religious studies is that religions routinely claim to deliver ultimate expressions of truth, often judging followers of other religions as inferior, or worse, dupes of some evil power. Ultraorthodox Jewish sects teach their adherents that the Jewish soul is superior to the souls of gentiles—dogma that many Jews accept with pride. Asian Buddhist sects for centuries approached the search for truth as if it were a competitive sport in which they excelled through one-upmanship. Fundamentalist Christians inform followers that people who do not believe in Jesus go to hell, including those who lived before him, never heard of him, or were raised to believe in another god. Similarly, Muslims tell their followers that Muhammad is the last of Allah's messengers and that Allah's final word must be heard and obeyed by all; for Islamic fundamentalists, this means the whole world must convert to Islam.

Organized religions have done much harm by professing the superiority of their followers and creating such divisive categories as true believers and godless heathens, God's righteous chosen ones and pagans, the heaven bound and hell bound, and the enlightened and unspiritual. Overtly, "us against them" distinctions attract congregants by psychologically empowering them. Covertly, they forge polarized perceptions and a distorted view of human abuses, catalyzing endless violence.

In addition, religious scriptures of all persuasions have imperiled humanity's freedom of thought and pursuit of liberty. Playing on fears of the faithful, scriptural writings exalt those who follow blindly, attack brave questioners who entertain honest doubts, and threaten dissenters with a lifetime of guilt. These writings work insidiously in the minds of the faithful who, intolerant of criticism, have gone on to incite witch hunts and religious wars, resulting in immeasurable bloodshed between religions and within them.

Historically, some of the greatest evils have emerged from displays of holiness. It was usually zealots, sure they had heard the voice of God, who fueled the fires of fear and hatred, directing them toward religious sects, ethnic groups, racial minorities, and women. Humanity is still suffering from the fanaticism of individuals influenced by canonized books espousing erroneous ideas, theologies based on superstition, unscientific cosmologies, false expectations, and unethical commands. And not surprisingly, wherever ethnic or racial minorities or women are treated as inferior, the landscape is parched with ignorance and fear. If there is a useful purpose served by religions that continue to disempower any portion of the human race, it can only be in inspiring us to prevent history from repeating itself.

God Without Religion examines the past effects of organized religion and offers more direct avenues to knowledge of God for the present and future. Chapter 1, "Worshipping by Wondering," explores our present understanding of God; this invitation to worship by wondering rather than believing opens pathways for questioning popular definitions of God while simultaneously observing the effects of belief systems on the human mind. Chapter 2, "A Bigger Picture of Human Progress," shows how we arrived at this point; challenging linear notions of progress, it introduces an ancient model of human evolution and devolution as a means for viewing both the rise of religion and humanity's intellectual and intuitive potential for universalizing God. Chapter 3, "An Alternative to Organized Religion," presents the theory of self, a nondualistic option for realizing knowledge of God; this theory portrays intuition as a verifiable, repeatable, and unbiased psychophysical science. Chapter 4, "Testing Today's Choices," weighs the merits of New Age spiritual movements, points out the pitfalls of modern approaches to Eastern spiritual traditions, and illustrates ways to expand the sense of self beyond narrow spiritual identifications.

Interspersed throughout each chapter are techniques to aid in the search for answers to spiritual questions—better answers than those furnished by organized religion. These techniques are universal, having been passed down in one form or another through mystical and philosophical disciplines. When practiced regularly, they help uncover not only better answers to spiritual questions but also better questions. And with better questions comes increased spiritual freedom on one's path to knowledge of God. Readers embarking on this path are advised to prepare for moments of discomfort following the release of one familiar belief after another. Eventually, in ceasing to identify with a narrowing belief system, your identity will grow, enlarged by the very questions you have embodied. And with your newly expanded identity you will be more knowledgeable in spiritual matters, for the more we question any aspect of life the better we come to know it.

Of the many ghosts from the past currently haunting humanity, few are as damaging as religion's outdated dogma and divisive practices. The dogma poses a barrier to intellectual and spiritual expansiveness, and the divisiveness a barrier to world peace. In vigorously challenging these walls until they crumble, we become the architects of our own thoughts, unfettered by conventional forms of worship and free at last to seek God from within.

CHAPTER ONE

Worshipping by
Wondering

"What Is God?"

God offers to every mind a choice between truth and repose. Take which you please—you can never have both.
—Ralph Waldo Emerson

Wonder is the gateway to knowledge. A person entering this gateway seeking spiritual knowledge would ask penetrating questions about the nature of God, and the more questions the individual asked, the more profound the answers would be, leading to deeper questions. Constantly challenging our conclusions and refining our knowledge of God prevents us from stagnating, both intellectually and spiritually. Simultaneously, these acts of wonder keep us engaged in perpetual worship.

It is also possible to worship God by believing other people's conclusions, but this approach erects barriers to intellectual and spiritual growth. Individuals who unquestioningly accept their inherited beliefs about God end up harboring a narrow view of themselves, humanity, and the natural world. Others challenge their inherited beliefs then hastily adopt the conclusions of a teacher whose answers to spiritual questions are more universal, encompassing expansive love, more people, and broader knowledge; but without testing these answers firsthand, worshippers are unable to personally experience them. In both instances, the acquiescence to others' precepts inhibits progress.

Worshipping by wondering does the opposite, continually revealing the next step forward. While wondering about God, a person advances because of the liberating knowledge she has gained through personal exploration. And the more questions she asks, the more inclusive her perspective will be because questioning erodes the barriers posed by beliefs. This means that each time the questioner integrates a more refined answer she expands not only her idea of God but also her sense of self. Step by step, refined answers broaden our spiritual identity by catalyzing intellectual and spiritual freedom.

A good starting point for wondering about God is to ask the question "What is God?" Answers to this question have historically incited violence between religious followers with clashing replies. However, seeking knowledge of God *without* religion eliminates preformulated answers that divide humanity into warring groups of people with differing beliefs. This question rouses even atheists, who piqued by curiosity will admit to having been swayed less by inquiring into the nature of God than by religion's poor answers. Though answers furnished by organized religions often lead to complacency and divisiveness, to call them "wrong" would belie the spirit of wondering. For atheists and religionists alike, the anguish a poor answer engenders can prompt further questioning.

In asking What is God? sincere truth-seekers resist the temptation to remain in a comfort zone and instead keep reaching for new answers. They recognize that the solace drawn from earlier convictions prevented them from contemplating more viable possibilities. They also see many answers that once furnished a sense of security as no longer useful, or worse, as stifling or superstitious. Rejecting pat answers, they embrace the uncertainty inherent in discovery and prepare to exchange old comfort zones for new understandings.

Asking questions about the nature of God is a path of scientific investigation. Just as material scientists investigate the outer universe, spiritual investigators seeking an understanding of God begin by exploring the inner space of the mind. In both endeavors, hard and fast answers suppress free thinking; hence, material and spiritual investigators alike, propelled by wonder, question their own answers and even doubt them. Wonder, it turns out, is not only a sure-fire method of inquiry into the nature of God but also a potent antiseptic for a mind flooded with accepted truths passed down for centuries by organized religion. Though the washing away of tainted views can be uncomfortable, it leaves the intellect free to exercise its potential and the eyes cleared of inherited myopia.

Unaware of the decontamination awaiting them, many spiritual investigators start asking What is God? in the context of the religious tradition that forged their earliest impressions of God. But they soon find that penetrating inquiries directed to religious authorities are generally discouraged because the religion's continued survival depends on wide acceptance of the answers already provided. For centuries the Catholic Church, for example, excommunicated or killed members who dared to question its dogma. Today, some religious authorities still use evocative words such as *heresy, devil,* and *Maya* to undermine the human propensity for wonder. Organized religion routinely capitalizes on the insecurity individuals feel when their views are at odds with the group persuasion.

Spiritual investigators meet with resistance from congregants as well, who inform them that the answer to What is God? emerges from faith. These encounters awaken a realization that religious faith leads to one answer only, whereas investigative perseverance ushers in a lifetime of questions and little interest in settling comfortably on an answer. It also becomes clear that faith based on religious dogma glorifies matters pertaining to destination, often resulting in a devaluing of human life and overdependence on a presumed afterlife, while spiritual inquiry celebrates the journey of life.

In pursuing answers to What is God? within the confines of a synagogue, church, or mosque, spiritual investigators begin to challenge their most deeply held beliefs. Many are startled to find the leader of the service is less a spokesperson for God than a human being with obvious biases. John Wesley, the founder of Methodism, exhorted his fellow Christians to save their money and grow rich—an instruction at odds with Christ's counsel to sell everything and give the proceeds to the poor. Now, as then, many members of the clergy profess narrow ideas of God that their parishioners either consciously or subconsciously internalize.

While plumbing for answers to What is God? in religious texts, spiritual investigators may be equally surprised to find the printed words and phrases are like inkblot tests: interpretations of them say more about the interpreter than about the books. To lessen the likelihood of mechanically projecting personal meaning onto a religious writing, it is important to read it with a discerning eye, override any feel-good interpretations instilled earlier in life, and study the historical context in which the work was written. It also helps to recognize that simply because they were recorded, words do not carry moral or divine authority. When it comes to gleaning knowledge about God, we can learn more by observing the habits of a bird than by blindly accepting the information furnished by religious texts, followers, and authorities combined.

The value in inquiring about God within the precincts of organized religion has more to do with clearing and focusing the mind—the instrument of investigation—than with realizing direct knowledge of God. In firing up the burners of discrimination to warm the test tubes of reason, for instance, it becomes possible to analyze limiting interpretations of God and unravel accepted truths. As both begin to fall away and investigators bring the question What is God? to more receptive arenas, as is suggested in Technique 1, further insights await their discovery. An answer to this question may give rise to other penetrating questions. Or the mind might silence an attractive yet incomplete answer, only to find a more complete answer coming to expression in a thought or event. Or it might come to pass that asking What is God? reveals more about the mind's conditioning than any conclusive answer ever could.

TECHNIQUE 1

Joining a Spiritual Colloquium

A profoundly helpful technique to practice while asking What is God? involves joining a colloquium of spiritual investigators. Together, participants in such a spiritual colloquium formulate increasingly sophisticated questions that challenge even those the great thinkers pondered. Sharing ideas in this type of setting inspires a deeper understanding of issues than is possible by contemplating the same questions in solitude.

Religions worldwide sponsor gatherings for their members. In the West, synagogues, churches, and mosques offer venues where like-minded people can hear a sermon, interact socially, and receive emotional encouragement; in the East, individuals can attend *satsangas* to receive guidance from a particular teacher. But in offering a supportive group identity, such gatherings tend to reinforce already shared belief systems and to inhibit innovative questioning.

In spiritual colloquiums, on the other hand, everyone is free to question, challenge, and doubt. Nonsectarian, they generally meet once or twice a week to discuss various issues. In some, participants alternate hosting the gathering in their homes or college dormitory rooms, preparing a relaxed ambiance that encourages members to speak from their hearts. Others hold meetings in a public location such as a library reading room or a park, an arrangement that helps focus their energy on the collective purpose.

Spiritual colloquium members ensure that their meetings are conducive to intellectual and spiritual growth. Instead of appointing a permanent leader to direct meetings, they take turns in the role of facilitator, who introduces the day's topic and moderates the discussion. Whether members sit around a large conference-room table or more casually in a living room, dorm room, or park, they position themselves for maximum eye contact. The ensuing discussion is animated and thought provoking, often initiated by the reading of a printed excerpt that elicits widely differing interpretations. Most religious, philosophical, historical, or dramatic books work well in such settings, where the contents are not likely to be construed with finality.

As the day's discussion proceeds, the facilitator keeps it on course. A useful compass can be found in the legendary distinction between a chicken farmer and an egg farmer: a chicken farmer regards fertilized eggs (generative answers) as a means for producing more chickens (questions), whereas an egg farmer views chickens (questions) as a means for producing more unfertilized eggs (nongenerative answers). The colloquium is like a chicken farm, where participants harvest new questions from fertilized answers and disregard crates of infertile answers since they are incapable of producing deeper questions. And spiritual investigators know that answers alone mean nothing while questions reflect back their depth of insight.

Most cities have such colloquiums. Notices of meetings can be found in the local newspapers, on bulletin boards at health food stores, and in alternative newsletters; also, librarians are often equipped to provide referrals, as are sales clerks at bookstores. Alternatively, you could start a colloquium. In seeking members, disregard such factors as age, gender, income, lifestyle, and religious background. The only criterion that matters is willingness to engage in open-minded investigation of human spirituality. Anyone unwilling to challenge their own notions, or fearful of having them challenged by others, may not be suited for your colloquium.

If meeting publicly with others does not appeal to you, consider participating in an online spiritual colloquium composed of people seeking to expand their ideas of God. Online formats allow you to either read bulletin-board messages on specific topics at the sponsoring Web site or have messages delivered to you by e-mail, to which you can then post replies. Live online chats about spirituality are also available. In addition to protecting your privacy, the online option allows you to link up with other spiritual investigators whenever you wish.

The company we keep, in person or online, strongly influences our spiritual growth. Associating regularly with people who are bogged down in dogma can contribute to more intractable beliefs and superficial attitudes. Joining with earnest truth-seekers whose spiritual questions are no longer answered by organized religion, however, can help eradicate obstructing patterns, setting the stage for accelerated intellectual and spiritual development.

Wondering about the attributes of God offers immense rewards on a personal level. After undermining a poor answer, spiritual investigators will never be able to return to it with the same conviction. On the other hand, any answer that withstands rigorous testing will strengthen one's spiritual foundation. Even if without widely accepted answers investigators never stop asking What is God? they will cultivate an unshakable spiritual foundation based on tested ideas. The more our spiritual foundation is infused with personal inquiry, the better equipped it will be to support a sense of self endeavoring to identify with more and more people.

Collectively, the ramifications of wondering about God are vast. With increasing numbers of people striving to incorporate all of humanity in their spiritual perception of themselves, fewer and fewer will be able to pervert the worship of God into violent religious crusades against people of differing backgrounds. With the passage of more time, any human being demeaned or impoverished by another's beliefs will be an affront to us all. Today, when millions of individuals are starving physically, emotionally, intellectually, and spiritually, wonder can single-handedly combat dogma, superstition, and divisiveness—the real enemies of humanity.

Gods Made in the Image of Men

And in that Heaven of all their wish,
There shall be no more land, say fish.

—Rupert Brooke

Historical images of God provide a pantheon of fertile impressions for the inquiring mind. In answer to the question What
is God? each religion has its own particular ideal—an icon,
name, or state of being—coupled with historical chronicles
and a series of instructions for the devout. Most religions
claim that their manner of showing devotion is inspired by
the will of God and therefore the best. They further assert that
God rewards the faithful for their piety and inflicts some form
of retribution on the unfaithful.

A survey of images used to portray God over the last thirty-
five hundred years reveals an uncanny resemblance between
them and the people who furnished them. Religions of antiq-
uity, such as Vaishnavism in the East and the cults of Mithra
in the Near East and Zeus in the Mediterranean, rendered
their gods in the form of humans, only larger than life, as can
be seen in ancient statues of Rama and Sita, Krishna, Isis and
Osiris, Apollo and Aphrodite, and other celebrated deities.
Scientific thinkers interested in the workings of the cosmos
viewed these male and female gods as personifications of
nature's power; and to ancient philosophers, feuding gods
symbolized the contending forces of nature. Early religions
also depicted their gods in dramatic stories of tribulation,
death, and resurrection, expressing the human longing for life
beyond death and freedom from physical limitations. From

the vantage point of spiritual investigation, these details indicate that the impersonal idea of God can be personalized into an image, or when needed, many images.

With the advent of monotheism, images of God came to mirror not only man's physical attributes but his tribal ideals and ideas as well. The Hebrew Bible, for instance, states that God created man in his image and woman from the flesh of man. This depiction of God, recorded by some of the men who wrote Genesis, introduced the ideal of God the Creator and All-Knowing Father. Through the written and spoken words of scribes and prophets, he promises the land of Israel, spiritual redemption, and the anointing of kings to be messiahs of Israel. The Hebrews, in turn, fancied the House of Israel to be God's chosen, God's son, and at times God's bride.

Spiritual investigators mining the question What is God? might regard this male figure as an incomplete answer based less on the impersonal idea of God than on a child's natural inclination to revere the father and on men's desire to serve the needs of their patriarchal society. Had the Bible been written by women, a truth seeker might point out, it would probably emphasize female imagery in the same way that religious writings emerging from societies more engaged with feminine attributes inspired the widespread worship of female deities such as India's Kali, Shakti, and Prakriti, and later through pagan influences in Rome, Christianity's Mary.

About two hundred years after the Maccabean uprising against the threat of Hellenization to their political and religious independence, the Hebrew culture spawned a new image of God—Jesus Christ. Early Christians, influenced both by the prophetic promise of a messiah-king who would lead the Hebrews to political victory and by the Greek idea of a demiurge, or intermediary between God and the world, considered themselves heirs to God's promises to Israel yet unbound to the injunctions of Mosaic Law. Like the Omnipotent Father ideal developed by the Hebrews, the Jesus image satisfied people's needs for a unifying, defining, and exclusionary worldview; it also held the dual promise of an end of times and eternal life. With the emergence of Jesus, God's word was made flesh.

Seekers challenging this answer to What is God? would detect a lack of historical authenticity in how the life of Jesus Christ is portrayed in the New Testament. The Gospels, which depict the tribulation, death, and resurrection of Jesus, are neither eyewitness accounts nor solely fact-based chronicles that might have been handed down through generations. Instead, they more closely resemble Greek dramas and legends from *The Egyptian Book of the Dead*.

The narrative about Jesus recorded between the middle of the first century and the fourth century in the Gospel of Matthew seems actually to have been written for enactment. Like the Greek dramas, it is rich with improbabilities; compresses events into a narrow time-frame to fit a series of scenes, a structure that allows for only minimal detail; and contains numerous incongruities. According to Matthew, after the Last Supper, Jesus and his disciples go into the wilderness for the night. As his disciples sleep, Jesus begins to pray. *We are told that no one hears his words, yet they are revealed to the reader.* While praying, Jesus is captured by a multitude and brought before the high priest of the Jews, as well as other scribes and elders. *Little explanation is given for this sudden nighttime gathering of religious leaders and false witnesses during Passover, when men were usually with their families, or for the lapse in time between any of these scenes.* Then witnesses come and testify that Jesus spoke of the destruction of the temple. *It is unclear where they suddenly came from.* The priests judge Jesus guilty of blasphemy for failing to deny claims that he was the anticipated Messiah, and the evening ends with Peter denying his companionship with Jesus. *But due to gaps in the story line, the reader is not told why Judas's betrayal could not wait until morning or about Jesus's experiences between this trial before the Jews and the one before the Romans; there is no word about Pilate's readiness to see Jesus and pass judgment; and no mention is made of preparations for the Crucifixion, which takes place immediately afterward.* Because of their drama-oriented presentation, Matthew's writings yield only a sketchy depiction of events that loses credibility as a historical account.

Probing further, a truth seeker will find inconsistencies in the Gospel of Matthew that suggest the image of God it portrays is based partially on expectations of the people living at the time. Matthew shows in Jesus's genealogy that his father, Joseph, was descended from David—a lineage conforming with the Hebrew understanding that the coming Messiah would be a descendant of King David of ancient Israel. Elsewhere he states that Mary was impregnated by the Holy Spirit. Thus, instead of choosing between Jesus being the scion of David and the Son of God, Matthew incorporates both ideas, despite their incongruity. This contradiction, among others, gives the impression that Matthew's depiction of the life of Jesus was influenced by Hebrew expectations.

Though Matthew gives Jesus the status of Son of God, to the Jews of Jesus's time all prophets were called sons of God—a title that did not imply virgin birth. It was perhaps because Matthew wanted to "sell" Jesus's messianic stature to the Roman people that he portrayed Jesus as the child of a god, just as the deities of the Hellenistic world were children of gods. Thus, Matthew fulfilled the expectations of the religious and also the political leaders of his day.

He seems to have accomplished this partly through intricate embroidery. Jesus was known as a Nazarene, implying he had been born in Nazareth. But Matthew, writing predominantly for the Hebrews, and Luke, oriented more toward a Greek audience, concocted elaborate and contradictory schemes to introduce Bethlehem as Jesus's birthplace—in keeping with an interpretation of the Hebrew Bible's prediction that the coming Messiah would be born in Bethlehem.

Matthew reached his intended audience through apparent mistranslation as well. Quoting Isaiah 7:14 in the Hebrew Bible[1] and loosely interpreting it as a prediction of Jesus's birth, Matthew writes: "Behold, a virgin shall conceive and bear a son" (1:23).[2] However, the original passage makes no reference to a virgin but simply reads, "Behold, the young woman is with child, and she shall bear a son" (7:14). If the young woman described seven hundred years before Jesus's birth had been a virgin, the Hebrew scribes of Isaiah's time would have noted this detail since a virgin birth would have been miraculous to them as well. Not only does Matthew, writing in Greek, subvert the Hebrew Bible, but compilers of the King James Bible later mistranslated the Isaiah text to agree with Matthew's description of events. By contrast, Mark and John, who were writing with different agendas for a general Roman readership, do not account for the virgin birth at all.

Further, Matthew 21:5, quoting Zechariah 9:9, describes Jesus as riding two animals at once, an ass and a colt. However, Zechariah 9:9, faithful to the rules of biblical Hebrew grammar, refers to only one animal, calling it by two different names. In this case the mistranslation in Matthew's story makes it evident that his writings, which are today regarded as the word of God, manufactured events in Jesus's life from incompetent translations of the Hebrew Bible.

Such inconsistencies, inventions, and mistranslations underscore the observation that the image of God portrayed in the New Testament is unquestionably fictional. On the one hand, this informs us that the centuries-old beliefs based on these stories have little historical foundation. On the other hand, it illuminates the means by which stories about the life of Jesus captured the imagination of his followers. Since the man Jesus and his message evidently failed to satisfy the messianic expectations of the Hebrews and the heroic aspirations of the Romans, Jesus the man had been made into the *ideal* of Jesus Christ. Consequently, the historical Jesus is largely unknown, while Jesus Christ is comparable in stature to the mythic gods of ancient Greece and Egypt.

The next major image of God, given fresh theological importance six hundred years after the execution of Jesus, was Allah, who mirrored back to the Arab world its receptivity to absolute monotheism and a rigorous rejection of false gods, idolatry, and sensual living. For years Arabs had expected a prophet of Allah would come to deliver a sacred scripture of their own. They considered themselves descendants of Abraham, along with the Jews, and they knew the stories of the Hebrew Bible and the New Testament, often weaving in colorful variations; but they were acutely aware that these scriptures were not of their people. Flocking in hordes to poets who, under the influence of spirits, would speak mysteriously of the future, intoning through rhythm and rhyme, they became intoxicated with thoughts of demons, possession, and soothsayers. And while these tribal people, like the ancient Hebrews, did not believe in an eternal afterlife, their disbelief prompted hedonism, possibly due to the lack of a formal religious law they could embrace. In short, the Arab world was ripe for a miraculous sign that the God of Abraham would take notice of them and fulfill their need for religious structure, pride in their spiritual worth, and freedom from the many gods, goddesses, and spirits that vied for their attention.

Though many prophets competed for their attention as well, the ideal of Allah finally congealed in the Qur'an, said to be dictated by the angel Gabriel to Muhammad, a middle-aged merchant who Muslims widely believe could neither read nor write. The Qur'an's stories are largely borrowed from the Hebrew Bible, yet similar to the early Gospels of the New Testament, it eschews immoral behavior, establishes a Day of Judgment, and for the faithful, promises resurrection in paradise. Throughout, it glorifies people who agree to call themselves Muslims and accept Muhammad as the last and greatest messenger of Allah.

Before long, Qur'anic teachings had penetrated beyond the borders of the Arab world. Like Christians and Hebrews who believed in the historical accuracy of their religious scriptures, many Muslims claimed the Qur'an contained the legitimate words of God. Convinced that Muhammad's illiteracy prevented him from prior knowledge of such subjects as God, Adam, Abraham, and Jesus, believers alluded to it as a sign of his purity of mind.

Spiritual investigators would challenge these assertions as well. They might point out that though Muhammad may not have read the stories in the Hebrew Bible, he could have heard them since he was well traveled and they had long since made their way across the Near East. Inquirers might then interpret his modified renderings of them as symptomatic of either his illiteracy or the cultural yen for improvisation rather than as proof that he heard them from an angel of God. It could even be argued that Muhammad's recorded revelations spread around the world not because they were miraculous but because their simplicity and unifying power quickly translated into political and economic advances for Allah's scattered followers.

Though most stories in the Qur'an adhere closely to the prophetic tradition of the Hebrews, Muhammad incorporated material depicting himself as other than a strictly God-inspired messenger. For example, at first he declared that his message was for his kin; then he felt commanded to share it with people outside his family; afterward he considered it his duty to preach in Makkah; and only later, fueled by people's increased receptivity to this angelically delivered faith, did he claim to be God's messenger to the world (6:92, 8:158).[3] In addition, soon after the Jews of Madinah rejected Muhammad as a prophet of God, his angry response to them showed up in Qur'anic references advising dissociation from Jews. For instance, while early scriptural material called for fasting during the Jewish holiday of Yom Kippur, he later reversed this instruction and instituted the month of Ramadan as the official Muslim fast (2:185). And whereas Muslims were initially instructed to face Jerusalem while praying, he changed the direction of prayer to Makkah (2:144, 149). These and other improvisations make it clear that the Qur'an, while rendered in the language of Allah's eternal commandments, contains guidance pertaining to the shifting circumstances of Muhammad's followers.

Among early Muslims, Christians, and Hebrews alike, the gods made in their image sooner or later reflected back social and political messages that today erroneously reverberate through all three religions as timelessly inspired truths. An example of this phenomenon is the belief in resurrection, a doctrine that first appeared in Hebrew thought during the Maccabean Revolt in the second century BCE. To entice men to fight in the revolt, according to the book of Daniel, the Hebrews were encouraged to martyr themselves for God's word and chosen people, in exchange for resurrection to eternal life—seeding a belief still embraced by Jews. The idea that martyrs are resurrected was later applied to Jesus's death, most likely because his Jewish followers, viewing him as a martyr, carried a nearly two-hundred-year-old expectation that he, like the Maccabean warriors they glorified, would be resurrected and ascend to God. The earliest biblical mention of his resurrection, appearing in Mark 16:6, sets forth a model of Jesus as the first Christian martyr to be resurrected; however, among early Christians the question of whether to accept Jesus's resurrection literally or symbolically was a fiercely debated political issue. Decades later, Church officials and theologians quashed the opposition, affirmed that Christ was physically resurrected, and established Church hierarchy as the only true conduit to God.

Six hundred years after Jesus's death, the Qur'an reiterated the "official" Judeo-Christian doctrine of resurrection, simultaneously making paradise richly sensual and mistakenly linking the promise of eternal life all the way back to Abraham and the patriarchs (2:260). Qur'anic references to the Day of Resurrection (3:161), combined with Muhammad's counsel, such as "What though ye be slain or die, when unto Allah ye are gathered?" (3:158), inspired a Muslim belief in resurrection in paradise after dying in warlike service to God's word and people. Muslims interpreting these ideas literally became willing, as did their Christian and Hebrew forerunners, to martyr themselves for their God and their people in return for resurrection to eternal life. Fundamentalist Muslims today continue the tradition, expecting suicide bombings to propel them to paradise. Regrettably, they believe that by acting on this doctrine they are following in the footsteps of Abraham, when in fact they are complying with a theological distortion that Muhammad unwittingly borrowed from later Hebrews hardpressed in military campaigns. So it appears that not only are gods made in the image of men but, in scriptural passages pitting man against man, the word of God articulates the sentiments of politically motivated men.

Once aware of the misconceptions and polarizing effects of religion's god figures, spiritual investigators might wonder how modern-day humanity can find a more embraceable and inclusive God—a universal God that can help us foster peace within ourselves as vehicles for world peace. For starters, we can recognize that the Hebrew Bible, the New Testament, and the Qur'an all project local human ideals and ideas onto the impersonal substance of God that their authors hoped would coalesce into personal form to fulfill their needs. Then we might strip away the layers of historical swathing in which they wrapped their mythic god images, watch the images expand back into universal substance, and make them our own.

Historical wrappings include all the events, dictates, and interpretations used to enhance acceptance of organized religion during its centuries of incubation, *whether or not they can be evidentially substantiated.* Actually, archaeological and textual studies have not corroborated many of the events portrayed in the Hebrew Bible, the New Testament, or the *hadith,* the records of Muhammad's life, though they do confirm that certain people and places existed. But indications that Moses, Jesus, and Muhammad existed does not imply that their lives proceeded as depicted in these texts or that their theological assertions are unequivocally true. At best, we can conclude that real people and places were used in otherwise mythological stories, most likely to give them a convincing context.

One example of a biblical event functioning in this way is the Exodus from Egypt described in the Hebrew Bible. There exists little evidence that the Hebrews fled by way of ten plagues and a parting of the Reed Sea, or even that they were slaves in Egypt. The entire story of the Exodus appears, from historical and archaeological studies, to be a myth designed to give a group of people a sense of importance, a feeling of solidarity, and a unique relationship to their ideal of God. Considering the countless centuries subsequently marked by observance of the Passover Seder, the myth clearly fulfilled its purposes.

Further, archaeological finds do not substantiate stories of the conquering of Canaan under Joshua's leadership or of King David's dispersal of the Philistines. These tales that gave the early Hebrews a sense of accomplishment are now considered historical facts in the minds of millions of people. Because of Joshua and David's purported victories, in combination with the Exodus account, Jews today pride themselves on being a people who survived four hundred years of slavery; who were freed by God, favoring them above all other beings in the universe; and who conquered a strip of land given to them by their God.

In fact, the ancient Hebrews, as well as the early Christians and Muslims, saw little point in unbiasedly recording events. To them, writing history meant sanctifying it, giving events cosmic significance by directing human attention to thoughts of God, glory, and good things for believers. Indeed, sanctified thoughts inspired by myths of the Hebrew Bible succeeded in enkindling the longevity of the Jewish identity by giving Jews determination, a sense of dignity, a system of values, and when fueling opposition in the form of anti-Semitism, a needed distance from others.

The problem is that in the attempt to sanctify history, organized religions ended up sanctifying one group of people at the expense of others, much to humanity's detriment. For example, though modern archaeological findings reveal that Canaanites of the time were culturally more advanced than the Hebrews, the Hebrew Bible depicts the opposite. Consequently, many of the European colonists arriving in America, influenced by the Hebrew Bible's mythic account of the chosen people's God-inspired triumph over the Canaanites, saw themselves as new Israelites whose destiny was to remove the "savage Indians," or new Canaanites, and take their promised land of the Americas. Similarly, evangelical Christians today, convinced by the New Testament that they have been chosen to "save" people of other faiths, send missionaries around the world to uproot entire indigenous populations of their traditions, all the while expanding the domain of Church influence. Any religious attempt to selectively glorify its followers for economic or territorial advantage imparts an ethnocentrism capable of corrupting their perceptions and treatment of others for centuries to come.

Religious attempts to sanctify history also end up erroneously glorifying one God image at the expense of others. For instance, in the 1960s Shrila Prabhupada, the founder of ISKCON (International Society for Krishna Consciousness), began teaching Westerners to worship Krishna by chanting the Hindu God's name, when Krishna himself had championed the freedom to worship any form representing the impersonal substance of God. Contrary to Krishna's own teachings, Prabhupada considered him to be the supreme representative of God, having apparently taken his words too literally in the Bhagavad Gita, a scriptural masterpiece dating back to about the fifth century BCE, where Krishna speaks on behalf of the infinite God. Rather than interpreting these words transpersonally, it seems Prabhupada mistook them for personal messages from the mythic King Krishna.

Christians who interpret Christ's words "I am the way, and the truth, and the light" (John 14:6) as personal statements make the same error of superiority. Whether or not Jesus was a Jew, had twelve disciples, uttered such statements, or was even born, pseudohistorical claims glorifying his words and deeds have little to do with the underlying image of Jesus Christ as a focal point of worship. Over the last two thousand years, this image has inspired such saints as Francis, Teresa of Avila, and Teresa Neumann to penetrate the divisive sheaths surrounding it and focus their hearts and minds on the expansive substance of God.

So it is that in unwrapping theology's historical assertions about God, we are left with purer images of God—as mythic figures that have invigorated centuries of worship among exceptional lovers of God and humanity. For individuals of a devotional temperament or interested in developing devotion, such images can still be used as focal points for worship and inward concentration of the mind. The image of Krishna, the Buddha, God the Creator and All-Knowing Father, Jesus Christ, Allah, or the Creator honored by Native cultures in the Americas is each a potential object of devotion capable of assisting worshippers in directing their awareness inward and expanding their hearts. In focusing heart and mind on the image best equipped to galvanize our devotion and secure our concentration, we actualize the spiritual ideals sought outwardly by the creators of God's many images.

On the path of spiritual inquiry, we can therefore embrace an expansive God by personalizing an image of God that secures our concentration and appeals to our hearts, establishing an intimate relationship with that image, then gradually identifying with it, as described in Technique 2. By giving the heart and mind a point of focus, this practice naturally awakens feelings of unconditional centeredness, contentment, and peace of mind. In the end, it helps us embody the very virtues we project onto our God.

 **TECHNIQUE 2**

Developing a Relationship with a Personal God

A relationship with a personal God, seeded by an intensely focused mind, awakens the heart to greater depths of intuitive awareness. For extremely intellectual people, this practice accelerates emotional growth and enhances receptivity. For highly emotional individuals, it strengthens the intellect, whose capacities are now called upon to convert the energy of reactive outer-directed emotion into inner-directed devotion. Great spiritual exemplars throughout history have used variations on this technique, devotionally surrendering to an inclusive God in one form or another to curb restlessness of the mind, in the process modeling service to others and universal love for humanity.

When a person's concentration on an ideal of God deepens with devotion, it produces physiological effects. Much as a moving current of electricity generates an electromagnetic field, nervous energy percolating in the dorsal plexus[4] through a devotee's intense devotion can induce magnetic properties along the spine. According to adepts, the continuous love of one's God ideal maintained in immobile positions yields a bliss intuited along the spine, which has drawn nervous energy magnetically from the senses, heart, and lung activity. It is for this reason that many adepts felt their love for God literally took their breath away.

To establish a relationship with a personal God, first decide on an image of God that your heart recognizes as universal, all-pervasive, and profoundly meaningful. (An image containing divisive elements, while equally capable of focusing the heart and mind, will give rise to a divisive attitude.) Many people select the image they were taught to identify with as a child, such as the Heavenly Father, Jesus or Mary, Allah, or a Hindu god or goddess. However, it is just as possible for a person born Jewish to emulate a modern-day exemplar of spirituality, a Christian to focus heart and mind on Krishna, a Muslim to idealize the virtues of Christ, a Buddhist to inwardly identify with God the Father of All, and a Hindu to adulate an infinite Allah. The point is to select the image you most admire not as a religious adherent but as a *human being.* Nor is it necessary to borrow from historical representations of God; mirroring the virtues of an expansive idea of God that humanitarians and scientists instinctively embrace, your chosen God can instead be impersonal love for others, the light of knowledge, or even the universe laid out before you.

Next, stripping away all devotional instructions and scripted prayers normally associated with your God ideal, begin to identify with it through active wondering. Raise questions and challenge beliefs with the virtues of your God ideal in mind, all the while surrendering your predetermined answers, conclusions, and the expected results of your worship. The ensuing colloquium will spark within your heart and head a new awareness of an unfolding relationship with others and the world.

To deepen the relationship, engage day after day in a dialogue with your God ideal. Perhaps ponder a recent experience, a book you have read, or a colloquium discussion, posing a few far-reaching questions it has inspired, then sit in silence contemplating the infinite qualities of your God and note any challenges that arise. The more you retrain your heart to look only to the embodiment of your inner God's virtues for happiness, the sooner you will view your outer-world circumstances as neutralized, free of gain and loss, bias, and conditioning. Once your relationship has grown endearingly personal and inspiring, you will naturally want to emulate your God ideal in every waking moment, minimizing distractions in order to do so.

Adoration of the inner God eventually becomes effortless, continuous, and intensely satisfying. You will know you have reached this point when you feel constantly centered in your God ideal, never lonely or bored, and aware that your image of God is expanding every day to accommodate more knowledge. Very soon, because you have endowed your God with cherished virtues and then concentrated on your God's containment of them, you will be exemplifying these virtues while expressing your unique perspective. And in loving a God that is a projection of your spiritual potential, you will deepen your love for yourself.

All along, the development of a personal relationship with an infinite God ideal expands the sense of self. This occurs because in epitomizing your inner universal God, you exercise your own potential for expansion. As a result, each time your receptivity to this personalized infinite substance of God comes to expression, inner barriers fall away and your sense of self extends ever outward to include others. Eventually you become a walking embodiment of your God without knowing it, automatically seeing yourself in others. No longer able to actively identify with a solely outer God, with whom a relationship would demand artificial rituals and a go-between, you embrace as inviolable this union with your inner God.

Gods of the past, made in the image of their creators, ultimately reflect their makers' sense of self. As such, they provide us with glimpses into the self-image of these populations—and by extrapolation, into our own self-image. The representations of God sculpted by ancient cultures suggest that the people of the times saw themselves as participants in the grand scheme of the natural world. Images of God portrayed by monotheistic cultures, whether visually descriptive of physical features or narratively expressive of ideals and ideas, point to a different understanding of the human self. Promises of paternal guidance "from above" and of a division between heaven-bound believers and hell-bound nonbelievers give an impression of people who considered themselves distanced from the cosmos and divided amongst themselves. In each instance, God was viewed as the property of a select membership in a centralized house of worship. The insular self-image that gave rise to monotheistic God images detached from a "fallen" humanity today breeds intense feelings of superiority over others and separation from a universal God, hindering spiritual investigation into the nature of the cosmos and the human self.

In tackling the question What is God? this narrow sense of self prompts one answer, while a more expansive sense of self, encompassing its inherently inclusive nature, propels another. People closely identified with a monotheistic religion often declare that God is a force "out there" ministering exclusively to individuals of their particular faith, often to the detriment of others. As their self-image expands, however, they're likely to arrive at a more pantheistic perspective, saying that the one infinite substance of God, the self-awareness inherent in the cosmos, underlies everyone and everything.

Expansion of the sense of self, the seedbed of all knowledge of God, engenders peace internally and also in the world. With an expanded sense of self, one hundred people may come up with a different image of God yet everyone would agree that each image merely provides a focal point of concentration for the heart and head to identify with the universal spirit of God. Though everyone in the world would probably arrive at a slightly different image of God to focus on, each reflecting a unique sense of self on its journey of expansion, these images would cease to cloak narrow interests and instead serve humanity as a whole.

Miracles and the Mind

Experience shows, without exception, that miracles occur only in times and in countries in which miracles are believed in, and in the presence of persons who are disposed to believe in them.

—Ernest Renan

For millennia, religion has been associated with miracles, viewed as instances when the laws of nature are temporarily suspended to prove God's power. Krishna is credited with everything from swallowing a forest fire to lifting a hill. The Buddha stops a raging elephant in its tracks. Moses's snake eats the snakes of Egyptian priests. Christ materializes enough fish and bread to feed throngs of assembled people. Muhammad, according to hagiographical accounts, is capable of splitting the moon. These miraculous feats have nothing to do with God, however, but rather with the respective religion's efforts to demonstrate the power and sovereignty of its ideal of God.

By encouraging the interpretation of events as miracles, organized religions sought to prove their claims and win converts. For example, during the widespread plague of the second century, many Christians survived due to their habits of hygiene and their communal style of living, though they attributed their endurance to the supremacy of their God. After the plague passed, tens of thousands of people converted to Christianity because they, too, interpreted the Christians' survival as miraculous proof of their God's protection.

People who interpret their circumstances as miraculous often end up bolstering their feelings of security in life. Upon landing a great job, a man may feel that God is on his side; if he doesn't get the job, he might decide that God is protecting him from what would otherwise have been an unhappy work experience. Similarly, whereas the ancient Hebrews were initially henotheistic, worshipping one god while accepting the existence of others, they became monotheistic following the loss of their worldly kingdom to the Babylonians in the sixth century BCE, when they determined that, instead of being squarely defeated by the Babylonians' gods, Yahweh had used the Babylonians as his instrument to punish Israel—a self-glorifying interpretation extending the dominion of their god over all people and all lands. Viewing Yahweh as the one universal god, the Hebrews could also pray to him anywhere, increasing their sense of safety in the world.

While human experiences viewed as miracles can furnish a sense of safety and security, these experiences, contrary to religion's claims, cannot validate a god's power. All they can do is *confirm beliefs we already harbor.* The more miracles we embrace, the more deeply entrenched our beliefs become, because we interpret our experiences through the filter of these beliefs.

Suppose, for instance, that a culture on a distant planet developed a religion complete with an image of God. Their ecstatic visions would have nothing to do with the power of their God and everything to do with the form epitomizing their local beliefs. In much the same way, a crowd of people on earth witnessing a vision of the Virgin Mary does not validate Christianity but rather reflects local adoration of the image of Mary.

Miracles experienced by people, either singly or in masses,

are informed solely by beliefs. Historically, the Virgin Mary did not appear to individuals until the image of the Virgin Mary had become a widely used icon, and she became visible to crowds only after her cult had grown in popularity. Nor has any image of God from one religion appeared to followers of another religion. The perception of supernormal events connected with any of the world's major religions, such as marble statues inexplicably drinking milk before Hindus or others bleeding before Christians, are likewise informed by the accumulated beliefs held by millions of people over many years' duration.

Religious authorities who interpret events as miracles are themselves guided by beliefs. These authorities either acknowledge apparent miracles or deny their existence, depending on whether the miracles support the religion's dogma. In the event that an apparent miracle conflicting with the dogma cannot be denied, perhaps because it has been witnessed by many people, the phenomenon will often be attributed to a diabolical force. A classic example of this type of demonizing occurred when Catholic theologians, unable to either take credit for or discredit parallel myths of other religions, such as the virgin birth of the Buddha, declared them works of the devil meant to trick humanity.

Not only are miracles used in dubious ways to increase one's sense of security and reinforce religious dogma, but they cast a dangerously misleading model of the universe—one that spiritual investigators would question. For one thing, assigning to God the cause for inexplicable events stifles the pursuit of knowledge. In the past when humankind was confronted with a mystery, God was usually invoked as an explanation, keeping people unschooled in the mechanics of nature. As a result, thunder was for centuries considered the rumbling of gods; rainfall, the outcome of angels opening the windows of heaven; insanity, the work of demons; and comets, the flaming swords or flowing beards of gods, the smoke of human sin rising to darken the heavens, or even omens of war. Today as well, interpretations of enigmatic events as the handiwork of God delay scientific advances, impeding inquiry into everything ranging from the incredible accounts of yoga masters to the thoughts we hear in our heads. A better definition of miracles would be events that have not yet been explained.

Spiritual investigators would also question the validity of presenting God as capable of overriding the laws of nature. Separating God from nature in this way at once transports God beyond the realm of human inquiry and discourages scientific research into the strange and wondrous phenomena misnamed "supernatural." In reclaiming events from this hinterland, we increase the likelihood of finding verifiable explanations for an abundance of supernormal phenomena; already, many bizarre events that have been scientifically investigated are found to result from quite calculable causes. And having accepted that the laws of nature are the unalterable will of the impersonal substance of God, we improve our chances of understanding God. With every insight into the enigmatic workings of the cosmos, we can then view ourselves as active seekers of knowledge instead of observers passively watching God disrupt the fabric of life to prove his existence. In fact, the very act of reuniting God with the natural world demonstrates a desire to understand more about both God and nature, of which we are a part.

Most significantly, spiritual inquiry into apparent miracles illuminates a profound connection between the human mind and events taking place in the world around us. Generations of human beings who in their ignorance perceived comets as signs of battle proceeded to actually engage in war—not because of the omens they thought they saw, but as a direct consequence of the thoughts they projected into the night-time skies. Moreover, group prayers for wellness are today repeatedly found to accelerate a person's recovery from illness. These and other effects of collective thought suggest that events interpreted as miracles may actually be products of the human mind at work. And from this broader perspective, all of life is miraculous.

In freeing ourselves from the idea that God authors miracles, we begin seeing the world differently and taking more responsibility for our thoughts and consequently our actions. Aware of the mind's capacity to shape outcomes, we notice that the world perceived by religious adherents is forged by their beliefs and, similarly, that supernormal events fail to occur in the lives of people who doubt such events. Christians, it has been said, will behold the face of Jesus in the bark of the same tree in which Hindus behold the face of Krishna. Spiritual investigators, however, might wonder if the bark contains healing properties, or perhaps the capacity to impart healing in response to thoughts projected onto it.

Once out of the grip of miracle-thinking, truth seekers realize they have been continually brainwashing themselves by interpreting their experiences through a limited sense of self. The world they now see becomes a reflection of a self no longer narrowed by religious indoctrination, instead claiming its membership in the vast realm of nature. Viewing the stratosphere—cleared at last of Elijah, Jesus, Muhammad, and other ascending saints representing humanity's skyward projection of hope in immortality—they observe heavenly bodies whirling through vast space. More and more, as we take science into our own hands, we can test the strange events in our midst, seek better models to explain them, then investigate those models. In a world perceived as less arbitrary and governed by cause and effect, we become increasingly more self-reliant as well. Having wrested the power of the mind from religions that exclusively centralize that power, we observe that improved personal and global conditions come not from a god above or from divine answers to human prayer, but from within us. The image we hold of God, used to focus the heart and mind, as described in Technique 2, merely intensifies and directs our prayerful thoughts.

Human thoughts projected outward reap observable effects. When those effects are considered miracle based, they disconnect God from the natural world, promoting ignorance and war. But when our thoughts affirm goodness and harmony in keeping with the laws of nature, that is what they usher in. Seekers can test the effectiveness of affirmation in their own lives by working with Technique 3.

 TECHNIQUE 3

Affirmation

Affirmation uses the power of the mind to gain needed things—such as good health, suitable employment, or caring friends—or to positively modify behavior. Affirmations themselves are like seeds in the soil of the mind, harnessing and directing energy otherwise squandered in daily routines. They are practiced by silently repeating a carefully worded thought or by focusing on the visual image of a desired outcome. In either instance, the phenomenon that manifests is the world's response to your focused mind, much as a blossom is the universe's response to a fertile seed.

Affirmations produce results because they create a vacuum in your experiences by establishing a contradiction between your thoughts and other thoughts. Nature, abhorring a vacuum, then fills it with the strongest thought or a combination of strong thoughts, thereby eliminating the contradiction. Provided that you persevere with an affirmation regardless of any sensory data suggesting it may not be fulfilled, thus overcoming all contradictions, your thought will eventually come to realization. Old-time religionists, aware of this phenomenon, explained it by saying, "Whatever you believe strongly enough, God believes also."

Ideally, affirmations are practiced to manifest an uncluttered, productive, and virtuous life. However, they can just as readily breed anguish. Depending on the particular thoughts or images seeded in the mind, they may either attract a lover or destroy a relationship, induce calmness or stir up restlessness, secure the essentials of life or generate material possessions in excess; they may likewise either eliminate or accentuate unwanted things and habits. For best results, temper the power of your mind with introspection, remaining continually aware of your desired outcomes and cultivating an increasingly expansive sense of self.

Also reevaluate any inclination you may have to manifest things or behaviors for the sake of personal happiness. The belief that we reap happiness after acquiring everything we want, or after changing our ways, places happiness in some eternally distant future and keeps it contingent on positive results. So if you learned from the self-help movement, for instance, that happiness derives from manifested affirmations for healing, romance, prosperity, or personal conduct, reevaluate your past accomplishments to see if they were instead *outcomes* of happiness. Experienced practitioners of affirmation, aware that unconditional happiness unfailingly fosters success in the external world, look deep within themselves for happiness before using this technique.

The successful practice of affirmation depends on three additional considerations. First, since your experience of the world will create the conditions for your affirmations to manifest, word them carefully to avoid ambiguity; state your true desires; and to tap into the well of unconditioned happiness within you, give voice to your most expansive sense of self. Affirmations shaped by a narrow sense of self often generate results that cause suffering and further narrow the sense of self. Second, keep your affirmations deliberate. Since spontaneous thoughts uttered in a heightened emotional state may produce immediate and regrettable effects, review many possible affirmations before choosing one to silently intone. Silent affirmations are generally more effective than spoken ones because they harness more intensity of concentration. Finally, couple your affirmations with daily actions that support their manifestation. For example, affirming that you will win the lottery, a thought sure to be pooled with millions of other such thoughts nationwide, can only start to bear fruit if you play.

To begin using this technique, write down the things or behaviors you want in your life. For each one, compose a single-sentence affirmation such as "I am eager to question and challenge new ideas," "I am physically robust," "I am a conduit for wealth and riches," or "I act in the highest service of others." Once you have arrived at your affirmations, keep them confidential. In sharing an affirmation with someone, you risk dissipating a portion of your initial determination. It is also possible to decrease the power of an affirmation by revealing it to someone who may then affirm its opposite. A listener's well-intentioned thoughts can have an equally adverse effect. For example, a seemingly positive statement such as "I hope he gets better" negatively affirms that the individual is not well.

The best affirmations for health of any sort—physical, financial, or emotional—unconditionally affirm vibrant well-being without assuming the need for recovery. This means that if you are ill, do not pray for healing but rather affirm that you are already healthy, for then your thoughts and outlook will automatically focus on well-being. And above all, persevere despite any counteractive thoughts in your midst. An affirmation for health that does not materialize instantly is contending with harmful thoughts, moods, and habits of living in either the present or the past; prospects improve with steadfast practice. On a much larger scale, the same is true of affirmations for world peace.

When you are ready to implement an affirmation you have composed, identify its function and adhere to the practice guidelines described below. Affirmations have a wide range of functions and can be categorized according to the following types:

Maintenance affirmations involve the basic needs of life, such as health, food, clothing, shelter, friendship, education, and peace of mind. This type of affirmation can be practiced upon rising and before sleep. If your maintenance affirmations remain the same from day to day, avoid repeating them by rote, for then they may not take root in your mind. Instead, practice them with concentration and depth of feeling.

Ideal affirmations target harmful habits and the acquisition of virtues such as patience, equanimity, honesty, and healthy living. This type of affirmation works to create both the inner and outer conditions needed to support the new habit or virtue. Careful wording will prevent the likelihood of triggering an adverse effect. For example, if you want to quit smoking, an affirmation that contains the word smoking, such as "I am not smoking anymore," can prompt your mind to affirm the habit of smoking. A better affirmation might be "I respect the cleanliness of my body"; this thought will help eliminate the habit if you believe that smoking pollutes the body. If instead you want to quit because smoking is an expensive habit, you could work with the affirmation "I respect money and spend it only on promoting my well-being." Ideal affirmations can also be used to remove good habits in the attempt to gain freedom from all habits. When you are no longer enslaved by good as well as bad habits, you will be freer to choose your thoughts and actions.

Visual affirmations orchestrate future events, ideally for the maximum benefit of all participants. This type of affirmation has endless applications—from preparing for a performance to making peace with a co-worker or directing a job interview. Alternatively, it can be used to excel in a competitive sport. The scene is visualized, after which it may or may not be put into words. We all engage in visual affirmations spontaneously; however, when practiced deliberately and with concentration, their power intensifies significantly. For example, before a scheduled meeting with someone you have experienced as cantankerous, you might visualize him being ornery and tell yourself to prepare for the worst, actually affirming that he will be in a bad mood. Persistently visualizing a harmonious exchange contributes to a more positive encounter.

Article affirmations make use of personal objects—representing such things as a positive attitude, health, success, or courage—to automatically instill in the mind the desired point of focus. When placed in strategic locations, such objects can

call forth the corresponding affirmations in just the right circumstances. The most widely used articles for affirmation purposes include altars, pictures of saints, beads, and phylacteries,
in keeping with the necessity to project universal ideals onto
devotional props. To retain their special significance, all such
articles need to be replaced or at least rotated from time to
time. Otherwise, those hung on walls or doors are likely to soon
blend in with the wallpaper and those adorning the body might
be mistaken for everyday apparel. For instance, the yarmulke, or
skullcap worn by Jews, is designed primarily to promote the
remembrance of one's personal God. If worn habitually, as is the
custom among most observant Jews, this article can eventually
lose its symbolic significance and be seen as just another gar-
ment to put on in the morning. But when intermittently alter-
nated, its original function can be restored.

Gratitude affirmations, extended either verbally or mentally, give thanks for the good things in life. Frequently thanking
God for the food set before you or for the roof over your head
affirms the place and value of these commodities, thus helping
to ensure that you are never without them. You might also
thank God for giving you things you are without. Using gratitude affirmations in this way corrects the beggar's mentality
that has us praying for something we do not have and thereby
affirming its absence in our lives. So if you need a vehicle but do
not have the money to buy one, rather than praying for a vehicle thank God for it, doggedly affirming its presence in your life.
Your experience of the world will respond and, having overcome contradictions, will make a means of transportation available to you.

Though all types of affirmations are empowered by depth
of concentration and perseverance, each has an optimal practice routine. Maintenance affirmations can be practiced year

round; ideal affirmations for one week, then rotated; visual affirmations for one to three days for isolated events, or for one week and then rotated for material desires; article affirmations for one month, or less if an object loses its symbolic value; and gratitude affirmations spontaneously throughout the day, to correct negative thinking and to fulfill specific needs. All affirmations other than maintenance affirmations need a rest period to allow the practice to take root in the mind and environment, and to keep the affirmations fresh and thus effective.

Affirmations require little time, no money, and prove that you do not need to rely on unpredictable external forces to secure the necessities of life. The seeds of contentment, whether directed toward material gratification or harmonious circumstances, are in the mind.

A model of the universe postulating God's miraculous interventions relieves us of responsibility for our actions. Indeed, it is nearly impossible to behave ethically in a world where "good" and "bad" outcomes are determined by the guest appearances of a deity that reflects our own beliefs. A model of the universe accounting for the power of the mind, on the other hand, teaches ethical living. It reminds us that the laws of cause and effect are operative, that forces emanating from our minds have an impact on others, and that we therefore have an obligation to monitor our thoughts. At times this may necessitate changing negative and fear-laden modes of thinking so we can make beneficial things happen for ourselves and others. Ever mindful of the thoughts we project into the world, we deepen our understanding of the infinite substance of God underlying the cosmos and our ideas of self.

Changed thoughts lead to changed actions. No longer bound by interpretations of the miraculous—which have historically been used to divinize not only religions but also nations, castes, ethnicities, individuals, and languages to be used for prayer—we can begin acting respectfully toward all our brothers and sisters worldwide. Then every time we witness an event that appears miraculous, we will know it is not God breaking the laws of nature to prove his existence but rather our minds pressing us into action to help build a better world.

Revelation and Reason

They [the clergy] believe that any portion of power confided to me will be exerted in opposition to their schemes. And they believe rightly: for I have sworn upon the altar of God eternal hostility against any form of tyranny over the mind of man.

—Thomas Jefferson

Claims of revelation suffuse the landscape of religious literature. Divine truths pertaining to both personal and societal aspects of life are received on mountaintops, in deserts, beside rivers, and beneath giant shade trees. Their presumed purpose is to offer undeniable proof of God's involvement with the human race, of divine guidance, and of the existence of an absolute authority. The problem is that acceptance of these claims cripples the human intellect.

In particular, revelation is used by religious leaders to assert their right to preach, as occurred with the founding of the Mormon Church, also known as the Church of Jesus Christ of Latter-Day Saints. In 1829, Joseph Smith claimed that apostolic figures announced he was to lead a new church. His statement, like all revelations, could be neither confirmed nor denied; while a bona fide prophet would presumably have known if Joseph Smith was lying, his listeners lacked prophets to call upon and therefore had to trust their own impressions of him. Smith also claimed that the textual authority for his revelations was the Book of Mormon, which he had translated from unfamiliar Egyptian hieroglyphics that appeared on gold plates mysteriously entrusted to his care. But his inability to produce these artifacts shed doubt on the likelihood of their existence. Even so, in that time of religious uncertainty and political unrest, not unlike our own, the Book of Mormon offered hundreds of people hope that God remained active in their lives, that America's soil was hallowed by the feet of Christ, and that events transpiring in the West at the time of Jesus's birth resembled those challenging the Hebrews.

To date, the culture and language popularly associated with the Book of Mormon remains unsubstantiated. In fact, archaeologists and secondary sources deny its validity as a historical document. All that can be said as of now is that the Book of Mormon borrows heavily from the 1611 edition of the King James Bible and reflects the religious ideas of Smith's era through parallels and plagiarisms. Yet despite the still uncorroborated revelations used to validate its origins, membership in the church has increased by nearly 20 percent over the last decade due to its proselytizing efforts, particularly in Utah and South America.

Present-day Mormons defend Smith's claims irrefutably through circular arguments. On the one hand, they say that use of archaeological studies to attack the authenticity of the Book of Mormon is unfair because such studies are inherently flawed. This argument ignores the fact that the Book of Mormon, based on flawed accounts of Jesus from the New Testament and mythic stories from the Hebrew Bible, is yet another historical artifact. Mormons counter such inferences by saying that their sacred book is revelation and so was not corrupted by historical events. The resulting circularity keeps Smith's revelation hidden in the haze of the indeterminable. But it is also true that while they reject discoveries refuting their beliefs, Mormons actively seek scientific data confirming them.

This example, among countless others from all religions, demonstrates that thought processes conditioned by revelation have difficulty penetrating the realm of probable knowledge. In fact, in subscribing to revelation religious followers surrender their inherent capacity for questioning, doubting, rational thinking, and other powers of reasoning. Without the relinquishment of reason, a component vital to self-reliance, they cannot have unquestioning faith in the revelations of organized religion.

Religious leaders use revelation not only to defend their right to preach but to legitimize social tenets, further incapacitating the human intellect—and with it, a well-functioning society. In the nineteenth and twentieth centuries, many ministers preaching in the southern portion of the United States believed that the right to own slaves was established in their holy books; some even felt that God had instituted slavery and that Jesus would have been a slaveholder. Indeed, slavery is permitted in the ancient texts of many religious denominations. However, mistaking for celestial authority the cultural attitude projected onto scriptural accounts shows poor scholarship. And perpetuating the sanctification of slavery provides grist for the mill of social injustice.

Whenever social ideals are predicated on past revelations of divine authority, religious adherents can easily justify not only slavery but disempowerment, rape, murder, war, and genocide. Jails around the world are teeming with religious men and women convinced that God authorized their violations. Similarly, the Holocaust was fueled by centuries of "divinely" inspired anti-Semitic doctrines. It seems the motivation to do serious harm often emerges from the conviction, born of revelation, that such an act constitutes a service to God and society—an interpretation mirroring earlier cultural projections of bigotry. In the end, though religious leaders believe that revelation inspires virtuous conduct, and though it does furnish examples of ethical behavior when interpreted by ethical individuals, it fails to support virtuous activity when we are faced with the real challenges of life and see vice as the more attractive option.

Religious leaders today, in narrowly identifying with scriptural revelation while proposing social ideals, compound the difficulties involved in sanctifying myths wrapped in codifications of past prejudices. For example, some ministers tell their congregants that for every choice in life there is a verse of revelatory scripture to guide them, when instead there are hundreds of conflicting verses from which they might choose—as well as countless alternatives in the world of nature. In instinctively internalizing scriptural codifications, congregants end up bringing narrow self-interests in the form of antiquated biases and hostilities to modern-day society. As if social progress weren't challenged enough by judicial interpretations of the law that sustain human prejudices, it must also contend with small-minded interpretations of revelation that perpetuate inhuman prejudices of the past.

Since revelation did not successfully address humanity's past needs for a unifying truth, there is no discernible assurance that it can fulfill our present needs for one. Nor is there a way to bring revelation to the province of constructive discussion and possible refutation, or to weigh and wrestle with the social ideals it spawns. In the spirit of investigation we can, however, move forward by uncovering present-day appeal for this dead-end path to truth, observing its limitations, and, like replacing burned-out lightbulbs or flat tires, finding a tenable substitute that serves human progress.

What prompts people to accept revelation without question, and how does this conditioning silence the intellect? One impetus for embracing revelation is the human tendency to romanticize the past. Against the gray backdrop of today's apparent chaos and cynicism, there is special allure in identifying with the heroic men and women of religious texts. Their lives may appear more black and white, and their days less burdened with complex decision-making. Idealizing these epic figures, many people see them as better and wiser than us, and their societies as more cohesive. Adoption of their revelatory perspective follows naturally. But while swept up in romantic illusions of the past, and having surrendered their own intellectual faculties, these individuals often fail to consider that their scriptural heroes and heroines, routinely shaped by social and religious forces often alien to our own, are mythic inventions of the human imagination.

Another reason people accept revelation is to avail themselves of a behavioral code, such as Moses's Ten Commandments. According to the Hebrew Bible, the tablets containing them were inscribed by God, leaving no room for argument in the minds of the Israelites—or in the minds of their contemporary successors. A point overlooked by many is that if the Ten Commandments are worth living by they do not require consecrated origins, and if they are not worth living by then no measure of authority can make them useful to humanity. Though it is the right of all individuals to weigh the merit of the Ten Commandments, what counts is whether these laws constitute an effective code of ethics, not whether they are intrinsically valuable by virtue of their presumed origin. Nor does the belief that God inspired Moses to write the Ten Commandments grant them authority. In fact, this belief fails to account for superior ethical systems that, in requiring people to attend to the root of behavior in the self, override the self-serving interpretations possible when commands are thought to be issued from on high.

Revelation also has a seductive psychological attraction for people yearning to be part of a collective, as was observed among Smith's followers in the early nineteenth century. Individuals who suffer from feelings of low self-esteem find that gathering with others under the auspices of uplifting revelation can almost instantly infuse them with feelings of belonging to something greater than themselves. In this sense, the vulnerability to religious revelation bears a striking resemblance to the susceptibility of depressed individuals to cult agendas.

Other people turn to revelation out of a desire to satisfy materialistic ambitions. A revelatory truth attached to the performance of mercenary tasks is believed to grant them dignity from the outside; on the inside, it allays remorse after the exacting of revenge, offering the palliative "eye for an eye" (Deut. 19:21). Individuals striving to work for the greater glory of God's revelations tend not to see that they are actually working for themselves. Nor are they likely to acknowledge that, as the history of the Roman Catholic Church demonstrates, when claims of revelation are violently defended as if power, property, or money are at stake, in fact one or more such elements usually are at stake.

Then, too, many people pattern themselves on revelatory examples of holiness in hopes of living an ethical life. After a while, however, they may mistake themselves for their heroes, whom they frequently perceive as having risen above the laws of morality to which others must answer. Exaggerated self-importance sparked by revelation is seldom acknowledged from within. Only in the wake of numerous pederasty scandals, for example, did it come to light that priests may have internalized the stature of the pope, who, according to revelatory dogma accepted by many devout Catholics, is at liberty to disregard human-decreed laws.

A common cause for embracing revelation in the twenty-first century is the desire to lend meaning to one's existence. The New Age penchant for channeling divine revelations is one such example. In crediting their spoken or "dictated" communications to a higher source, mediums derive an elevated sense of their own purpose in life. But according to the cosmological structure mediums have adopted, their angelic messengers are little more than disembodied human beings; and based on the messages themselves, it appears that these beings may be no more evolved than their embodied transmitters. Curiously, few mediums recognize the similarities between the messages they channel and their own beliefs, ideals, and thoughts, or that a message is not authoritative by virtue of the manner in which it is communicated.

A second example of the hope for revelation to infuse life with significance is the tendency to sanctify weekends. Many religious followers have little tolerance for unreasonable concepts during the workweek, yet at worship service they seem to turn off their critical faculties and let instinct take over. Suddenly apprehensive about leading an unanalyzed existence, weekend worshippers may have no qualms about agreeing wholeheartedly with a sermon or prayerfully invoking their God's selective beneficence. Few, if any, notice this lack of communication between their hierarchy-based instincts and their more discerning intellect. Of course, if the faithful had the same high standards for their religious thinking as they do for their practical weekday concerns, revelation-based faiths could not stay in business.

A third example of the draw to revelation can be seen in

the multitudes of Westerners who, raised on revelation, seek to enhance the significance of their lives by unquestioningly taking up Eastern practices onto which they have projected revelatory holiness, such as yoga, Zen and other forms of Buddhism, and tantra. To many practitioners, such exotica ends up imparting exactly what they were hoping for. But the West's mystification of Eastern religions has repeatedly led to the commercialization of ideas, an outcome to which most practitioners remain oblivious. For example, yoga has become disconnected from nearly every spiritual and philosophical consideration, and distorted into a system of physical culture. Zen—currently associated with archery, tea ceremonies, passive forms of meditation, and other sense-bound activities— has been transmogrified by the addition of outer rituals and paraphernalia. As for tantra, it is often grossly misconstrued as a means for consecrating sexual promiscuity.

Perhaps the most compelling attraction to revelation is fear of the devil, revelation's own personification of spiritual ignorance and suffering. As is to be expected, submissions to revelation promise a swift escape from this dispenser of adversity. But what is the devil? Conflating the Judeo-Christian ideals of Satan and God, some Islamic literature asserts the devil is an angel that loves God so completely he cannot bear the thought of anyone else loving God. But if God is in everyone, this would mean the devil so loves everyone that he would strive to prevent human beings from loving one another, which is in fact God's way of testing people's love for him. One means by which the conflated devil-God might accomplish this goal would be to create potent distractions in the world, such as excess wealth, that can tempt people to be too preoccupied with warring to bother loving God in one another. A more insidious ploy would be to inspire divisive and conflicting revelations of God's will that sanctify people's wars over wealth by instilling fear of the devil. Both methods are geared toward preventing humanity from thinking deeply about life and from identifying with one another.

Once caught in the devil-God's revelatory trap, people's fear of the devil becomes fear of anything that might threaten the justification for wars fought over wealth. Ironically, many religionists come to define the loss of trust in revelation as spiritual ignorance and the absence of wealth as suffering, which at once pleases the devil and confirms God's suspicion about being unloved. The inevitable outcome of this reversal is entrenched beliefs and intensified wars, thereby increasing humanity's inventory of fears. In the final analysis, fear of the devil draws individuals to revelation by allowing the narrow sense of self to sanctify its narrowness through inverted nomenclature: calling ideas conducive to expansion "the devil" and ideas promoting narrowness "God."

To avoid succumbing to the vice grip of this devil and to assure God that we love him in others, we would reject the notion that God communicates to humanity through a small group of "the enlightened faithful," especially since it is so easy to counterfeit revelation. And to gain sanctuary from revelation's duplicity—that is, to take refuge from a self-image already narrowed by fear—we would expand our sense of self. Even when fear of the devil is simply fear of the unknown, as is most often the case, it can be overcome by rejecting the influence of fearmongers and getting in touch with the fearless, expansive self. In each instance, we achieve success by shining the light of investigation into the darkened recesses of the intellect, illuminating our inherent love for truth and the essential unity of the human race.

All these incentives for accepting claims of revelation—

from identifying with heroic individuals to overcoming fear of the devil—can be satisfied *at no cost to the intellect* by turning instead to reason. When guided by reason, we approach problem solving through direct evidence rather than handed-down claims of truth. We sift, analyze, and reflect on large quantities of data, then draw conclusions consistent with our observations. Because it is evidence based, reason forces us to think clearly, precisely, and unbiasedly; to develop ever-increased mental agility; and to arrive at original hypotheses, skills crucial in today's shrinking world. It is through the cultivation of critical thinking skills that we are able to penetrate the realm of probable knowledge blocked by the reliance on revelation.

Spiritual investigators would point out that revelation asks us to silence the voice of reason, the faculty of knowledge that speaks to us directly and informs us about bogus claims. They would argue that seeking truth is not a spectator sport requiring us to pit one person's revelation of God's will against another's. Nor is it about downloading conclusions from someone else's experiences. Instead it's about coming alive with questions—taking in content through the lens of our own experience and subjecting it to the light of reason by challenging every possible assertion. Progress is assured because in engaging reason, the herald of global unity, we expand our sense of self.

But coming alive with questions takes practice when reason's operating instructions have been obscured by revelation. Among those of us accustomed to revelation's biases and busily mortgaging the future by mining the past, it can be hard to know how to begin. In such instances, the first order of business is to decondition embedded patterns of thinking and perceiving (see Technique 4). Through deconditioning, it becomes possible to stop regurgitating revelatory ideas we have absorbed secondhand and begin developing our own thinking skills, and with them, a new verve for questioning.

 **TECHNIQUE 4**

Reading, Writing, and Reflecting

To elicit the truth of something or resolve contradictory ideas, freethinkers of the past engaged in dialectics, a form of dialogue that can be practiced with others, as in a colloquium, or individually. When practicing on our own, we engage in an inner dialogue that trains us to challenge our thoughts and question our perceptions. The more thoughts and perceptions we dispute, the better prepared we are to lift the veil of conditioning that has separated us from our inoperative reasoning faculties and distanced us from others.

This technique involves reading books that help expand the self, writing down questions they inspire, then reflecting on them. Contemplating your questions within the larger context of an author's questions allows you to uncover biases in both. Though it may seem futile to try to overcome conditioning by posing questions that have been shaped by it, comparing your views with those of intellectual and spiritual giants can immediately broaden your perspectives.

When selecting reading material, look for books that depart from your usual frame of reference. Include titles by men and women alike, as well as people of different ages, nationalities, and historical eras. Also read religious texts with which you are unfamiliar or about which you have not yet formed an opinion. If you decide to read the Bible, choose a translation other than the one you are accustomed to, or study Greek or Hebrew then read the Bible as it was originally written. The more translations you delve into, the more questions you will be able to formulate for inner dialogue.

Seek out a variety of genres, as well. Most classics, whether fiction or nonfiction, provide food for thought. If you enjoy romance novels, however, a valuable catalyst for inner dialogue might be Murasaki Shikibu's *Tale of Genji,* which at least furnishes a historical glimpse into the perspectives of other cultures. Provocative reading material can also be found amongst the writings of America's Founding Fathers, some of which have been suppressed because they challenge traditional ideas about religion. Thomas Jefferson, for example, thought of himself as being in the church of his mind, freed from the constraints of manufactured beliefs.

To further your liberation from customary patterns of thinking and perceiving, read several books that examine the same subject from different perspectives. Exposure to a range of views on any topic will increase your breadth of comprehension. This enlarged perspective will have you weighing the relevance of each and arriving at your own viewpoint, which may change yet again as you gain even more exposure.

Because books have a way of becoming good friends, choose wisely and embrace them open-mindedly. If you don't know quite where to begin, visit the library, read book reviews, or seek recommendations from trusted others. To make a book your own, scribble freely in the margins; decorate pages copiously with question marks and exclamation points; highlight segments worth returning to; and tuck in clippings, bookmarks, and other inspirational oddities. Once personalized in this way, a book is more likely to keep you engaged with its contents.

The writing portion of this technique awakens critical thinking skills. Writing just anything distances us from content that would otherwise remain in the head and largely inaccessible to us. It follows, then, that drafting questions inspired by reading material provides a chance to actually see our legitimate concerns, doubts, and fears so we can later work through our conditioning. And indeed, the questions appearing on paper open portals of insight into thoughts and perceptions we did not know we harbored.

To begin, while reading a book you have selected for inner dialogue, keep a writing tablet beside you and jot down questions that come to mind. You may wonder, for instance, how the author's worldview, life experiences, or assumptions differ from yours, or what sorts of conditioning the author has undergone. Allow plenty of time for composing your questions since some may cause initial discomfort as your self-image expands beyond its usual contours. Just as more time is spent digesting a meal than eating it, so are more hours needed to assimilate ideas after reading about them. Ideas that are well absorbed through questioning become part of who we are. At that point we start to view the world through them, using them to interpret the sensory data that come our way.

Once you have finished each chapter, begin reflecting by contemplating or writing several possible answers to the questions you have posed. Engaging with your questions in this way allows you to rigorously evaluate them. In contemplating every question, do your best to arrive at a personally meaningful answer. If a question does not profoundly affect you, dig more deeply and fearlessly into your mind for a better one. For instance, if your answer to the question seems to justify a desire, question the desire. If you have difficulty determining whether the desire is of a narrow or expansive self, see how it affects your perceptions of people you know. Remember that desires themselves are neither narrow nor expansive but rather become so upon mirroring one's self-image.

While reflecting, you are likely to encounter dialectic pushes and pulls. In such instances, look for a truth beyond these contradictory answers. For example, in examining clashing images of God, find a truth large enough to encompass them all. You will know you have arrived at a viable truth when you begin living it and observing how your self-image incorporates the interests of more and more people. Of course, the most viable truths open themselves to new challenges and questions as time passes.

With practice in reading, writing, and reflecting, you will be able to identify any attraction you currently have to revelation and how it has co-opted your ability to lead an intellectually and spiritually honest life. To question what revelation posits as unquestionable is to begin courageously thinking for yourself— a leap into the future for a self that may have spent years fearfully adhering to revelatory truths. Ongoing use of this deconditioning technique delivers the fearlessness that investments in revelation only imitate.

To reason, the world of revelation is a game of make-believe while the world of critical thinking is an outward projection of an expansive idea of self. Departing from René Descartes' dictum of "I think, therefore I am," reason reminds us, "From the idea of 'I am (the self),' all thinking arises." And while it cannot on its own confirm the infinite substance of self, in showing its kinship with that substance, reason paves the way for the finite sense of self to eventually expand its parameters to infinity through communicating with others as equals.

As such, reason provides handrails to a more just and

magnanimous society. Critical thinkers gauging the worth of an idea appraise not its presumed source but rather its effect on humanity, which can be observed and repeatedly tested. Claims exempted from rigorous testing—such as Muhammad's Gabriel, Joseph Smith's golden plates of hieroglyphic writing, a religious devotee's view of holy scripture as the word of God, or a modern-day medium's divinely relayed messages—merely reinforce the understanding that revelation does not exist, that revelatory claims are by their very nature subversive, and that everything has its source in someone's mind. A wise prophet, then, is not a recipient of sacred truths delivered from on high but simply an individual whose God-given faculty of reasoning has empowered a sense of self expansive enough to awaken intuitive perceptions. Every one of us can be a prophet of reason, a freethinking philosopher dedicated to replacing graft and bigotry with generosity and a global identity.

Religion and Spirituality

What do I want?
I want to free the earth, to free mankind.
I want to do away with everything behind man
so there is nothing to see when he looks back.
I want to take him by the scruff of the neck
and turn his face toward the future!

—Leonid Andreyev

The ideals of religion and spirituality—its timeless counter-part—are the same: both aspire to assist human beings in leading a virtuous life. The methods applied by religion, however, too often prevent followers from living those virtues. When ideals degenerate into belief systems, as they have in organized religions worldwide, adherents argue over them, kill for them, and die for them, yet rarely embody them.

A major drawback of organized religions is that instead of simply offering their members effective techniques for leading virtuous lives, they demand something much easier to muster: a profession of belief. To be a member in good standing, an individual is not required to be dedicated to a lifelong search for truth. It is not sufficient to be devoted to a universal ideal of God day and night, affirming expansive ideals for oneself, others, and the world; to be charitable materially, empathically, and educationally; to live simply and renounce sensory excesses; and to be humble and happy. Nothing is enough if you do not profess belief. But beliefs themselves cannot prevent unethical conduct. On the contrary, they tend to inhibit embodiment of the very virtues they espouse, by imparting a false sense of satisfaction.

Religious self-satisfaction is displayed in overt and covert pardons for conceit. Ultraorthodox forms of Judaism excuse worshippers' belittling displays of superiority stemming from their all-consuming immersion in study of the Hebrew Bible. Christianity, according to a prevailing interpretation of the New Testament, promotes missionary work in the name of the "only" Son of God. And Qur'anic references claim that Muslims, who call themselves slaves of God, are followers of the only true religion in the world. Content with thoughts of being chosen, saved, or truer to God than everyone else, people are unlikely to develop moral responsibility, much less avoid repeating unethical acts in the future. Spiritually minded individuals, on the other hand, strive not to enhance pride and arrogance but rather to acknowledge and dislodge them.

A second factor undermining the embodiment of virtues by religious followers is the belief in atonement, by which their misconduct is thought to be annulled. Jews, during Yom Kippur, are said to make amends by deeding the consequences of past transgressions to this day of ritual fasting and prayer. Catholics who confess are viewed as ceding the consequences of mortal sins to penance prescribed by the Church. Christians believe their sins are forgiven after confessing belief in Jesus Christ. And Islamic jihadists are not only pardoned but rewarded for violations against humanity. Such notions of atonement go further than failing to inspire virtue; they end up compensating people for their lack of virtue. Moreover, the belief in one person, such as Jesus, willingly suffering for the sins of others at liberty to continue their violent actions serves neither the cause for ethical living nor the desire for self-betterment. Spiritually inclined individuals, however, have no desire for God or an innocent savior to free them of the consequences of their actions; they would sooner look within and free themselves of the ignorance that prompted them to err in the first place.

A third challenge to virtuous living among the devout is that since their inception religious groups have repeatedly failed to model the ideals they teach. For example, though Jews, Christians, and Muslims in theory worship the same monotheistic ideal of God, they have fought one another over differing interpretations of God's word, each believing that God is exclusively on their side. The sectarian them-or-us dogma of these "select" groups of God's children has propelled a long history of conflict and of viewing war as its inevitable solution.

Why, one might wonder, do millions of people—many of whom seek to live a virtuous life—embrace religions that in the name of a belief condone such superiority, irresponsibility, and exclusivity? It appears that narrow self-interests reflected in the profession of belief has been a recipe for humanity's self-image to become still narrower.

Not all the fault for humanity's belief in irrational dogma lies with religion, however. Human factors also play a part, such as vulnerable individuals believing nearly any absurdity if it is repeated with enough fervor. Children, because of their impressionable minds, are particularly susceptible to this type of indoctrination. And since it is during childhood that the beliefs supporting exclusive religious identities are traditionally propagated, they can easily remain entrenched in the mind.

Another factor impairing the ability to assess religious dogma is the reassurance drawn from membership in a group. A belief somehow seems credible if thousands of others subscribe to it, particularly the belief that other groups are not as deserving of God's grace. Loyal to the gestalt of the group, individuals borrow from its numbers a myriad of justifications for unethical behavior.

In addition, human beings have a survival instinct wired into the primitive reptilian complex (R-complex) of the brain, a feature shared by crocodiles. The R-complex registers sensory information in terms of survival needs and is responsible for aggressiveness, the attraction to rituals, and the maintenance of social structures based on strata of authority—all features of organized religions. If you are within range of a stampede, this portion of the brain signals you to get out of the way. Similarly, if your R-complex records sensory input indicating that your survival depends on adherence to a particular religious dogma, it will signal you to cling to it. Unfortunately the R-complex, attentive only to our immediate physical needs, cannot assist us in identifying with individuals whose sense of survival is informed by other beliefs.

The most convincing explanation for why religious dogma is embraced by so many people may simply be apathy. Organized religions, by providing their followers with answers, suppress the urge for personal investigation—a tendency as natural as a child's questioning. The idle acceptance of answers can have us believing wholeheartedly in irrational dogma of all sorts, such as the doctrine of eternal heaven and hell promoted to reward and punish humanity. Few Christians ask themselves whether a fair God would compensate finite actions committed in one brief lifetime with infinite heavenly or hellish consequences. Even fewer admit that if passage to eternal heaven were secured by a belief, a just God would at least start out everyone with an equal opportunity to believe rather than blessing a small number with birth into a family of believers.

One presumed political consequence of this doctrine

occurs in the New Testament at the end of Matthew, where Jesus commands his disciples, "Go therefore and make disciples of all the nations, baptizing them in the name of the Father and of the Son and of the Holy Spirit" (Matthew 28:19). Spiritual investigators might argue that Jesus could not have made this statement because the doctrine of the Trinity was not developed until the third century or ratified until the fourth. This line of verse, they might add, represents not Jesus's call for his disciples to prepare themselves and others to be rewarded with a passage to heaven but rather the efforts of later politicoreligious authorities to promote a missionary agenda of conversion.

A later example used to support the doctrine of heaven and hell appears in John 14:6, where Jesus states, "No one comes to the Father except through me." Zealous evangelical leaders generally interpret this statement to mean that if you don't believe in Jesus you are going to suffer eternally. But in lazily accepting this explanation, congregants fail to account for the transpersonal meaning of the passage. Indeed, when mystics entered into an ecstatic state their utterances would be absurdly megalomaniacal if understood in any context other than a transpersonal one. Long before Jesus, Krishna claimed that though people might believe they were worshipping other gods, they were really worshipping him, the infinite God beyond all local deified images. Sufi mystics also identified with God in moments of rapture. Likewise, if Jesus actually made the statement cited in John 14:6 or declared, "Before Abraham was, I am" (John 8:58), transpersonal interpretations are most apt to render a sensible meaning. Personal interpretations, hinging on an acceptance of Jesus's words as literal announcements of a heaven accessible to only a select few, promote a narrowing of identity, missionary imperialism, and an exclusionary worldview.

People wishing to lead a just and good life embrace religion for other reasons as well, few of which awaken an understanding that the profession of belief in irrational dogma and the perpetration of injustices go hand in hand. Often it takes the discrimination of spiritual inquiry to see that despite their purported attempts to inspire ethical behavior, religious doctrines tend not to benefit humanity. For example, those encouraging us to do good so that we might be saved in this lifetime or another instead foster self-serving actions. Self-serving Western believers who attempt virtuous living do so to secure passage to heaven; and they strive to avoid injurious action not necessarily because it inflicts suffering on others but out of fear that they themselves might suffer retaliation. Injustices hidden from view are thus easily ignored. Self-serving Eastern believers, faithful to the Indian doctrine of reincarnation, behave virtuously to ensure a higher rebirth, often dismissing the unhappiness of others with such platitudes as "It's their karma," "It was meant to be," or "I accept things as they are." Such sanctified indifference ensures that injustices even in plain view will be routinely discounted. In identifying with our own narrow desires to the exclusion of others' needs, we end up not only mistreating others but affording ourselves only small pleasures and short-lived happiness.

Spiritual investigators might conclude that for the ethical advancement of humanity we are obliged to assess religions according to whether their values benefit humanity, as opposed to whether their beliefs empower us and allay our fears of death, appeal to our social and economic survival instincts, or claim to be beyond the necessity of proof. Individuals who still feel compelled to adopt religious beliefs might at least consider choosing those that are nondivisive and nonexclusive—that is, beliefs that best unite humanity.

A more enriching option would be to embrace spirituality, a path to expansion that actively avoids the profession of belief and therefore freely allows for the embodiment of virtues. Spirituality, at once progressive and exceedingly ancient, more easily invites the perception that virtue is its own reward for it automatically leads to the betterment of humanity. People embarking on a spiritually centered life base their actions not on simplistic models of personal reward and punishment disseminated by centralized authorities, but on broader ethical considerations that benefit present and future generations.

A criterion useful in assessing the ethical value of an idea is its effect on the body, emotions, and intellect. An idea that improves one person's physical, emotional, and mental hygiene is regarded as a thought that, if entertained, would enhance the larger body of humanity. For example, a person can determine the ethical value of the doctrine of heaven and hell by the physical, emotional, and mental havoc it wreaks on him or the peace it brings. If thoughts of this doctrine elicit within him fear or impressions of injustice, he would deem it a spiritually unhealthy idea for humanity to entertain. Thoughts of an eternal life to come, he might feel, generate perceptions of a life that is never quite here and hence a devaluing of this life; and the fear of an eternal hell, provoking sentiments of an unfair God, may stifle creativity or produce unhealthy explosions of suppressed creativity. Even emotionally neutral ideas can generate turmoil in the body and mind, such as the notion that the earth forms the center of the cosmos, that a monotheistic God created the world nearly six thousand years ago, or other concepts that contradict the preponderance of empirical evidence presented to the mind.

Ethical considerations, then, are nothing more than health considerations. They are not inscribed in a book or on a stone; rather, they are experienced within the human organism and society. A person living a spiritually centered life would say ethical thoughts, emotions, and actions are registered inwardly because the human organism is subject to the laws of nature—the only will of God we can know firsthand. From this perspective, it appears that cleanliness is next to godliness not because the statement was included in one of John Wesley's sermons but because a clean organism is one that lives in accordance with the laws of nature. Just as we avoid disease by bathing regularly, eating healthful foods, and practicing sound mental hygiene, so do these health-supporting customs keep us receptive to the positive and negative effects of ideas. The same holds true for our emotions and thoughts, which are best kept clean through the dislodging of those that generate discontent, conflict, or myopic images of the self. Ultimately, the only sacred book is the opus of nature, which teaches us how to live.

While ethical considerations inform virtuous actions, ambitions of the narrow sense of self can sometimes take the upper hand. Because of our conditioning, it is easy to gravitate toward conduct geared solely for personal gain, including the pursuit of pleasure at someone else's expense. The question of how to determine right from wrong conduct has baffled philosophers for centuries. Aristotle and others conclude that life is too spontaneously organic for a set of rules to work in every circumstance. Still others point out that though general principles such as moderation and nonviolence can be universally applied, such ideals on their own do not free people from the desire for narrow-minded personal gain. To ensure that our actions are virtuous, spirituality asks more of us, encouraging us to eliminate the desire for small personal rewards by disengaging from the results of our actions (see Technique 5). This pragmatic approach to expressing embodied virtues can assure us that our actions will indeed benefit humanity.

 **TECHNIQUE 5**

Nonattachment to Results

Virtuous conduct, behavior expressed for its own sake rather than for short-lived personal rewards, flows naturally from people unattached to the results of their actions. This nonattachment may come intrinsically, as it did for Mother Teresa of Calcutta and Mohandas Gandhi, or from practiced forgetfulness of the narrow sense of self. In either instance, the resulting actions are called selfless because they derive from an identification with the larger self of humanity instead of the narrow self of the individual. So selfless were Gandhi's actions, and so extensive his kinship with human beings, that through nonviolent resistance he succeeded in winning India's independence from British control and in bringing about pioneering social reforms.

Whereas the real saints of history manifested social change by working for human beings, people less allied with humanity manage to do little for our species. New Age enthusiasts claiming that spiritual masters they know identify with the entire cosmos often discover many do not even identify with their own students. As a result of ignoring humanity while proclaiming unity with the universe, these individuals' ideas engender no more love than does the promise of an eternal heaven.

To learn nonattachment to the results of your actions, begin by looking within and distinguishing universal aspects of your being—the sense of self, your spark of awareness, the planet you inhabit. Looking within gives you an intuitive knowledge of your inherent oneness with humanity; looking outside yourself may only give you information about your separateness from others, thereby heightening a narrow investment in outcomes.

Second, after taking any action, model yourself on your chosen ideal of God or spiritual perfection, and proceed to interpret the event through the lens of your expanded identity. In doing so, you will notice that the outcome, whatever it may be, is neutral as far as a narrow sense of self is concerned. Soon you will be able to regard all results—short-term gains and losses, comforts and discomforts, praise and blame—with the equanimity born of service to others. Even if your house burns down, the instinct to grieve over personal losses can give way to an evaluation of the event's effect solely on your ability to serve others and seek truth. The capacity to look even-mindedly on our immediate accomplishments and catastrophes, including impending death, inspires a desire to alleviate the pain and suffering of others rather than obsess over our own discomfort.

Third, cultivate an ability to keep your attention focused on what you are doing at any point in time. Whether you are eating, showering, or conversing with a child, concentrate on the actions rather than the personal advantages that may ensue. The more proficient you become at resisting the mind's tendency to gravitate toward narrow goals, the easier it will be to imbue your actions with an expression of your larger self. Instead of eating for your own satisfaction, you may soon be eating to care for a body that is working for others. You might even begin taking better care of your body since you will no longer regard it as a vehicle to satisfy the pleasures of a narrow sense of self.

Fourth, pay close attention to the effects your actions are having on other people by observing any changed ideas of self they might exhibit. This will deepen your awareness of whether others are truly benefiting from your behavior. Until the expanded sense of self is well established, old habits of the narrow sense of self can easily justify its myopic ambitions, such as the exploitation of millions of people in the interest of making millions of dollars to donate to a religion that fails to admonish exploitation. In such instances, any illusions of benefiting humanity will reveal themselves when you look at how your actions influence your sense of identity and that of people close to you.

Finally, practice nonattachment to results in a broader setting by deciding on a course of action or volunteer project that allows you to serve others unconditionally—preferably people with beliefs or cultural traditions unfamiliar to you. For example, Jews who volunteer at the local Jewish Community Center, while demonstrating selfless actions for the benefit of those with whom they already identify, would embody increased expansion and the capacity to assist still more of humanity by serving at a Muslim center instead, or perhaps a place with no religious affiliation. The farther outward you reach, the more expansive your identity will be, and the greater your potential for effecting change in the world.

If you are tempted to bring religious ideologies to people with different beliefs, steer clear of proselytizing. No matter how helpful you intend to be, such actions will alienate you or cause estrangement within the community you are serving.

Swami Vivekananda, Professor Bingham Dai, and other Eastern philosophers rigorously disapproved of the nineteenth- and twentieth-century missionary campaigns to preach Christianity to poverty-stricken people in India and China. The starving Hindus in India were indeed hungry, but not for religion; the Chinese converts, given monetary compensation for undergoing Christianization, were dubbed "rich Christians" by their fellow countrymen. In the Americas, where children of Native cultures were treated to a bed and meals in exchange for listening to sermons, entire generations were uprooted from their long-standing customs and traditions.

To ensure that actions taken in your broader setting are in fact selfless, first intuitively expand your sense of self beyond interpretations informed by your beliefs and desires. Next, detach from the results of your forthcoming actions, aware that nonattachment works only when you are no longer invested in the benefits. Then whatever you do will be in the interests of everyone whose identity you've encompassed. But even if you uncover either selfishness or a desire to help people with whom you already identify, half the battle is won, for you will have recognized your limited sense of self. You can then practice expanding your identity to include more and more of the world's population.

Religion, through its profession of belief and its system of rewards and punishments, often keeps its followers chained to the interests of a narrow self, while spirituality liberates the self to unconditionally place its powers in the service of humanity. As spirituality gains ground, we will one day see in the symbols of religion—the Star of David, the cross, the crescent—the divisiveness they reflect; then the idea of an absolute religious authority that indulges human pride and arrogance will seem absurd. Instead, people will take responsibility for their own authority over their minds, worshipping by wondering about the natural laws to which we are all bound. Nurtured by this progressive spirituality, we will look upon the natural world as a house of worship, the book of nature as sacred scripture, the laws of nature as God's commandments, the resonant effects of thoughts on the human organism as the voice of God . . . and our lives will be our prayers.

Terrorism in the Name of God

There were two "Reigns of Terror" . . .
the one wrought murder in hot passion,
the other in heartless cold blood;
the one lasted a mere months, the other
had lasted a thousand years;
the one inflicted death upon ten thousand
persons, the other upon a hundred millions;
but our shudders are all for the "horrors" of
the minor Terror. . . .

—Mark Twain

The human race has experienced a long history of bloodshed because of organized religions' political and economic interests. The use of God to sanctify conflicts over land and sovereignty beginning in biblical times continued with Muhammad's conquest of Arabia, Genghis Khan's invasion of Mongolia, the Crusades, the Inquisition, the French Wars of Religion, and the settling of colonial America. Ever since, monarchs, generals, and popes have condoned brutality by divine decree if it served their interests. Religious leaders, too, have prayed for military victory and seldom advocated questioning war's social destructiveness, while houses of worship, anticipating financial rewards from armed conflict, have repeatedly failed to promote goodwill and peace on earth. Piloted by political and economic ambitions, organized religions continue to subvert ethical principles and advocate violence in the name of God—an obvious contradiction.

Recent events illustrate the extreme ways religion can be

used to vindicate violence. On September 11, 2001, America was made painfully aware of how Arab terrorists sanctify death and destruction. In fact, the American media portrayed the World Trade Center attacks as acts instigated solely by Islamic fundamentalism rather than in large measure by the political firestorm gaining intensity in the Arab world. In retaliation, the United States launched two wars, toppling the governments of Afghanistan and Iraq and destabilizing the regions, killing uncounted thousands of innocent civilians and paying the price in thousands of American casualties, as well as fanning the already hot flames of Arab and Muslim hatred for America while claiming to promote "God's gift" of freedom.

Despite the divine dictates cited on both sides of this growing conflagration, its roots are more political and economic than religious. Arab distrust and contempt for the West goes back hundreds of years, perhaps to the Muslims' early-seventeenth-century expulsion from Spain. Later, at the start of the twentieth century, Arabs perceived the colonizing French and British as cause for their hardship; then beginning in the 1950s, they viewed the United States as the personification of evil. Americans were corrupt, Arabs believed, because they supported corrupt Middle East regimes and played war games with civilian lives, exploiting the region's natural resources for their own economic gain. Though such grievances were largely justified, the Arab world was too disorganized to muster an effective diplomatic response.

The mid-twentieth century also ushered in attempts to unify the Arabs socially, efforts akin to Muhammad's mission over a thousand years earlier. After secular ideologies, such as Gamal Abdel Nasser's pan-Arabism, failed to resonate in the Arab world, exclusionary monotheism consolidated poor and

relatively uneducated populations with incontestable revelations from the Qur'an. Following the addition of social services, fundamentalist organizations succeeded in galvanizing
millions of people to the banner of jihad, a crusade in devotion to Allah. In the hands of Hamas, Osama bin Laden, the
Iranian clergy, and other extremists, Islam was soon trans-
formed into an instrument for unifying Arab resentment
against the Christian West and Israel, in the process exploiting
jihadists for political and economic gains.

A striking parallel can be seen in America, where fundamentalist Christianity found receptivity among impoverished
and poorly educated residents of the Bible Belt, who had felt
disenfranchisement since the post–Civil War shift in economic dominance from a North-South to an East-West axis. Here,
too, exclusionary monotheism lent vigor to extremist political
agendas, empowering millions through social programs aimed
at increasing their voting power. In this instance, violence of
the disenfranchised was directed against people viewed as corrupting the moral fiber of America—because of skin color,
reading material, sexual orientation, or positions on abortion
and other personal-choice issues. Church life, offering its own
ideals of virtue, gained moral authority over a wide range of
circumstances to prepare God-fearing worshippers for the
"end times" described in the Book of Revelations.

With increased government programs in the 1930s, cor-
porations favoring unchecked capitalism aligned themselves
with evangelical leaders and Dixiecrats, widening the gap
between the electorate and legislators. Then, like the fundamentalists under the jurisdiction of politically motivated
Islamic leaders, evangelists were directed to consider the perceived moral character of political opponents a public religious issue. The impeachment proceedings for President

Clinton disclosed the degree to which fundamentalist Christianity was poised to align itself with unrestricted corporatism, funneling money into military and pharmaceutical coffers, media deregulation and the resulting decline in journalistic standards, legislation restricting income mobility for the middle and lower classes, and eradication of environmental statutes. Later, in an ideologically driven response to 9/11, fundamentalist Christianity joined with Israel in portraying Islam as evil, revealing the extent to which America's fundamentalist Christians, like their Arab counterparts, had again employed religion to sanctify political and economic missions. The result: in the Middle East and the West, monotheistic religious messages increasingly contradict the aspirations of humanism and expansive spirituality.

Israel's brand of exclusionary religious fundamentalism also is associated with political and economic agendas, fueled by interpretations of the Hebrew Bible that forecast the imminent arrival of a messianic leader who will fight to "reestablish" the borders of a mythical biblical kingdom called Greater Israel. To Jewish extremists, war is not only inevitable but necessary for the fulfillment of God's word, a belief demonstrated by an ultraorthodox Jew's assassination of peace advocate Yitzhak Rabin, Israel's eleventh prime minister. Like evangelists and jihadists, fundamentalist Jews incite divisiveness through expressions of bigotry, even against secular Jews; by appealing to people with limited education; by considering themselves legislators of morality; through striving for an electoral majority by following the letter of the biblical commandment to be fruitful and multiply; and by condoning violence in the forms of occupation of Arab territory and retaliation for Palestinian violence.

Everywhere, religious fundamentalism's defense of violence has incubated heinous crimes of increasing magnitude because of its long, unchecked history in thwarting creativity, gaining control over thought, weakening education, disseminating fear, and stifling the questioning process. Worshippers today, unwittingly conflating religious ardor with temporal ambitions, contribute directly or indirectly to the killing of thousands of people, the enactment of inequitable global trade agreements and social policies, degradation of the natural world, and the cultural obsession with strictly materialistic goals. Because organized religion interprets morality in term of political and economic goals, even an apolitical religionist's involvement has political ramifications. And wherever an unchallenged religious authority with extremist beliefs capitalizes on disenfranchisement, poverty, and the lack of a spiritually inclusive education, that involvement can spark acts of terrorism in the name of God.

The way to curb organized religion's political agendas and potential for abuse of power is by undermining the concept of religious authority. This can be done by embracing spiritual inquiry, with its premise of critically examining any truths proposed as sacred. Such an attitude naturally results in an expansive sense of self that can automatically diminish unhealthy social conditions and thus uproot the underlying causes of sanctified terrorism.

Truth seekers on the path of spiritual inquiry may find that behind the battle cry "My God is greater than your God"—uttered by religious authorities in dominant societies as well as terrorists—lie divisive interpretations of God that terrorize the human psyche with a sense of self so narrow it is unable to identify with many others. Seekers might also observe that it's just as likely for a dominant society to glorify war and vilify terrorists as it is for a disenfranchised minority to glorify terrorism and vilify their perceived oppressors. The greater terrorism, one might conclude, is the enemy within us all: the narrow sense of self that sees violence as a solution to conflict. And the way to combat this violence is by sacrificing narrow self-interests that thwart our ability to implement more life-promoting solutions.

Before beginning, it is natural to wonder to whom or what these personal interests are best sacrificed. In general, sacrificing for the glory of God is dangerous because definitions of God, especially monotheistic ones, often reflect a narrow sense of self. For instance, fundamentalists of all religions eagerly make personal sacrifices for the sake of fellow believers without considering the larger interests of humanity. Similarly, missionaries who seek to convert people of other cultures may claim to have humanity at heart in their sacrifices, but actually they have projected onto humanity their own narrow sense of self. Likewise, Islamic suicide bombers who strongly identify with the suffering of their people perpetrate acts of violence that mistake their projected personal interests for humanity's interests. Too often, sacrifices made for the glory of God are simply sacrifices made for narrow self-interests. When the goal is humanity's freedom from terrorism, personal interests are best sacrificed not for God but for humanity as a whole, as described in Technique 6.

 **TECHNIQUE 6**

Sacrificing Personal Interests for Transpersonal Interests

Sacrificing one's own interests for transpersonal interests prioritizes the needs of humanity. Transpersonal interests might include a more equitable distribution of wealth, a healthier environment worldwide, better education for more people, and mitigation of conditions that breed war. But until the narrow sense of self is dislodged through self-evaluation, sacrifices for any universal ideal will probably be of little benefit. Clear signs of the narrow self are exclusionary religious views, ideologies that depreciate human life, "us and them" perceptions, an unwillingness to take on challenges, lack of empathy for people of other cultures, and unwillingness to consider ways in which they truly want to be helped.

The first step in sacrificing personal interests for transpersonal ones is to explore pressing concerns around the world, perhaps through a global colloquium. Without coming together to share information and perspectives, it is easy to see conditions primarily from a narrow point of view and continually project our individualized interests onto the world, sometimes thinking we are saving people whom we are actually exploiting. A forum for dialogue about the concerns of people worldwide can alert participants to the exploitive policies leading to religion-based conflicts and terrorist attacks.

Ideally, the shift in focus to transpersonal interests will encompass concerns of the volunteers whom terrorists recruit. Understanding their exploitation at the hands of terrorists and factors contributing to their vulnerability can transport us beyond vengeful reactions to their horrifying assaults on civilians. Responding to terrorism with violence or indifference only breeds further violence; a more advantageous response is to increase public awareness of the underlying issues, protest injustices, and exemplify the principles of the expansive self in daily life. Sacrificing personal interests for transpersonal interests means to transcend the narrow sense of self and actively identify with more and more portions of the human race, steering humanity away from self-destructive patterns through increased dialogue.

For a more harmonious and peaceful world, it is essential that nations sacrifice personal interests for transpersonal interests. An economic boon in one country is not good for anyone if it negatively affects the health and well-being of citizens of another country. To prevent such occurrences, and ensure the positive impact of a country's policies on world conditions, citizens would work for social changes that benefit everyone. Possibilities include advocating for projects that satisfy the needs of the disenfranchised instead of allowing fundamentalist religions to fill the vacuum; supporting politicians who value alternative forms of energy; conserving energy so there are increased resources for world use; making sure trade agreements are not only honest and fair, but reflective of the wealthier nations' spirit of sacrifice; and leaving a healthier environment, the source of all wealth, to future generations.

On a more individual level, sacrificing personal interests for transpersonal interests can be approached in many creative ways, none of which entails deprivation. For example, instead of seeking happiness through wealth and possessions, you might pursue happiness through gradually sacrificing excess goods, living a simpler life, and sharing your surplus with those in need. If you would prefer to help others indirectly by giving to a charity, make sure not to donate to a group with hidden social agendas you disapprove of. If you own a business, recognize its impact on the community and environment, and consider sacrificing some of your profit for the good of the earth and humanity.

Other ways to sacrifice for transpersonal interests without renouncing a healthy lifestyle include participating in nonviolent protests, fasts, or vigils to bring public attention to various injustices and refusing to shop at stores or own stock in companies that are irresponsible. Sacrificing for a cause will expand the sense of self as long as the cause benefits a large number of people without discrimination. To make such personal sacrifices easier, more enjoyable, and more publicly effective, seek like-minded friends who will join you in your efforts.

To shift your focus more to transpersonal interests, educate yourself about people of other cultures. Information gleaned through reading, travels, or documentaries may spark an empathic response, encouraging you to help them improve their lives. Whereas the small self, unable to identify with the human race, may have you convinced that you do not personally cause global conditions of poverty, lack of education, damage to the environment, divisiveness, or terrorism, the empathic larger self assumes responsibility for them. To mitigate these conditions, you might sacrifice your desire to promote personal values and beliefs while traveling abroad unless asked, or forgo any inclination to abuse the world's natural resources and labor pools.

If through education and dialogue you sincerely arrive at transpersonal interests, it is likely they will soon replace your personal interests. You will then seek to satisfy your personal interests by working for transpersonal ones. For example, your transpersonal interests may prompt you to support regional farmers both at home and overseas by shopping for groceries with them in mind and voting for politicians who promote fair trade and fiscal responsibility in a global economy. Or you might feel strongly about making material and spiritual education available to everyone.

With increased awareness of transpersonal interests, you will understand how they can guide everyday decision-making. Then you will see that, in stark contrast to sacrificing one's life in martyrdom to God, it is possible to dedicate little pleasures and comforts of the small self to the altar of humanity. In time, you will automatically replace the old ways of doing things with new ways that are more socially and environmentally responsible because they reflect the interests of more people. Instead of only watching travel videos to learn about humanity's diverse experiences, you might imagine living in other parts of the world and actually identifying with these people; identifying with others means acting every day in anticipation of switching places with them the next day. And rather than generating needless waste, you might minimize packaging and reuse and recycle as much as possible, using fewer fossil fuels as energy sources and generally striving for self-sustainability. As sacrifice becomes habitual, your interests will begin to reflect those of an increasingly larger radius of people, at which point you will know inwardly that everyone is a victim of injustice and violence and everyone is responsible for it. In this sense, sacrifice is a proactive spiritual technique used to expand the sense of self.

As your interests shift to reflect global interests, people around you will mimic the nonviolent patterns of living you are establishing. Viewed from this perspective, sacrifice is a force for positive social change, inviting even enemies to embrace its principles. Patterns of nonviolence, like patterns of violence, impel others to exhibit a similar psychophysiological disposition. Both are contagious, exciting effects that can last for generations.

The more you sacrifice, the more you will be inclined to sacrifice, because you will be empathizing with more needs of humanity. In turn, the more you replace divisiveness with respect, the more you will know that your sacrifices are successfully combating injustices and encouraging universal harmony. By embracing sacrifice, we at once dislodge personal patterns of violence in ourselves, join with others who want to positively direct nonviolence, and pave the way for world peace.

Terrorism in the name of God is yet another example of what can happen when people become alienated from their inherent intellectual and spiritual powers. In this instance, the projection of exclusive images of God, refusal to question tradition, and surrender to an absolute authority may lead to a torrent of trained killers eager to extinguish their lives for a cause in which no one is immune to attack. Though individually, armed zealots, like other devout worshippers, tend to demonstrate great religious conviction, when they come together to serve an elite religious minority their spiritual sacrifices can become corrupted. Creative visions of past spiritual and philosophical luminaries have often turned into dictates for military activists, imperiling the intellectual and spiritual evolution of the human race. Even the view espoused by organized religion that the earth is a fallen world and that Christ will soon descend to save the righteous has the potential to endanger societies through divisive dogma and shortsighted policies. Because of the apparent inability of institutions entrenched in tradition to unify people's spiritual power, humanity is now on a destructive course that threatens world habitats, harmony, and peace.

Worshipping by wondering is a means by which we not only question belief systems devised by elite groups to pervert spiritual ideals, but also reclaim our inherent intellectual and spiritual powers. Showing devotion to a more universal God by wondering, we open our eyes to the natural world; simultaneously, we examine the past, challenge political and economic agendas of the present, and gradually change our direction. Instead of worshipping divisive religious myths based on projections of cramped self-images, we can expand the sense of self narrowed by sectarian beliefs and broaden our intellectual and intuitive perceptions until the ideas of self and ideals of God include everyone and everything.

CHAPTER TWO

A Bigger Picture of Human Progress

The Cycle Theory

I do not believe in the indefinite
progress of Societies;
I believe in man's progress over himself.

—Honoré de Balzac

Gaining a broader perspective on human history, humanity's relation to the cosmos, and the meaning of life helps us reexamine truths we have inherited. A wider viewpoint of this sort provides both a good foundation for questioning and resources to investigate intuitive self-knowledge. But questioning accepted truths of the past is challenging due to our cultural traditions. In regard to religion the difficulty is compounded by the assumption that organized religion is a divine dispensation, or at the very least, an integral and unalterable component of human life. Seeking God without religion seems impossible when religion is viewed in this way. However, by looking at the bigger picture of human progress it becomes possible to discover how today's dominant organized religions fit into a cyclical context, challenging the notion that they have a fixed place in human destiny.

Many scientific thinkers have been intrigued by the seeming fluctuations in human progress, as characterized by the rise and fall of various civilizations and the attendant advances and declines in human knowledge. In his book *Cosmos,* Carl Sagan remarks on the diminishing number of Ionian scientists from the time of the Greek philosopher Thales of Miletus, born in the seventh century BCE, to the era of Hypatia, a mathematician, philosopher, astronomer, and physicist born in Alexandria in 370 CE. He further characterizes the scientific attitudes of earlier philosophers like Thales, Democritus, and Anaxagoras as superior to the later approaches of Plato and Aristotle because their methods more often agree with modern science.

Ironically, Sagan points out, seeds for a scientifically and philosophically progressive world were planted over twenty-three hundred years ago in Egypt, where Alexandria's many libraries were a bastion for the advancement of knowledge. But in the first century BCE, after attracting such thinkers as Euclid, Erastosthenes, and Aristarchus, Alexandria's great library was subjected to warfare and fires, suffering the loss of tens of thousands of scrolls, many of which contained recorded knowledge of the ancients. Due to the survival of its smaller libraries and museums, Alexandria remained a seat of learning for a few hundred years, but rioting between local pagans and Christian sects eventually led to the ransacking of these last repositories of wisdom. In 391 CE, following a final clash between pagan sciences and religious ideology, Alexandria's museums and libraries were destroyed, whereupon Roman emperor Theodosius ordered them razed and had churches built on their sites. Hypatia, one of the last of Alexandria's notable scholars, was brutally murdered by followers of St. Cyril, Archbishop of Alexandria, in 415 CE.

Noting the lapse of over a thousand years between the death of Hypatia and the work of Copernicus and other progressive thinkers, Sagan asks why the seeds of knowledge sown in Alexandria bore no scientific fruit. He then speculates that the rise of religious dogma, the decline of Roman culture, the failure of Alexandria's scientists to challenge the assumptions of political and religious rulers, and science's lack of popular appeal all prevented the masses from valuing scientific and philosophical inquiry and helped usher in the Dark Ages.[1] Sagan's yearning to inspire a quest for knowledge resembling the one prevalent during the era of Alexandria's famed libraries prompted the television series *Cosmos,* aired in 1980.

Questions concerning the periodic acquisition and loss of knowledge also occupied the minds of ancient Vedic Indians, who offered an alternative view in a cyclical model of human progress called cycle of the ages. These stargazers, who likewise measured human progress by the acquisition of knowledge, proposed their cycle theory via an oral tradition that was eventually recorded in a text called the *Manu Samhita,*[2] after centuries of astronomical investigations into the relative capacity of the human race to fathom the mechanics of the universe and the mystery of self-awareness. Ancient Babylonians and later Chaldeans, Hebrews, and Greek philosophers adopted models paralleling ancient India's.

In their cycle of the ages, Vedic astronomers predicted that humanity's potential to investigate the cosmos and the self, and thus acquire both material and intuitive knowledge, underwent predictable periods of gain and loss that could be calculated thousands of years into the future. As unlikely as their claim appears to be, it may offer an explanation for the advances and declines in human knowledge not only in Alexandria but throughout the world. For example, the decline in Ionian science from the time of Thales to the era of Hypatia and its ensuing resurgence culminating in the European Enlightenment may have been accurately predicted by the cycle theory. Still, the value of this theoretical model is not so much in the possible explanation it gives but in the questions it raises, the context it offers for the study of human history, and the practical parameters it provides for assessing humanity's current progress.

According to the cycle theory of the ancient Indians, two ages of the gods—which Western astronomers call one Great, or Platonic, Year—equal one full cyclical precession of the equinoxes. In one Great Year, one age of the gods is an evolutionary period and the other is a devolutionary period. All told, in one Great Year the world passes through four ascending ages and four descending ages which, together with their Sanskrit names, are termed: Iron (Kali), Bronze (Dvapara), Silver (Treta), and Gold (Krita). The cycle theory applied an average precessional rate of 54", meaning it takes roughly 12,000 years to pass through the four descending ages and another 12,000 years to pass through the four ascending ages (see the illustration titled "Cycle of the Ages," on page 87).[3]

The cycle theory asserts that humanity's periodic gain and loss of knowledge is caused by a galactic magnetic field generated by a subatomic substance called prana, which affects, among other things, the human cerebrum and nervous system. The influence of this subtle magnetism can be illustrated by the following analogy. Suppose an experimenting scientist constructs a colossal sphere in which he builds a gigantic roller-coaster and places a single powerful light source at the center. You are in the sphere and it is floating in space, reducing to zero all gravitational and electromagnetic influences outside its perimeters. The only way you know where you are in the sphere is by the relative brightness of the light source as you move toward and away from it. The scientist then hands you a book, which you take with you to a seat on the roller-coaster. At times during the ride, the light source is too far away for reading, while at other times it is closer, so you take advantage of brighter periods to read as much as you can, learning about such topics as your role in this experiment, the other riders, the roller-coaster's movements and composition, the size of the sphere, and the electromagnetic spectrum emitted by the light source.

In this analogy, you represent humanity, the book represents knowledge of the cosmos and the self, the sphere is our galaxy, and the seats of the roller-coaster are planetary systems, one of which is the earth's. As moons revolve with planets and planets with suns revolve around common centers of gravity, according to the cycle theory so does our sun revolve

with a twin star in roughly 24,000-year cycles as both revolve around the light source at the galactic center. The Gold and Silver ages signify portions of the ride where the solar system is relatively close to the light at the galactic center, allowing humanity to accumulate knowledge. During the Iron Age, humanity is at its greatest distance from the center, able to understand little about either the cosmos or the self. Each age has an ascending arc during which the earth moves toward the light, and a descending arc when it moves away from the light. As the earth moves toward the light, humanity evolves because the galactic center has a pronounced magnetic effect on the nervous system, permitting individuals to reach more elevated levels of intellectual and intuitive expression by enlivening previously dormant portions of the cerebrum; these higher age humans are generally able to transcend earlier limitations in their comprehension of the cosmos and the self. By contrast, as the earth moves way from the light, humanity devolves, becoming more encumbered by physicality.

According to the cycle theory, 11,501 BCE marked the most recent start of four descending ages, signaling the earth's journey away from the galactic emanation and humanity's loss of intellectual and intuitive acumen. This arc of slow degeneration lasted for 12,000 years, making 499 CE the low point in exposure to galactic magnetism and the onset of the period Western historians call the Dark Ages. Thus, the cycle theory states that humanity's loss of knowledge began about 12,000 years before the notorious assault on science and learning that culminated in the destruction of the libraries of Alexandria.

In 500 CE, the cycle began its present arc of four ascending ages. The first, the ascending Iron Age lasting 1,200 years, was marked by humanity's general inability to fathom anything beyond the grossest properties of matter. The second age, the ascending Bronze Age, or era of space annihilation, which began in 1700 CE and will last for 2,400 years, is the current period. Assisting humanity's emergence from the darkness of the preceding millennia, it will usher in rediscovery of the finer atomic substance and electromagnetic forces necessary to surmount obstacles posed by vast distances.

Intriguingly, historical events since 500 CE seem to reflect the characteristics attributed to these two ages by ancient Indian astronomers. The decline of the Roman Empire, epitomized by the downfall of Ionian and Alexandrian science, left the Western world in a near permanent state of war and ignorance, with hardly a recollection of past societies or future possibilities. Beginning in the early eighteenth century, scientists made major discoveries about electrical, magnetic, and cosmic forces; greatly broadened the understanding of astronomy; invented the microscope; and developed breakthrough theories on the refraction of light. Additional technologies for overcoming the limitations of space were quickly developed and utilized on a global scale. Today, just over three hundred years into the ascending Bronze Age, we have television, telephone, radio, trains, cars, airplanes, satellites, rockets, powerful telescopes, and the Internet—all designed to overcome constrictions imposed by vast distances.

In 4100 CE the Bronze Age will cede to the ascending Silver Age, the era of time annihilation, which will last for 3,600 years. During the Silver Age, humanity will learn to control prana, the superfine fundamental substance that underlies gross atoms and is responsible for a vibratory-based universe manifesting laws of nature in variable dimensions of time. Concurrently, the subtle magnetism emitted from the center of the galaxy and responsible for cerebral enlivening will also become measurable.

Finally, the ascending Gold Age, to begin in 7700 CE and last for 4,800 years, will mark the true age of enlightenment for the human race and annihilation of the limits to scientific and spiritual knowledge imposed by perceptions of cause and effect. During this era, the finest substance of elementary causal ideas underlying prana will be intuited, opening doors to widespread knowledge of the substance of self. Ancient Indian philosophers called the substance of self infinite truth, existence, awareness, and bliss. They considered it the omnipresent and omnipotent Infinite Being within which the entire cosmos exists as only the reflection of an idea.

In approximately 12,500 CE, at the end of the ascending Gold Age, the sun's current 24,000-year cycle will be complete, signaling the start of a new descending arc through the Gold, Silver, Bronze, and Iron ages. During this time of devolution, knowledge of the cosmos and self will be almost completely obliterated from humanity's memory. Such knowledge, it seems, is therefore gathered not in the service of ever-evolving societies but rather to provide for the expansion and expression of the sense of self.

As hard as it is to imagine human progress influenced by forces emanating from the center of the galaxy, the cycle theory can be partially tested by looking at knowledge acquired by societies preceding the Roman Empire and the attendant destruction of the Library of Alexandria. In terms of mathematics, the numerical system of positional notation we use today, complete with the zero, was utilized in India thousands of years before the rise of the Roman Empire. Today, the West refers to numbers as Arabic numerals, but in Arabia they were called *al Arqan al Hindu*, Hindu numbers. In fact a Hindu mathematician, Vedic priest Baudhayana (c. 800 BCE), enunciated the so-called Pythagorean theorem more than two centuries before Pythagoras. Later, Babylonians employed positional notation but did not understand use of the zero until it was imported from India; moreover, their computations were based on the limiting sexigesimal system. Even so, Babylonians were more sophisticated mathematically than Greeks of the descending Iron Age, while the Greeks, in turn, were more sophisticated mathematically than the later Romans, whose calculations were limited by cumbersome Roman numerals.

Ancient India's mathematical accomplishments were paralleled by scientific achievements. Advances in astronomy had sprung from an introduction of the lunar and solar partitioning of the zodiac, the theory of epicycles, the division of the day into twenty-four hours, and the asymmetric circuit of the sun.[4] Like Erastosthenes of Alexandria, ancient Indians did not consider the earth flat—a notion taken up by a large portion of humanity during the descending Iron Age—and they also had sophisticated knowledge of human physiology, phonology, pharmacology, and psychology. Thus, the relative dating of mathematical and scientific achievements in the ancient world appears to substantiate the cycle theory.

From a broader perspective, the cycle theory explains why societies everywhere degenerated. For example, though some unknown society preceding ancient Egyptian culture must have provided supportive knowledge of how to build such architectural triumphs as the pyramids and the Sphinx, most of ancient Egypt's roughly four-thousand-year history entailed stagnation and decline, its devolution beginning as early as the twenty-fifth century BCE according to many historians. By the sixteenth century BCE, Egypt was practically a dead civilization, even though it lasted nearly another two thousand years. By 499 CE, the darkest point in the cycle theory model,

Egyptian society was gone, leaving no decipherable clues regarding its foundational civilization.

Another society reflecting the degeneration of a declining age is that of Rapa Nui (Easter Island). When discovered in 1722 by the Dutch admiral Jacob Roggeveen, Rapa Nui's Polynesian inhabitants had neither the ability to carve giant statues, nearly a thousand of which carpeted the island, nor the capacity to navigate the seas, another of their ancestors' achievements. In a degenerate phase, overpopulation and overexploitation of resources had led to wars, cannibalism, and a decline in knowledge and social order. Inhabitants of the island, claimed historian Arnold Toynbee, had "begot in each generation ruder and more incompetent offspring."[5]

The Mayan culture experienced a similar fate. Despite its rich inheritance in knowledge and traditions from the ancient Olmec, the Mayan culture, possibly originating as early as the second millennium BCE, underwent a steady increase in population and hierarchism during the darkest portion of the cycle. The Maya had erected immense public buildings at the heart of magnificent city-states and excelled in astronomy and mathematics, building observatories and developing a vigesimal numeric system inclusive of zero. Their comprehensive calendar, likely influenced by the Olmec, rivals our own and is today the most sophisticated and precise in all of Mesoamerica. But as the Dark Ages advanced and warfare increased, the Mayan civilization could not survive the chaos, the increase and subsequent dramatic loss of most of its population, or the destruction of its rain-forest ecosystem. With the rise in power of priests who controlled more and more aspects of society, sacrifice became prevalent, along with bloodletting and other rituals infused with fear of supernatural forces.

The decline of Roman civilization led to a similar break-down in the social order and ultimately the spread of Christianity throughout the Roman Empire. Philosopher-rulers like Marcus Aurelius had given the Christian cult little attention while the society was still robust. Toynbee wrote that the Greco-Roman historian "would diagnose both the Christian Church and the Barbarian warbands as morbid affections which only appeared in the body of the Hellenic Society after its physique had been permanently undermined by the Hannibalic War."[6] At that point the so-called Barbarians had been unjustly turned into slaves for a degenerating society, whereas world-denying and hell-threatening Christianity spread exponentially after Constantine apparently found it useful in reestablishing order and stability. Toynbee thus concluded, "The Athens of Pericles dwindled to the Athens of St. Paul."[7]

When human history is viewed in light of this ancient model of progress, it invites evaluations not only of mathematical and scientific knowledge but of theological and philosophical systems as well. For example, Hebraic thought concerning an afterlife degenerated from an emphasis on social conduct to the promise of an eternal beatitude coupled with the violence-producing doctrine of martyrdom and resurrection. This doctrine, appearing in the second century BCE during the descending Iron Age, replaced the Bronze Age emphasis on a moral code not associated with an eternal heaven for which people must kill and die.

Another example of degeneration in eschatology can be found in India's doctrines of caste and rebirth. In ancient India, caste was to be determined by conduct and character, but over time it came to be determined by birth, promoting an attitude used to justify social oppression. And while the doctrine of reincarnation had once espoused a progressive spiritual evolution, it degenerated to the point of supporting the decadent caste system through the reasoning that upward evolution did not always occur. Consequently, a person born as an uneducated peasant remained so; kept from studying the Vedas as a result of previous births, the individual was considered lucky not to have been born as an insect, plant, or demon. Today, freethinking Hindu scholars are attempting to rectify the caste system in the face of considerable opposition from those still benefiting from the social privileges it confers.

The Buddha, teaching his fellow ascetics during the descending Iron Age, sought to revitalize the ancient tradition of yoga, challenge priestly abuses, and offer a universal approach to spirituality. A few centuries later, Emperor Asoka normalized Buddhism, providing the masses with an eclectic and accessible dharma, a sociospiritual pattern of conduct. As the Dark Ages proceeded, Buddhism spread to East Asia, where the Buddha's message was further distorted and even contradicted. Now in the West, the Buddha's yogic technique and ascetic discipline are often misinterpreted by a consumer culture raised on monotheism, and the alliance forming between Buddhism and psychology offers followers a path not to universality but to increased self-absorption in which the effects of psychotherapy are now mistaken for enlightenment.

In China, the gradual degeneration of Confucianism came to full expression in 213 BCE, when the Ch'in emperor Shih Huang Ti burned the books of the "hundred schools," representing freedom of thought. Soon the past, so revered by Confucius that he had attempted to reestablish the ancients' sociophilosophical heritage, was rejected. At this point the humanism of Confucius could no longer offer a social solution to the endless strife of warring feudal states. The goodness of human nature propounded by the philosopher Meng-tzu was replaced by Hsun-tzu's view of human beings contaminated by violence, selfishness, and materialism. With this triumph of the Legalists, pragmatic Han Fei-tzu, who valued the state over the individual and considered even the relationship between parent and child tainted by selfish ambitions, had instituted a social remedy in strict adherence to laws based on reward and punishment—an approach still in effect today. Attempts to return to Confucianism during the Han dynasty were marred by the zealous New Script School which, paralleling the early church's treatment of Jesus at about the same time, deified Confucius and produced forgeries of his teachings in order to procure wealth and power.

Many devolving cultures of the past acknowledged the decline they were undergoing. Early Chinese writings allude with awe to knowledge of the ancients and its gradual loss; the *Mahabharata* of ancient India tells of the powerful technologies and vast knowledge of earlier Vedic generations; even the ancient Greeks and Hebrews kept alive legends of an earlier utopian state, as in the stories of Atlantis and Eden. But though these and other ancient cultures experienced themselves in a declining age, modern historians wisely do not apply the term "Dark Age" to them, due to their store of knowledge and perhaps because of an embedded belief that the acquisition of knowledge progresses linearly—a conclusion supported by recent centuries of rapid scientific advancement. Yet according to the cycle theory, in assessing the advancement of knowledge one cannot separate material knowledge from self-knowledge since humanity's awareness extends toward both equally. The widespread ignorance of atomic matter during the Dark Ages, for instance, paralleled global spiritual myopia.

Some philosophers, like historians, also apply an expectation of linear advancement to historical events. Georg Wilhelm Friedrich Hegel, for one, maintained that Christian monotheism was the culmination of religious thought. By contrast, the cycle theory reveals that monotheism and the exclusivity it promotes are products of intellectual and spiritual degeneration, with Christianity forming during the darkest period of recent human history. So it seems that the loss of scientific and theological knowledge during the descending Iron Age imprinted humanity with an expectation of linearity that scientific progress has reinforced.

It also appears that along with loss of knowledge, the cycle theory itself degenerated during the descending Iron Age. Distorted in earlier Indian, Babylonian, and East Asian sources, inaccurate versions of the theory emerged in the writings of Plato, Virgil, and Shelley. An Iron Age version appearing in the East most likely fueled the popular Hindu and Buddhist belief that today's world remains in a stage of degradation likely to last for tens or hundreds of thousands of years—a picture very different from that presented by the untarnished cycle theory, in which the last downward arc ended in 499 CE.

This distortion persists even though humanity's knowledge is advancing in the scientific manner associated with an ascending Bronze Age. Perhaps influenced by centuries of ignorance, many students of Hinduism and Buddhism conclude that present-day wars, corporatism, and consumerism prove we are in an extended Dark Age. Instead, such social characteristics could just as easily result from implementation of early ascending Bronze Age technologies that make the lingering myopia of the Iron Age more apparent and destructive. Similarly, today's environmental problems likely derive from scientific advances outpacing spiritual ones—another phenomenon to be expected in the early centuries of an ascending Bronze Age, during which relatively few scientists serve as custodians of most of humanity's material knowledge. Having recently emerged from the Dark Ages, we are at a crossroads: we contaminate the biosphere with carbon emissions and mercury, for instance, but we are aware of the dangers due to our expanding knowledge of meteorology and biochemistry.

Nevertheless, the twenty-first century departs radically from the descending Iron Age with its increased emphasis on magic, pseudoscience, and ethnocentric theological projections. So obvious are the advances themselves and hopes for a better tomorrow that in scientifically progressive societies around the world, younger generations view conservatism in the face of promising change as stagnant and "old guard." Signs of balanced progress include the following: the large amount of knowledge accumulated through the scientific method in a relatively short period of time, the widening interest in living in harmony with the natural world, recent tendencies to challenge past religious truths, the care for the plight of women still oppressed by religion, and the struggle for other human rights, as well as animal protections. Simultaneously, the grip of divisive organized religion is weakening as the ideal of a global sense of self strengthens; progressive forms of medicine are becoming more popular; science is no longer thwarted by popery; and the philosophies of ancient people are being widely explored and respected. The knowledge humanity needs for a scientifically and spiritually advanced world seems to have reemerged and simply needs to be made globally available through a progressive form of education that holds nothing sacred but the search for truth. Even though humanity has a long way to go until it is free of past ignorance, appreciating the incompleteness of our knowledge signals progress over the surety of religious beliefs.

The cycle theory, while offering an interesting approach to the study of history, leaves many questions unanswered. For example, aside from ancient scientific textual references, megalithic observatories, and pyramids standing in places warm enough to have sustained human life during the higher age's ice age, why is there little material evidence of higher age technology? The *Mahabharata* refers to flying crafts, described as remnants of both a space- and time-annihilating technology. But if Gold Age humanity had had such technology, we would expect to find physical signs of it today. Some people might point out that the cycle theory accounts for advanced civilizations such as Atlantis, where humanity's ability to fly became legendary, but without hard evidence the reverse possibility could also be true—that the legends of these ancient societies were fantasies born of the cycle theory.

Comparing aspects of the cycle theory with theories of modern science raises other issues. Paleontologists David Raup and Jack Sepkoski discovered that extinction rates seem to rise dramatically every 26 million years as the earth is hit by comets and asteroids. Astrophysicist Richard Muller further theorized that periodic extinctions may be caused by a star, which he named Nemesis, revolving with our sun in 26 million-year cycles and pulling the earth out of its normal cone of protection against comets and asteroids, making the planet vulnerable to extinction-level events.[8] The cycle theory likewise proposes the existence of a binary star, but instead of revolving in 26 million-year cycles and causing destruction with each one, it is said to revolve with the precessional and every thousand revolutions herald a new day of Brahma. This would place our sun's binary closer to the solar system than

Nemesis. Finding such a dark dwarf star might help confirm the cycle theory and possibly account for the gravitational variance recently found in our solar system.

Perhaps the most startling comparison between the cycle theory and modern science concerns the cycle theory's claim that radiation emitted from the center of the galaxy affects the evolution of intelligent life in all solar systems. Since the ancient Indians who proposed this subtle radiation did not say it was emitted spherically, they may have experienced it is as being beamed along the galactic plane, possibly explaining why they likened the center of the galactic spiral to the navel of the god Vishnu. If this was their understanding, it might be compatible with the modern scientific measurement showing that our solar system lies unusually near the galactic plane, to an accuracy of .001 degrees—perhaps contributing to intervals of a magnetism that stimulated the nervous systems of life forms on earth or the development of our sophisticated cerebral structure. If so, the sun's proximity to the galactic plane and the presence of intelligent life on earth are directly related, making humanity all the more rare and precious.

Other comparisons between the cycle theory and modern science are more problematic. For example, the cycle theory's mathematical calculation for ages is apparently at odds with modern calculations for the precessional. Its model of 12,000 years of devolving and evolving ages adds up to a 24,000-year precessional; by contrast, the current precessional rate results in a cycle closer to 26,000 years. This discrepancy raises questions about whether the precessional rate changes over time and, if so, the elements factoring into such variation.

Consideration of the relationship between the cycle theory and evolutionary theory raises additional concerns. Does the cycle theory imply that the bridge between the intellect of modern man, Cro-Magnon, and apes is to be found not in a missing species but in periodic evolutionary boosts? Did the human intellect receive evolutionary boosts from the ascending ages or was it sparked by a more active lifestyle resulting from decreased temperatures caused by the cooling of the sun? Though such intriguing questions cannot be answered with certainty, posing them opens doors of possibility, broadening our perspective on human progress through the ages.

Despite its limitations, the cycle theory offers an explanation of human evolution and devolution that is based neither on the whims of vengeful gods nor on sheer randomness. The people who proposed it were looking for global causes to account for a worldwide disintegration of human societies and galactic forces contributing to the evolution of intelligent life in any solar system. That is, they were seeking general knowledge by asking several small questions, unlike Dark Age theologians who asked grandiose questions and arrived at provincial answers. In this sense, the cycle theory bears the stamp of scientific thinking and highlights stark contrasts between humanity's distant past, its recent dark history, and its potential for positive change. As such, the theory can indeed assist in evaluating humanity's scientific and spiritual progress.

Use of the theory's model of progress furnishes insights into the ongoing dominance of organized religion despite the degree to which it runs counter to contemporary predilections for scientific and freethinking investigation. For one thing, organized religion continues to foster Dark Age beliefs in magic and superstition that impose a fear of questioning degenerate dogmas, such as Transubstantiation, the Roman Catholic doctrine that bread and wine convert into the body and blood of Christ during the Eucharist. Further, organized religion consolidates power in "select" individuals, relying on proselytizing and unquestioned faith to spread its beliefs. Since the majority of people today identify with a religion from the Veda-based Hindu-Buddhist traditions or the Hebrew Bible–based Judeo-Christian-Islamic traditions, many other degenerate theological and social doctrines continue to exist, including martyrdom and resurrection, as well as oppressive caste systems. The cycle theory informs us that such degeneracy continues because these dogmatic religions—formed, ironically, around philosopher-mystics like the Buddha and Jesus, who challenged religious superstition—have a common enemy: the material and intuitive sciences that grant individuals the freedom to challenge all accepted truths. Organized religion, it seems, remains dominant in this scientific age because knowing how to operate technological devices like computers, cars, and cell phones does not inspire an active investigation of beliefs.

Organized religion endures primarily by affecting social conditions and codifying cultural biases. Today's organized religious groups worldwide have thrived where others failed because they adapted to the ever-changing social needs of their followers, often enforcing beliefs within the populace through social incentives, ideological education, and coercion. They also addressed the common need for a sense of purpose and place in the world, helping followers define themselves in relation to others, mark rites of passage, and ensure economic survival. But throughout it all they undermined the spirit of questioning.

As the human race continues to evolve in the acquisition of knowledge, Sagan's hope for social and spiritual change may yet come to pass. Commenting on our hardwired ability to shape our institutions, Sagan remarks, "About two-thirds of the mass of the human brain is in the cerebral cortex, devoted to intuition and reason. . . . We have brilliantly deciphered some of the patterns of Nature." Describing the challenge before us, he adds, "Our global society is clearly on the edge of failure in the most important task it faces: to preserve the lives and well-being of the citizens of the planet. Should we not then be willing to explore vigorously, in every nation, major changes in the traditional ways of doing things, a fundamental redesign of economic, political, social and religious institutions?"[9]

Sagan makes it clear that since the human race has inherited both knowledge and ignorance, the continual reaping of ignorance from the past is an alterable fate. Just as mathematicians no longer limit themselves to Roman numerals but use ancient positional notation, humanity need not restrict itself to provincial organized religions but can explore its inheritance of universal spiritual ideals. The cycle theory may suggest that evolution of intelligent life is dependent on galactic forces; but it also stresses that knowledge is the highest aim of life, implying that organized religion is a product not of some perfect Supreme Being but of fallible human beings who were relatively ignorant of the workings of the cosmos and their own self-awareness.

Though science has dramatically progressed from the days when Copernicus revolutionized perceptions of the world and self by suggesting that the sun was the center of the solar system, our generation may never be able to confirm or deny that a magnetism emanating from the center of the galaxy enlivens the cerebrum. Fortunately, the cycle theory need not be proven for it to inspire timely questions prompting practical solutions to a religiously divided world. Challenged by the theory's radical views of the world and self, we can begin to satisfy our social and personal needs in more unifying ways.

Moving Past the Dark Ages

*The means by which we live have outdistanced
the ends for which we live.
Our scientific power has outrun our spiritual power.
We have guided missiles and misguided men.*

—Martin Luther King

Constant reexamination of traditional patterns of thought has furthered humanity's social and spiritual progress. It makes sense, then, that questioning assumptions born in the Dark Ages and gleaning advice from understandings embedded in the cycle theory might help us resolve conflicts in today's political, economic, and religious institutions. Balancing knowledge of the infinitesimal atom with knowledge of the infinite substance of self may also go a long way toward curbing humanity's new capacity for self-destruction.

In recent centuries, humans have gained an understanding of electromagnetic forces and begun dissolving the barrier of space. Previously, people were relatively unable to traverse great distances or even conceive of an airplane, radio, or missile though the necessary materials for them existed. Also, individuals lacked interactions with cultures around the globe, making it difficult to identify with them. Adding to the obstructions imposed by great space were organized religions' competing attempts to control the heavens so they could control the imaginations of believers, often through projecting a cosmos populated by a host of heavenly angels singing praises to God.

Today, the race is on again to control the skies, this time with weapons of combat and instruments of surveillance. Our military reach over vast distances has outpaced our ability to live in peace with diverse cultures. And yet, with our sense of identity extending farther than the range of modern weaponry, world harmony would be within reach. So it seems that while overcoming the limitations of space has the potential for oppressive military consequences, the mastery of space also dissolves communication barriers between cultures. Indeed, in contrast to the looming shadow of powerful weapons and spy satellites, grassroots movements are already utilizing technologies like the Internet to bring people together and share information. The better the understanding is between people, the more the self can expand since the whole world is only a phone call, plane ride, or mouse click away.

The expanding sense of self, in turn, is apt to shape the implementation of new technologies, completing the feedback loop. And once individuals are able to identify with all people, including future generations, uses of technology, naturally reflecting this broadened base of responsibility, will no longer threaten the survival of the human race.

Another potentially valuable use of space-annihilating technology is in the creation of privately funded programs that afford young adults from all cultures the opportunity to see the world and work side by side for extended periods with people of every nation to promote world peace. Traveling freely might also encourage children to expand inner awareness instead of spending years staring into today's foremost space-annihilating technology: the television. Excessive entertainment can dull the intellect, discourage learning, and narrowly define the self by standards of material success reflected in the lifestyles of popular entertainers who focus on money, fame, and sex appeal.

To further instill global harmony, societies could agree to standardize measurements and modes of communication. For example, people of all cultures might concur on the importance of implementing the metric system and a global currency, and of promoting a universal language as a second language. Since the use of English is already widespread, citizens of wealthy countries utilizing it as a primary language could both fund English instruction around the world and promote the study of other languages at home. Wealthy philanthropists seeking to encourage world peace through expansion of the sense of self could also help introduce students in all cultures to a greater awareness of history and ethnic diversity.

The adoption of a universal calendar would contribute enormously. While the time of day has been standardized worldwide and calibrated according to a cesium-beam master clock, currently Jews, Roman Catholics, Eastern Orthodox Christians, and Muslims all have different calendars based on local historical events, lives of notable individuals, or the creation of the world according to their particular belief system. A calendar based instead on the equinoctial precession could help universalize the passage of time since this cycle belongs to no religion, nation, or race, and is scientifically calibrated to the most universal yardstick—the motion of heavenly bodies. In lieu of the Sanskrit terms, we could name our ages and number our years by the changing pole star, a universally accepted astronomical event.

During the Dark Ages the inability to agree on a universal calendar resulted largely from political, cultural, and religious sectarianism, often reflecting a false sense of superiority. Arnold Toynbee writes that the Christian Church "succumbed to the egocentric illusion . . . of treating the transition from one [society] to another as the turning-point of all human history."[10] And though other religions created calendars reflecting their beliefs, none was as successful in globally enforcing its dating system. Consequently, the sun's sidereal passages are numbered according to the birth of an enigmatic personage upon whom the Christian Church projected irrational hopes and fears. But unlike past cultures that produced these calendars, ours requires interactions with other cultures; in fact, survival today is *dependent* on peaceful exchanges between all people of the world. A universal calendar would propel us in this direction, helping us expand the sense of self by reminding us that we are all part of the same human family and by keeping us focused on broader ideals of progress and greater harmony of purpose.

In addition to a universal calendar, moving past the Dark Ages requires a new relationship to its myths and other inventions. The ancients apparently lived without having to machinate personal points of reference. According to the cycle theory, there is no beginning or end to the cosmos since the substance of the universe is complete, reflecting a pantheistic eternal existence perpetually in motions of ebb and flow like the rhythms of a dancer. By contrast, Dark Age humanity, frightened by a cosmos whirling in continuous cycles, gave creation historicity by fashioning myths about a confined beginning and end of time. Ethnocentrically placing themselves at the center of a cosmos created by God primarily for humans may have helped them gaze at the vastness of the night sky without being horrified by the nearly empty space. These myths defined God as a creator separate from the fallen forms of creation and regarded the purpose of human existence as a striving to regain God's favor and divine presence for a future ascent. End-time prophetic scenarios, such as the Day of Judgment, the resurrection of the dead, and Armageddon to vanquish evil after which a vengeful God and the righteous would triumph, reflected the Dark Age need for stable points of reference to mark the end of humanity's supposed exile.

Thus, while higher age cultures of the ancient world viewed terrestrial and stellar cycles of birth, death, and rebirth as gyrations affording all of life the opportunity to expand, the Dark Ages spawned myths of the world as a stage for a cosmic battle between light and darkness, with human souls at stake. In the Christian tradition, Paul's belief in an imminent end to the world not only shaped doctrines of the early church but still negatively influence Christians who pray for the second coming of Christ.

Myths of historicity were often portrayed in stark dualistic terms such as light and dark, or good and evil. One of the first religions to make its followers aware of the perceived conflict between good and evil was Zoroastrianism, a Persian religion founded in the sixth century BCE by the prophet Zoroaster. Possibly borrowing the idea of twelve-thousand-year arcs of degeneration and regeneration from the original cycle theory of ancient India, the religion claimed that Zoroaster was born at the turning point of a battle in which the forces of good gained the upper hand. After an additional twelve thousand years of battle, Saoshyant the savior would come and rid the world of darkness. Followers of Zoroaster believed that his birth, not astronomical calculations, heralded the beginning of the ascending ages of goodness. But Saoshyant's victory day marked the last day of history.

Other religions followed suit. Rejecting the idea of eternal cycles, cults formed in the Near East around the hope that human action could accelerate the arrival of the glorious Day of the Lord, even if that action meant killing heretics and infidels who stood in the way. These cults developed into monotheistic religions, each of which determined that its followers were dearest to God and its efforts the most fruitful in returning to a state of grace. Jews, claiming to have made a pact with God and hoping for the coming of their Messiah promised by Malachi, composed prayers of praise to a God who seemed like a vain king. Christians, intent on partaking of a new covenant with God through the blood of Jesus Christ, cultivated liturgies to inspire humanity's escape from the clutches of original sin and eventual return to beatitude. Muslims, purporting to have the word of God's final messenger, Muhammad, divided the world into believers and infidels to convert the human race to Islam.

The cycle theory became a particular source of anxiety for the Far Eastern traditions that inherited it. Some manipulated the cycle to revolve around the coming of fantastic individuals who would put an end to evil. For Buddhists, the savior is Maitreya, who promises to overcome humanity's evil with love; for Tibetans, Maitreya will emerge from Shambhala during a time of chaos to summarily usher in a golden age; for Hindus, it is Kalki, who will come at the end of the world and defeat death, darkness, and other dualities. Many Eastern religions determined that the best recourse was to escape this fallen world and be reborn in a better one, such as Shangri-la, a Pure Land, Krishna loka, or heaven, instead of pursuing an outer search for knowledge of the world and an inner one for knowledge of the self. The creators of these myths failed to analyze human motivation and to acknowledge that where life is portrayed as effortless, few efforts are made, even in the pursuit of truth.

East and West alike entered the Dark Ages devaluing their multibillion-year-old world. Striking parallels between their end-time prophecies show that whereas higher age civilizations both reduced the dualistic forces of good and evil to a relative play of nature and respected the universe's capacity to function according to set laws of nature, they themselves saw the world coming to an end and evil instantaneously eliminated. Further, their attitudes reveal that a society's cosmological sense of time is embedded in its sense of morality. In both hemispheres, belief in end-time models promoted fear of evil and moral absolutism, depreciation of the natural world, and divisive eschatology, all of which disrupted the harmonious survival of the human race.

In today's progressive age requiring more sophisticated, universal answers to life's questions, spiritual seekers overlook the Dark Age penchant to invent ethnocentric time schemes, fabled places, and fantastic individuals holding the key to human salvation, preferring to reinterpret past myths as mere parables for personal enlightenment. They also recognize that good-versus-evil theologies and other end-time models fail to serve humanity's best interests. The dangerous myths that haunted darker minds can be expunged by observing the cosmos without religious projections, exposing ourselves to the bigger picture of human evolution and devolution, and learning to accept the cycles of time as cultivated in the practice of Technique 7.

 **TECHNIQUE 7**

A Meditation on Cycles

By meditating on cycles, we learn to accept them and change our perception of time, expanding our sense of self while making long time-spans seem shorter. Ultimately, we learn to see ourselves in universal terms and actively transcend the prevailing conditionings of our era, a significant accomplishment considering that even thinkers like Plato and Aristotle were subject to the assumptions and superstitions of their age.

To begin, sit in a meditation pose with eyes closed and

attention focused on the forehead, mentally aware of your breathing, which represents the cycle of existence that began with your birth and will end with your death. As you breathe in oxygen and breathe out carbon waste, realize that life and death are in the body and that breath is born from both. Breathing is a cycle we accept as part of the human microcosm.

While "watching" your breath with your attention focused on your forehead, allow other cycles to come to mind, such as day and night, the moon and the tides, the seasons, the zodiac, and the equinoxes. Calculate your birth date in terms of the cycle theory (2000 CE was roughly 300 Bronze Age). Gain a perspective of your lifetime within the current ascending precessional arc. Explore what the concept of endless cycles means in relation to your finite life and how it challenges your sense of self.

As you continue to watch your breath, imagine yourself in a spaceship approaching the speed of light, the only absolute in this world of change. You are in the captain's chair aware that with each breath, years are going by for the rest of humanity. As you go faster, almost becoming a light ray yourself, picture a million earth years going by with every breath.

Next, contemplate the idea that relative time is a function not only of velocity but of the mind. To start, regulate your breathing by taking long, full, and slow inhalations through your nostrils, holding your breath for a few moments, then exhaling through your mouth. While regulating your breath, picture yourself approaching the speed of light by accelerating your mind in concentrative stillness so your breaths can encompass increasingly vast time-spans. As your mind becomes more and more focused, imagine that with every breath an hour goes by, then a day, and finally a month of human activity.

Now, move your attention up the spine to your brain while inhaling and, after holding your breath for a few moments and focusing on the gentle pressure at your forehead, down the spine to your tailbone while exhaling. At the same time, imagine that with every breath one year passes: six months with the inhalation and six more with the exhalation. Can you imagine galaxies being born with your inhalation, sustained for billions of years as you hold your breath, and gradually dying with your exhalation? When your breathing dramatically slows and your mind begins to melt away in perfect concentration on the forehead, hours may feel like moments and you can experience entire ages coming and going with your breaths.

The ancient science of intuition compared the human spine and brain to the four ages, with the cerebral and medullar plexuses representing the Gold Age, the cervical and dorsal plexuses representing the Silver Age, the lumbar and sacral plexuses representing the Bronze Age, and the coccygeal plexus representing the Iron Age (see the illustration titled "Anatomy of Intuition," on page 113). According to these scientists, humans untrained in controlling the energy that flows in the spine and brain can know only what is dictated by the age in which they live. So they devised techniques such as this one to direct nervous energy to the brain and enliven the cerebrum and its outer layer, the cerebral cortex, allowing practitioners to see the universe through the eyes of a Gold Age human being.

Once you cease to battle time and begin accepting the cycles of life and the changes they bring, you can expand your sense of self by imagining yourself extending across the universe with your slow, even breaths reflecting cycles of phenomenal existence. Finally, if you center your attention on the cerebrum, gradually reducing the influence of time as you increase your intuitive capacity, you can shoot through the roof of impositions that time places on your faculties of perception.

The recognition of cyclical patterns illuminates a fundamental difference in cultural backdrops between the East's Veda-based religions and the West's Hebrew Bible–based religions, and helps explain the growing interest in Eastern thought among Westerners in the current progressive period. Interestingly, even though Vedic India predates the Hebraic tradition by only several thousand years, that brief span of time spelled the difference between a higher age and a dark age. And though Hinduism and Buddhism gradually formed and declined thousands of years later, their roots in the higher age Vedas may explain why these religions are now receiving more attention in the West and how they created cultures more contemplative than European societies.

Also intriguing is the fact that while Eastern higher age spiritual pursuits degenerated during the Dark Ages into methods of mind-numbing meditation, outer rituals, and abject surrender to one's fate, wars of faith rarely appear in the East. In fact, the Chinese were able to place Buddhism, Confucianism, and Taoism peacefully side by side. The climax of antagonism between Hinduism and Buddhism came in the ninth-century CE writings of Adi Sankara who, seeing the degeneration that had crept into Buddhism, worked to assimilate Buddhists back into the fold of Vedanta, the ancient philosophy taught by the Buddha. The conflict between Hinduism and Buddhism helped prepare for the emergence of one of the world's greatest philosophers, suggesting that though the two religions diverged and degenerated, their roots in the higher age Vedas inspired a potential for peaceful resolution in the East.

By contrast, wars of faith have run rampant in the monotheistic West, precipitating endless violence and strife. Not even Jesus's universal ideals could prevent Christianity's participation in the Crusades, the Inquisition, conquistador

ANATOMY OF INTUITION

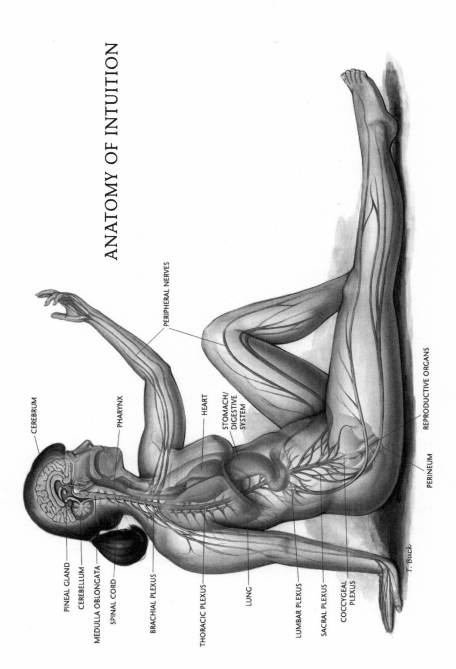

CEREBRUM

PINEAL GLAND
CEREBELLUM
MEDULLA OBLONGATA
SPINAL CORD

PHARYNX

BRACHIAL PLEXUS

PERIPHERAL NERVES

THORACIC PLEXUS

HEART

STOMACH/
DIGESTIVE
SYSTEM

LUNG

LUMBAR PLEXUS

SACRAL PLEXUS

COCCYGEAL
PLEXUS

REPRODUCTIVE ORGANS

PERINEUM

T. Buck

expeditions, antiscientific trends, colonialism, disrespectful missionary campaigns, slavery, pogroms and the Holocaust, and two world wars. Islam, for its part, promotes jihad by formally dividing the world into a realm of believers and a realm of war. The ongoing antagonisms triggered by these religions are unsurprising considering that their roots stretch back not to the higher age Vedas but to the Dark Age Hebrew Bible, a book that recounts a tribal war god's ambition to be regarded as God of the universe.

With the years 700 BCE to 499 CE marking a time of devolving societies according to both the cycle theory and historical records, the religions established during that time must be carefully scrutinized if we are to move past their accepted truths. In view of the dangers humanity is presently facing as a result of their perpetuation, failure to question them is tantamount to consenting to murder. Blind acceptance of end-time scenarios, for one, turns these plot lines into self-fulfilling prophecies.

Just as science has rapidly erased centuries of religious antagonism toward scientific investigation, so might spirituality, when approached methodically, quickly remove the darkness of religious myths. If the cycle theory is right, the responsibility for casting off this darkness has been placed squarely on our shoulders; and supported by a global awakening to the self's capacity for expansion, we will have accomplished what earlier generations could not. If the cycle theory is faulty, we can still effectively embrace its promise as our own expansive self-fulfilling prophecy.

Avenues to Knowledge

It is said that desire for knowledge lost us
the Eden of the past;
but whether that is true or not, it will certainly
give us the Eden of the future.

—Robert G. Ingersoll

Before humanity embarks on its next upgrade by balancing material knowledge with self-knowledge, the spiritual explorer might bear in mind a few guiding questions: What is knowledge? Do beliefs, sensory information, and thoughts constitute knowledge? What distinguishes self-knowledge from material knowledge? Can the mind uncover the meaning of existence and other absolutes? The rigorous examination exercised while facing these questions gradually erodes religious faith and helps construct, in its stead, a base for investigating the seemingly divergent avenues to material knowledge and self-knowledge.

A good way to begin investigating the nature of knowledge is through a historical review of knowledge acquired in the West. The modern scientific method was born in the fifth century BCE in Ionia, where ancient Egyptian and Indian influences inspired a surge in philosophical and scientific investigation. Spurred on by Ionia's cultural diversity, freedom from conformity, and widespread literacy, coupled with its citizens' inclination to challenge ideas, Greek philosophers pronounced the cosmos knowable by the human intellect. When Ionian science began showing signs of decline in the work of its early exemplars and their disciples, magic, organized religion, and pseudoscience gained footing. Philosophers like Plato divorced spirit from matter. Pythagoreans preferred thinking about the heavens rather than observing them, a tendency later echoed by Christian theologians who considered Aristotle and the New Testament authorities on astronomy. While Pythagoras and Plato advanced science, they also undermined scientific investigation by suppressing facts that did not fit their theories, projecting perfect worlds that disagreed with empirical evidence, and refraining from objective experimentation.

The onset of the Dark Ages ushered in an incapacity to critically assess authoritarian declarations, which became so intense that reason was soon decried, blind faith exalted, and theological inconsistencies sanctified as divine mysteries. Answers to the question What is God? originated in faith, leaving little room for the unbiased pursuit of knowledge for its own sake. Theologians inattentive to their motivations devised ethnocentric models describing the workings of the world and humanity's place in the cosmos, many of which still retain their authority. Theological models implicitly asserted that there is more meaning to humanity's material existence than sensory organs alone can verify, but then fostered the world-demeaning belief that the material universe and ephemeral human beings are imperfect and that a changeless meaning should be sought apart from matter. Few theologians entertained the possibility that there may be more meaning to matter than meets the eye or that matter might arise from the changeless world of infinite being, or God.

In the fifteenth century, belief in magic began to give way to a rebirth of the Ionian spirit of science, breaking the shackles religion had placed on it. Scientists uncovered worlds hidden in matter, theorizing an inherent simplicity and unity in nature and rejecting the theological tendency to view natural forces as projections of a local god. Traveling past edges of the known world in search of greater universal truths, scientists focused on unbiased investigations, in contrast to theologians who defended scriptural models through faith.

Today, centuries after these conflicts between science and organized religion, disagreements still exist. Despite recent scientific successes in revealing the mechanics of the cosmos, organized religions, popularized mystical traditions, and New Age spiritual movements largely reject the scientific method: religionists tend to pursue a doubt-free faith; mysticism enthusiasts often confuse mystified anecdotes, ecstatic and cathartic exercises, and coded languages for avenues to infinite knowledge; and New Age adherents routinely romanticize exotica and esoterica, whether or not they constitute tested knowledge.

At the same time, there is reason to question the scientific method for it repeatedly confirms the intellect's limitations in knowing the cosmos absolutely and directly. Not only is knowledge based on sensory data unable to furnish a final verdict regarding the substance of the cosmos, but the finite intellect cannot fathom an absolute truth, making it impossible for material science to give enduring and universal meaning to human existence. In other words, as tempting as it may be to regard the discovery of a universal constant as the equivalent of direct knowledge of the universe, information about *how* the cosmos operates should not be mistaken for an understanding of *why* it exists. The best that science can offer in the search for universal meaning to human life is a question mark. Still, science effectively assists in analyzing data to extract useful information, predict events, explore technological pursuits, and examine beliefs advocated by organized religions.

Secular humanists, too, played a significant role in critiquing theological models. Paralleling advances in science, outspoken philosophers like François-Marie Voltaire, Robert Ingersoll, H. L. Mencken, and Bertrand Russell, repulsed by the dogma of religious institutions, used critical thinking to raise important questions about the meaning of existence. And despite the efforts of religions to suppress their works, these and other secular humanists partially wrested the monopoly on spirituality from religion. However, due to religionists' sensitivity to criticism, a misplaced tolerance for religious beliefs, the prevalent entertainment culture, and low educational standards, relatively few people were exposed to these philosophical challenges and religion largely remained the assumed root of goodness and truth.

Eventually, though the Catholic Church had fought against early scientific advances threatening the validity of its worldview, the appearance of unquestioned technologies promised a futuristic new world. In response, humanity began to speed along the avenue to material knowledge while faltering on the avenue to self-knowledge, which was obstructed by the prevailing Dark Age perspective mired in greed. For people influenced by the "why" of world-demeaning theologies, superstition, and exclusionary belief systems, technology became their modern version of magic capable of satisfying desires and solving problems. But the deficiencies in self-knowledge led to shortsighted applications of this technology, often resulting in machinery of murder that caused crises increasingly more difficult to resolve. Many applications were made with convenience and profit in mind. Deforestation was preferred over the cultivation of hemp; pharmaceutical drugs were promoted as miracle cures; power to cities and fuel for transportation were dispatched without regard for their environmental impact, causing catastrophes and wasting resources on dangerous or dead-end technologies that profited an elite few. Because scientists most influential in these programs often fought as "hired mercenaries" in a technology-driven economic war zone, the implementation of science for purposes of advancing expansive self-knowledge to this day has not been actualized.

Twenty-first-century humanity has instead inherited the struggle between Dark Age religious myopia attempting a last-ditch effort to claim the world as God's kingdom and the more recently awakened reasoning of secular humanists who see God in humanity. But with today's advanced weaponry, fundamentalists on all sides may have the capacity to decide the world will be God's kingdom or nothing.

This global struggle is mirrored in America, a microcosm fighting its own ideological war. Here, Thomas Jefferson's secular humanism has penetrated the hearts and minds of millions, while followers of religious fundamentalism still dream of culturally winning the civil war against Lincoln's enduring spirituality. However, all Americans can win the battle against narrowness by gaining self-knowledge and using it to inspire humanitarian ideas of God and country. Increased self-knowledge, manifested globally, could then guide new applications of science and offer a universal meaning to human existence that is in keeping with both reason and the innate capacity of the heart to identify with all of life.

The first step in investigating the avenue to self-knowledge is to reject biases and refuse to accept anything on authority. As children, we picked up initial information about the world from the ideas of parents, peers, teachers, and religious leaders. Buried within the storehouse of this limiting information are beliefs passed down to us as truths. As we age, misguided ideas of self become firmly rooted and used to assess views introduced over time. Meanwhile, the world deceptively confirms our ideas simply because we use them to interpret sensory data. To counteract these early influences and question the nature of self, it is necessary to gain a wider perspective on human nature, culture, and history. For example, if you wish to focus on the idea of God, self-study begins with an investigation into the many ideas of God that humanity has developed. Similarly, to grapple with the idea of mortality, self-study calls for observing life before deciding on beliefs about death. With sincere questioning, self-study eventually reveals that ideas of the self have their roots in conditioning and notions of finitude.

The second step in exploring the avenue to self-knowledge is to differentiate between intuition and cognitive instruments employed for gathering knowledge of the world, such as the senses, feelings, and intellect. Sensory information, acquired about an object, for instance, assumes an individuated sense of self observing the world but is incapable of revealing anything about the underlying substance of self. Feelings establish awareness of a world reflecting the beliefs of an individuated self. The intellect interprets the sensory data, as do feelings, though they can trump the intellectual response and color it. But while each generation of material scientists builds upon the work of its predecessors, a million generations of scientists relying on five senses, feelings, and an intellect would be insufficient for acquiring significant knowledge of an infinite self. Even if the substance of self were quantifiable, its measurements would have to pass through the senses, feelings, and intellect; but the senses register little of the world, neither feelings nor the beliefs they reflect constitute direct knowledge of the objects inspiring them, and the intellect interprets that meager data according to a conditioned idea of self. Sensory data, then, even when aided by microscopes and telescopes, provides little information for the self to make any final determinations regarding the nature of its own cognition or presence in the cosmos. Intuition, on the other hand, penetrates the sense of self in order to derive knowledge of the infinite substance of self.

The third step in appraising self-knowledge is to recognize, through reason, that infinite self-knowledge represents a human potential that transcends the finite knowledge of an expansive self identifying with all of humanity. While earlier steps on the avenue to self-knowledge may expand the idea of self beyond historical codifications of religious, racial, and cultural prejudices, they cannot help us realize the infinite substance of self behind all seemingly individuated selves since they are taken in the footwear of finite faculties. Guided instead by intuition, we move beyond an expansive sense of self and begin identifying with the infinite substance of self underlying the cosmos.

These three steps gradually reveal that neither religious faith nor the sensory world is sufficient for ascribing an absolute and universal meaning to human existence. Meanings based on faith show a strong contradiction with reason, the sense of justice, and the ideal of the expansive self. And meanings drawn from sensory data cannot be entrusted with finality because the conditioned sense of self precedes and naturally interprets sense perceptions. Each of us, as it were, eats from the tree of knowledge of good and evil—the branching afferent nervous system that bears the dualistic fruit of sensory data—and we are tasked with tempering this inherently deceptive relative knowledge.

Since the mind retains conditioning and deciphers senso-

ry data within the parameters of space and time, our ideas of
self and our judgments of other ideas are largely predicated on
finite self-encoded standards. Only by developing intuition—
a nonfinite avenue to knowledge—can we distinguish these
standards from actual knowledge of the substance of self.
Otherwise, subsequent information arriving through the senses, feelings, or intellect will continue to reinforce adherence to
one or another finite idea of self. Aesop's fable "The Lion and
the Statue" illustrates this point:

> A man and a lion were discussing the relative strength
> of men and lions in general. The man contended that he
> and his race were stronger than lions by reason of their
> greater intelligence. "Come now with me," he cried, "and
> I will soon prove that I am right." So he took the lion into
> the public gardens and showed him a statue of Hercules
> overcoming the lion and tearing his mouth in two. "That
> is all very well," said the lion, "but it proves nothing, for
> it was Man who made the statue."[11]

Human beings interpret information according to biases,
wishes, and limited frames of reference. Labels and statues, as
well as religious symbols, theologies, and philosophies, may
name and define aspects of life, but they can never reveal anything directly about existence, much like the equation $2 + 2 =
4$, which is a relative mathematical definition rather than
absolute knowledge. In extreme circumstances, even this
arithmetic breaks down. According to Albert Einstein's special
relativity theory, the speed of light is an infinite barrier, and
when it is approached by two colliding spaceships, their relative velocity, no longer derived by adding their individual
velocities, would be more nearly reflected in the computa-
tion $2 + 2 = 2$. Similarly, in realizing the infinite self, finite

statues, names, and definitions of the world become useless.

Wondering about God eventually reveals that the self projects itself into every decision, belief, and action in which it participates. And unless the self is questioned, conditioning will continue to program it and keep it small. Through questions emerging from the finite self it is impossible to realize an infinite self, but asking What is God? leads to the question What is self? as the questioner probes her fluctuating sense of identity and comes to intuit her underlying universal self. Hence, advanced steps along the avenue to self-knowledge can no longer be based on the examination of human-made idols of the world since doing so would at best only uncover the self who made them and the self who is examining them. But once truth seekers learn to utilize the sophisticated avenue of intuition, outer investigations will be coupled with positive and progressive inner realizations of the substance of self.

Though science is unable to provide absolute knowledge of the cosmos, progress along the avenue to self-knowledge is compatible with the scientific method, which employs reason, imagination, and the recognition that all theories are invariably tested according to the assumptions associated with a sense of self. As many prominent scientists have shown, to be great in the quest for knowledge, seekers must challenge what others take for granted, embrace the value of intuition, and nourish an expanded sense of self. To question accepted truths about the world, celebrated scientists would inwardly ponder the data accumulated in laboratory experiments. Johannes Kepler, for one, used such data to challenge assumptions made by Aristotle's self circumscribed by ideas of planetary perfection. Kepler arrived at his second law of motion through this insight, but because his mathematical ability was not sophisticated enough to prove it, he did not understand why it was true. Similarly, Einstein arrived at his special relativity theory by feeling it viscerally after challenging an accepted theorem; upon realizing it within, he proved it mathematically. Newton's genius also reflected a freedom from tradition and prejudice that allowed him to see the world differently and gift to science the calculus that could compute motion.

The scientific investigation of material knowledge complements the search for self-knowledge because both essentially have the same goal: knowledge. Regardless of the avenue to knowledge, the word *God* nobly represents the knowledge of everything, though ironically it is used most often to indicate the unknown or hide the ignorance of belief. The knowledge scientists and spiritual investigators seek when they ask What is God? differs only by orientation: acquisition of material knowledge derives from outward observation, while intuitive knowledge results from inward observation. Where God is the cosmos to the physicist, God is the self of the cosmos to the spiritual seeker.

Further, material and spiritual investigators alike have developed tools for broadening the range of the senses in making discoveries. Due to telescopes and accelerators, material scientists can now study everything from vast galaxies to subatomic particles. Similarly, ancient spiritual seekers devised techniques for finding answers to What is God? without sensory limitations by focusing on the instruments used for gaining knowledge: the senses, feelings and intellect, and intuition of the self. While scientists use these faculties to study the world, spiritual seekers study them to understand how the self and world are constructed. The result is knowledge based not on conditional sensory data but on the mechanics of a sense of self seemingly individuated from the one self of the cosmos.

Technically, these mechanics involve the intuitive capacity of the nervous system, which is enlivened so that the cerebrospinal axis no longer relies on sensory data, feelings, or the intellect to reap knowledge of the self. And the unraveling of that awareness allows the intuited self to encompass the substance out of which the physical world is erected.

Spiritual seekers and scientists also view the physical world in much the same way—as if through the eyes of a physicist. Some Indologists and modern physicists have discovered that the ancient intuitive investigations found in the Vedas were probably considered by their authors to be works on the physics of a cosmos made up of a superfine substance. And while physicists theorize about substances beyond the confines of everyday space and time by deeply penetrating matter, spiritual seekers encompass material phenomena as by-products of the infinite substance of self through intuitive realization.

To the spiritual seeker, a sort of intuitive scientist, infinite self-awareness includes an awareness of matter, though it is very different from the awareness gleaned through the senses. At the same time, the substance of self does not qualify as pure spirit, which would imply the existence of a spiritual world "out there" separated from this gross one. To begin gaining awareness of the mechanics governing the formation of a sense of self, students of intuitive practices are generally asked to observe the gross personal phenomena of which they are aware, such as breath, thoughts, emotions, or the flow of nervous energy, all the while developing an individualized understanding that the self is supremely physical, though of a composition more subtle than atoms and waves of prana. As advanced practitioners, they can then conclude firsthand that the substance of self is the foundation of the physical universe. Or conversely, if the substance of self has been designated nonphysical, which is certainly reasonable, then the universe can also be considered immaterial despite sensory evidence to the contrary.

Since spiritual strivings have a great deal in common with scientific quests, it seems odd to find so few intuitive scientists in our scientific age. One reason for today's dearth of intuitive scientists is that with scientific sensibilities and religious beliefs still at odds in cultures, genuine science and spirituality remain unintegrated in individuals. Another difficulty is the inability of the senses, feelings, and intellect alone to absolutely prove or disprove any theory, leaving even scientifically educated people vulnerable to a sense of self so narrow it remains unaware of a preponderance of inherent contradictions. A Christian fundamentalist theoretical physicist may have no qualms about burning fossil fuels to drive to work, using petrified wood for bookends, or taking his daughter to a museum to see dinosaur skeletons while believing the world is only a few millenniums old. Relative inconsistencies are likely to thwart human spiritual progress until it is discovered that the human body, as host to a sense of self, is the ultimate laboratory, because all knowledge is dependent on it.

So, while material science and intuitive spirituality parallel each other in the bigger picture of human progress, for individuals they function as diverging avenues to knowledge, and development in one does not imply advancement in the other. For progress to occur along both avenues, an individual would need to consistently balance scientific knowledge and self-knowledge by building on past scientific discoveries and intuitively realizing that the human body hosts a sense of self that is substantively connected to the selves of all things. Declaring that atoms have arranged themselves in patterns allowing humans to feel, sense, and think neither explains anything nor gives an enduring meaning to existence. But questioning the mechanics of feeling, sensing, and thinking might reveal the science of intuition, the substance of self that underlies an apparently individuated human identity, and the unifying "why" that humanity seeks to know.

The view of human progress afforded by the cycle theory reveals the urgency of pressing beyond Dark Age constraints in our spiritual investigations. With this in mind, balancing the two avenues to knowledge calls for a mission similar to Kepler's, Einstein's, and Newton's. Just as they questioned and discarded past scientific assumptions, individuals can question assumptions about their existence. The more we learn about the self from within instead of relying on superficial intellectual explanations or religious dogma, the closer humanity will come to an expansive knowledge that illuminates both the forms and forces of the cosmos and the subtle substance of self.

CHAPTER THREE

An Alternative to Organized Religion

A Theory of Self

Men seek out retreats for themselves in the
country, by the seaside, on the mountains. . . .
But all this is unphilosophical to the last
degree . . . when thou canst at a moment's
notice retire into thyself.

—Marcus Aurelius Antonius

Humanity today faces the challenge of investigating the path of intuitive knowledge for a more unifying concept of self. Arriving at a comprehensive theory of self, however, is difficult since the sense of self influences every form of inquiry and is by nature biased. Another dilemma is that whereas past philosophers like Georg Wilhelm Friedrich Hegel and Karl Marx proposed theories of human history, a theory of the human self must take into account their research, as well as scientific discoveries and other present-day knowledge. Ironically, a good place to begin searching for a theory of self may be in views of the ancients concerning the cosmos and the self, perspectives uncolored by today's social complexities and therefore perhaps capable of helping us find an alternative to organized religion.

The ancients observed that human beings, as well as all other living things, are driven to reach for infinitude, as was seen in the widespread hope for an eternal afterlife, desire for progeny, and instinct for self-preservation; in the endless quest for knowledge and greater awareness; and in the yearning for lasting happiness. This observation prompted the simple theory that the underpinning of the universe was infinite existence, awareness, and bliss, and that human compulsions reflected the presence of an underlying substance of self motivating individuals to achieve a more expansive sense of self and ultimately some kind of immortality.

Today, for good or ill, we live in a world that tends not to see the drive for realizing an infinite existence, awareness, and bliss as a primary motivating force. But an expansive sense of self with no hope for an infinite apotheosis promises no personal immortality, no omnipotent God to love us eternally, no chance of reuniting with departed loved ones, or any glory other than working for the love of humanity during one brief life-span. Whether due to selfishness or an inherent drive for infinitude, most people are not content to live for all of humanity with death ensuring eternal oblivion. Desperately desiring an escape from finitude and mortality, they seek promises of eternal paradise, reincarnation, or enlightenment to motivate them emotionally and spiritually. To satisfy this craving, many adopt religious beliefs. Yet even if religion's future rewards are real, the human longing for infinitude remains unfulfilled in the *here and now.* As a result, both those who do and do not identify with promises of organized religion will continue to seek infinitude in many ways—from fairly benign approaches that have no benefit to others, as in cosmetic restorations of youthfulness, to more destructive ones that harm others, as in political or economic domination.

Perhaps the most destructive way to seek infinitude is through exclusionary beliefs that narrow the sense of self, instill feelings of superiority, and justify tyrannical ambitions. Far from satisfying the drive for infinitude, exclusive promises of immortality exacerbate the difficulty in developing an expansive sense of self by giving believers a rationale for exploitation and violence toward others.

For the progress of society, religious institutions that seduce the drive for infinitude with dangerous promises must therefore be replaced; they cannot simply be removed, because no amount of deconditioning and reeducation will stamp out the drive for infinitude any more than they can abolish mortality. Moreover, religions must be replaced by something that can both satisfy the drive for infinitude and universally instill a larger sense of identity. While the philosophy of an expansive finite self does not grant complete satisfaction, seekers investigating an avenue to intuitive knowledge might come to know the source of the finite self and subsequently find gratification by directing their drive for infinitude inward.

Though the finite self manifests in physical bodies, its source eludes investigators, who invariably end up grappling with the age-old question of how bodies can have sensory awareness, to whatever degree, of the cosmos from which they emerged. Scientists throughout history have attempted to postulate how matter organizes itself to think, believe, feel, and act. They have found that life is dependent on the presence of nervous energy, suggesting that the life of the body is not in gross organs of perception but in subtle motions of energy and awareness. From this perspective, a human being's sensory apparatus would be considered dead were it not for the energy flowing through it and the faculty to interpret sensory data. The senses, then, are necessary for awareness of the phenomenal world and of an experience of self circumscribed by body consciousness, but sensory awareness cannot be the source of the finite self when it is not even its own source. Neither can the sense of self be its own source, for if it were it would not be in constant flux.

While energy pouring into the senses from the cerebrospinal axis connects the brain to the sensory world, the human sense of self can theoretically survive without sensory faculties, legs and arms, genitals, and even internal organs as long as the nerve plexuses in the spine and brain remain functional; excessive damage to the spine and brain leads to death of the body. In effect, both life and the sense of self depend on the spine and brain and are inseparable, even during sleep or a coma. Modern science has discovered, however, that the finite self is not merely a physiological by-product of the spine and brain, indicating that while a sense of self relies on the spine and brain, self-awareness cannot be limited to them. What, then, is the source of the finite self?

This quandary was addressed by a theory of self that derived from the ancient Vedas and eventually—through the philosophies of Samkhya, Vedanta, and Yoga— evolved into the science of intuition. According to the theory, the spine and brain operate like a receiving set, intuiting a sense of self; as for the self, it relies on the cerebrospinal apparatus to manifest yet is not its by-product. This theory makes it clear why every spiritual and religious tradition emphasizes the importance of surrendering to the infinite: because the individuated human self is merely a localization of an indivisible infinite self, meaning that satisfaction depends entirely on recognition of its infinite nature as opposed to its seemingly finite one.

Technically, the ramifications of this theory are vast. For one thing, according to its premises the brain could not be entirely responsible for conceiving thoughts; instead, it would store raw impressions contributing to electrophysiological patterns of language, and the cerebrospinal axis, in its entirety, would house other patterns eliciting an intuited sense of self. In other words, rather than articulating the mind's thoughts directly, the spine and brain intuit the mind as an attribute of the individuated sense of self. At the same time, a thought entertained over and over again records an electro-physiological pattern in the cerebrospinal axis that, informing the intuitive capacity, helps define the sense of self. It also appears that though complex thought presupposes complex language composed of impressions recorded in the brain, language could not directly convey thoughts. Mental or vocalized sounds might intimate thoughts, but articulations of them would only approximate their meaning, and in another mind the same sounds might evoke different thoughts. That is, only when the magnetism of someone's spine and brain supports the intuition of a particular sense of self would a corresponding thought arise in the mind. In effect, we could not share thoughts directly through articulation; we could only share magnetism, and our magnetism would be expressed in our thought patterns, as well as in our words, beliefs, feelings, and actions. It is no wonder that ancient ascetics prized the company of their masters over books, which could only hint at the magnetism involved in authoring them. From this perspective, intuition could no longer be called the "sixth sense" but would instead be regarded as the single avenue to knowledge, which when directed outward divides into currents that feed the five senses and by which all knowledge is a form of self-knowledge.

This theory of self has repercussions in both the organic and inorganic worlds, indicating that the ability to intuit a sense of self is not limited to human beings. And indeed, about a hundred years ago the East Indian physicist Jagadis Chandra Bose discovered that plants have a nervous system equipped to intuit a limited sense of self and are capable of reacting to their environment and having an emotional life.

According to Bose, even though human beings genetically have a far greater awareness and thought capability due to the intuitive power of the sophisticated human spine and brain, all animals and plants have nervous systems that can intuit a sense of self, and even a piece of tin has a self of sorts that reacts variously to external stimuli and requires periodic rest. Bose concluded that despite harboring a seemingly infinite number of diverse selves, the cosmos holds the promise of indivisible unity.[1]

Viewing the cerebrospinal axis as a complex receiving instrument also allows us to imagine how the movement of nervous energy in our bodies determines where we focus our attention and where the resulting physioelectric patterns produce magnets of awareness that define the sense of self. Wherever nervous energy is directed by thoughts, beliefs, feelings, or actions, awareness follows. In other words, what a person thinks, believes, feels, or does causes shifts of attention that then determine the individual's sense of self. And just as some radio stations broadcast only songs of a specific genre, different bandwidths of the cerebrospinal radio may intuit only certain ranges of thoughts. Certainly, energy flooding the senses promotes sensory awareness and ignites thought and memory arising from prior patterns of conditioning, while energy surging through sexual organs awakens sensual consciousness.

To test how various aspects of the self are affected by electromagnetic patterns, note your enhanced awareness of portions of the body that have contact with your hands in the following exercise. First, place your palms together at the chest, where they instinctually go in prayer, with fingers extended outward like antennae, increasing receptivity of the emotive heart; in time, a sense of self infused with heightened feelings may emerge. Then place the tips of your fingers on your temples as if you were preparing to think, naturally boosting receptivity of the cerebral plexus corresponding to the intellect. Pressing your palms together at the center of the forehead, where it is common to knit the brow in concentration, you may be able to experience an intensified feeling of focus. Finally, place your palms, one over the other, at your abdomen to increase a sense of power or drive. While practicing this exercise, you can discover firsthand how each plexus receives a different bandwidth of self that together contribute to a well-rounded sense of self containing all these characteristics.

As fascinating as this ancient theory of self is, its usefulness today depends on its ability to satisfy humanity's drive for infinitude, as well as its universality. First, it is important to understand that shifts in awareness, too, obey the principles of electromagnetism. This means that just as moving currents of electricity produce magnets in a power plant, currents of nervous energy traveling away from the cerebrospinal plexuses produce physiological magnets in the body. Such magnets are formed by focusing attention on the senses, for example, or on habits and past trauma, the palate and stomach, the genitals, discomforts and desires, emotional and intellectual reactions to stimuli, or memories. These physiological magnets of awareness, external to the centers of intuition in the spine and brain, condition and narrowly define a person's thoughts and ever-shifting sense of self.

It is because of this narrow range of information transmitted to the cerebrospinal receiver that the individuated sense of self misinterprets sensory data and misidentifies the body as the source of its thoughts and identity. The narrow self might then do such things as hoard, steal, consolidate power, or claim divine authority to bring pleasure and happiness to a self circumscribed by the body—all in a misguided attempt to reach for infinitude. According to the ancient theory of self, however, the searchlights of the senses and other faculties of finite satisfaction can be turned to focus on their inner source of awareness and thus expand the sense of self. Once the power of the cerebrospinal receiver is enlivened by this flow of nervous energy along the spine, the bandwidth of self expands and the intuitive individual, no longer identifying solely with the body, eventually realizes the infinite source of the self. In this way, the ancient theory does indeed assist in satisfying the drive for infinitude. And its model of the human organism as a "body electric," housing physiological magnets of awareness, frees the study of self from cultural, philosophical, and theological biases and places it in the larger context of physiology and physics—making the theory universally applicable and practicable.

The effectiveness of the theory hinges on its success in helping practitioners establish a physiological magnet within the intuitive centers in the spine and cerebrum. With such a magnet in place, awareness, concentrated on the highly sophisticated plexuses and away from the conditioning of the senses and outward-flowing faculties of cognition, compels the brain to intuit the all-pervading "broadcast" of the infinite substance of self underlying the various cosmic substances. In this broader context, the ancient theory of self can be adopted for our times and expressed as follows: *Intuitive faculties enlivened in the cerebrum produce a nonfinite self-knowledge in which the individuated sense of self is recognized as indivisible from the infinite substance of self.*

This aspect of the theory has in fact been tested in the practices of ascetics of all religions. One practice involves keeping the body motionless to assist in establishing a cerebrospinal magnet by minimizing the flow of energy in outer body parts. Because lying-down positions were found to discourage magnetization of the spine, ascetics of many traditions began regulating currents of nervous energy in the spine while in a motionless upright position. This common meditation pose persists today though its intended purpose of cerebrospinal magnetization is generally overlooked.

Another practice through which religious ascetics control energy is fasting. On a physiological level, abstaining from food saves tremendous amounts of nervous energy that can then be directed inward through prayer or other concentration methods to magnetize the intuitive centers in the spine and brain. Fasting, a way to die a little to the body and the senses, naturally introverts awareness by decreasing the activity of the sympathetic and parasympathetic nervous systems.

A third practice ascetics use to conserve energy is the observation of silence. Physiologically, speaking employs small muscles that expend more nervous energy than larger ones. Conversation also expends energy, through the acts of listening, responding intellectually and emotionally, and forming electrophysiological memories in the brain. Thus, silence has traditionally been invoked to create a buffer between the sensory world and the spiritual aspirant's sense of self.

In addition to silence, nighttime is viewed as an aid to intuitive practices. Ascetics often stay awake at night since darkness naturally introverts the attention and ensures a less active environment. Though human beings and animals may be sleeping nearby, their patterns of energy are found to be submerged into the lower spine, further assisting ascetics in turning their own attention inward. Remaining awake and disciplined at night makes it easier to overcome habits and to direct nervous energy into the spine for spiritual pursuits.

Ascetics throughout history have realized the need to dislodge old patterns, especially those conditioned by society, in order to create new channels of energy for development of the expansive sense of self. Rumi, the celebrated Sufi poet, described this principle colorfully when he advised readers not to allow the snake of a habit to become an unstoppable dragon through laziness, lack of discipline, restless company, or indifference, all of which have physiomagnetic consequences. A habit, from this perspective, is a pattern of energy in the body and brain. Whereas a weak habit—the snake—is easy to dislodge, a habit made powerful by repetition—the dragon—is not.[2]

To remove or prevent new forms of social conditioning, ascetics often turn to solitude. They have found that proximity to the magnetism of others affects their sense of self even in the absence of direct communication. Ascetics of the past often remained single because romantic interests pulled their attention outward and sex used considerable nervous energy. By contrast, the solitary life freed ascetics from the influence of other people's patterns of thinking and living.

Today, such practices are generally followed on retreats. Fast-paced living forges a discrepancy between daily exigencies and the ideals of a spiritual life, and for the devout of every tradition retreats offer an environment that enhances introspection and meditation by minimizing distractions. Periodic retreats to isolated locales are beneficial also for individuals accustomed to having their nervous energy and attention drawn outward by television, radio, the Internet, work, school, friends, and family. However, such getaways are superfluous for a bona fide ascetic whose powerful cerebrospinal magnet allows for the immediate withdrawal of awareness from the senses in any setting.

Advancement in sensory introversion is attained through the added cultivation of psychophysical components belonging to the theory of self, which many belief systems impede. For example, the theory of self postulates that focusing on universal images of God directs energy to the intuitive centers in the spine and cerebrum. Worshippers who embrace exclusive and divisive images of God are unable to go deeply inward because their images of God are tinged with worldly ambitions, fear, or other extroverting concerns. By contrast mystics, accustomed to focusing inward, have traditionally adopted more universal ideals of God. In fact, great mystics from every religion explicitly referred to God as the infinite self because they intuitively found no God other than the all-pervading infinite substance of self. Even the nontheistic Buddhist doctrine of no self affirmed the indivisible substance of self by denying its apparent individuation.

Religionists who place all their faith in prayer, chanting, and reading scripture might consider how purely psychophysical ascetic exercises based on the science of intuition can enhance knowledge of God. Though devotional prayer elicits motions of nervous energy, when the focal point used for inward concentration is an all-encompassing image of divinity it can draw such energy away from the senses and back toward the spine. In other words, even though prayer is widely considered an intimate religious rite it is actually a psychophysical activity causing nervous energy to flow in sense-introverting patterns—another illuminating discovery made in the distant past. This means that churchgoers as well as aspiring ascetics who lack the intensity of devotion necessary to sit for hours in concentration on an image of God can, by practicing psychophysical techniques of intuition along with modest expressions of devotion, find themselves on a par with Saint Francis and other great lovers of God. The two processes represent essentially the same dedicated effort in concentrated soul-searching and result in the same feeling of intimacy with the larger self, intuited within. Where the yearning for immortality is concerned, psychophysical considerations override any rituals codified by tradition and history.

Other ancient psychophysical ascetic practices overlooked among religious practitioners intent on externalizing their images of God are breathing techniques for focusing attention inward. According to the theory of self, the most sophisticated technique to invigorate and magnetize the spine is breath regulation coupled with the active drawing of nervous energy toward the cerebrospinal plexuses. Breathing techniques were devised to create revolving currents of nervous energy that magnetized the spine, pulling in the energies that normally feed the breath, heart, senses, and mental restlessness, thus centering the attention totally in the spine and the brain.

Ascetics of the past, knowingly and unknowingly, weighed the merit of their practices by assessing each one's psychophysiological effect on the spine and brain. Today, we can likewise measure the value of religious rituals against a cerebrospinal yardstick, replacing those that fail to enliven cerebrospinal activity. Everything we think, feel, and do—even just glancing at a tabloid beside the grocery store check-out counter—contributes to a pattern of energy in the spine and brain, which then influences one's intuited sense of self. Aspiring ascetics, like those of the past who gained knowledge in the science of intuition, can perfect similar practices to help center attention on the spine and brain, as described in Technique 8.

℘ TECHNIQUE 8

Commonsense Asceticism

The ancients devised methods for gradually mastering energies of the body, approaching asceticism as a means to harness nervous energy. But in the Dark Ages, many of these sophisticated methods fell out of practice, whereupon ascetics gravitated toward extreme behaviors, wearing hair shirts, self-flagellating, and martyring themselves. As a result, the word *asceticism* now conjures up images of saints surviving on water and dates for fifty years, monks living in cloisters and eating only bread crumbs, sadhus lying on beds of nails, anchorites living atop pillars, or dervishes staying awake continuously.

While religionists of the past often glorified ascetics who gave their lives to God in these dramatic ways, today we are wisely motivated by the ideal of balanced living. In fact, few people outside of organized religion are interested in asceticism, seeing it as life denying. Lacking a viable theory of self, they do not recognize how possible it is to live a balanced life by incorporating commonsense ascetic practices to minimize exertion and stress and to grow spiritually.

The following practices, which derive from ascetic traditions of every religion, provide balanced living regulations for three necessities: food, speech, and sex. Moderating your use of these necessities allows you to harness the freed energies and direct them back into the spine, while ensuring that you are not overindulging in them to find any "lasting happiness" they cannot provide. Moderation essentially means restraining oneself to amounts slightly less than desired so the body and mind gradually learn to live with less, to avoid the imbalanced behavior that comes with excessive indulgence, and to cease obstructing expansion of the sense of self.

Limiting food intake begins by adopting a diet that excludes the consumption of animals. This practice saves tremendous amounts of nervous energy otherwise expended in digestion and clearing the body of excessive waste products, prevents recurrence of aggressions found in animals that hunt and eat other animals, and promotes health and longevity.

The moderation of food intake also includes periodic fasting. Research shows that fasting not only has health advantages but also, by freeing nervous energy normally used for digestion, effectively jump-starts intuitive practices. For optimal benefit, periodic fasting includes sufficient fluid intake and lasts from one to three days a few times a month. Other fasts entail eating only fruits, leafy greens, and nuts (optional) for a week or two each season, or eating standard fare but only one or two meals a day for several days a week. After years of regular fasting, you may be able to comfortably maintain yourself with less food even when you are *not* fasting.

Moderating speech, another aspect of a balanced life, liberates the nervous energy normally used in thinking and articulating. While the practice of silence contributes to peace of mind, speechlessness maintained out of anger or hurt feelings only draws the liberated energy into increasingly narrow patterns of irritation or sensitivity. Initially silence can be practiced every day for twelve hours, starting from a few hours before sleep to a few hours after rising, or for a full day once a week. Extended periods of silence, coupled with sense introversion, assist in cultivating an intensely focused mind, as well as the capacity to harness restless thoughts and direct their energy back into the spine for the pursuit of self-knowledge.

Silence practiced in combination with solitude has additional spiritual benefits: freedom from the influence of company that may inhibit the will to question patterns of belief, uproot habits, and advance intuitively. Solitude is best approached moderately at the start, by remaining in a quiet place for a few hours one day a week. Over time, solitude may be observed for a few hours every morning or evening. During more extended periods of solitude, special precautions should be taken to avert violent catharses. With the removal of comfortable references, prolonged solitude practiced without proficiency in concentration techniques can cause fading patterns to overload the psyche before finally resolving into currents of energy to be directed toward the spine.

Celibacy, the third aspect of balanced living, has historically been practiced by ascetics to attain freedom from sensory limitations. Celibacy taken to extremes, however, can be very unhealthy. Social scientists have found that puritanical attitudes toward sex, imposed by either organized religion or society, often lead directly to violence, misogyny, and psychological difficulties, as well as preoccupations with pornography and fanatical forms of sexual misconduct.

Candidates for celibacy in moderation are therefore people with a balanced attitude toward sex. Infants and adolescents who are given plenty of love and physical affection to support their emotional growth are more likely than their deprived counterparts to develop healthy, normal sexual appetites later in life. Similarly, in households lacking prohibitions against premarital sex youths are less likely to associate sex with violent emotions.

Despite beliefs to the contrary, if you have a healthy attitude toward lovemaking, periods of celibacy can improve your sex life, instill greater respect for your partner, and conserve energy for inward focusing. You can begin to practice celibacy for one week a month, perhaps during the menstrual cycle. Over time, you might observe sixteen or more weeks of celibacy a year. Additionally, men might consider ejaculating less frequently when progeny are not desired.

The important point to keep in mind while developing commonsense asceticism is that the necessities of life are just that—necessities. Making too much or too little of them fosters imbalances. As the theory of self suggests, enormous amounts of energy are available when needs are regulated by never completely satisfying them yet also not ignoring them. Regarding sex, for instance, energy conserved through celibacy can be easily wasted in sexual frustrations resulting from excessive abstinence. Regulations in practices involving food, speech, and sex alike guarantee the slow removal of poor living habits and promote a balanced life that encourages spiritual investigation.

Truth seekers subscribing to this theory of self in lieu of projecting their spirituality outward toward a centralized religion, will find that the multitude of energy patterns triggered internally by thoughts, beliefs, feelings, and actions can instead be centralized along the spine for greater access to intuitive knowledge. Then the body becomes the house of God, and the cerebrospinal axis the altar. Seekers embracing this theory of self may also discover that despite an inherent longing for personal immortality, any hope for its emergence is unreasonable: the body dies and returns to the elements, and no belief in resurrection, heaven, or Judgment Day can possibly reconstitute it. At the same time, since division within the infinite substance of self is a prior causal idea, the eventual dissolution of a plant, animal, or human being does not affect its earlier individuated sense of self, which could still be intuited by another body. In effect, we may all be intuiting ever-expanding selves that were previously intuited by the nervous systems of other bodies. Meanwhile personal immortality, which by definition exceeds the reach of time-bound individuated selves, is secured not through hope but through the transpersonal substance of self that remains forever free of division. Satisfaction in the here and now comes from intuitively knowing this infinitude rather than merely piecing together the mortal self gleaned from sensory data.

Beyond the realm of causal ideas, there has never been an individuated self, nor could there ever be anything but the infinite and indivisible substance of self. The cosmos, like an iceberg of prana with a visible tip of atomic matter floating in a sea of causal ideas, in which the sea and the iceberg are made of the same infinite substance of self, can only know itself as one indivisible being despite its multifarious appearances to our senses. Consequently, from the vantage point of the theory of self, the doctrine of individuated selves, while useful as a model, is nonviable, leaving us with the challenge of imagining a reality far wider and wiser than any that holds out the promise of personal immortality.

Going Straight to God through Energy Control

At some point, the body and mind together become fundamentally aware and convinced that the energy by which the body is pervaded is the same as that which illuminates the world and maintains alive all beings.

—Joseph Campbell

In ancient mystical traditions, intuition was a highly guarded science whose techniques were not so much invented in any one locale as continuously rediscovered and communicated from age to age and place to place. The techniques involved accessing the path to the brain via the spine by controlling the body's energies. By the time the Bhagavad Gita was written, in about the fifth century BCE, Indian techniques of intuition were already ancient. Today, the science of intuition is called pranayama, meaning energy *(prana)* control *(yama)* in the service of sense introversion, the name fittingly given to it by the Indian yogis who codified its techniques.

India, home to the oldest continuing civilization on earth, was a mecca for seekers of knowledge in the ancient world. India's Vedic Aryans systematized many spiritual and secular sciences after exhaustively investigating the human mind through the lenses of spirituality, physiology, and psychology, as can be seen in Sanskrit's wealth of technical nomenclature. So extensive is this body of knowledge that it encompasses every mystical system known to humanity, and pranayama was the Indian yogis' priceless pearl, their spiritual science par excellence.

In developing pranayama, ancient yogis studied the relationship between patterns of nervous energy and awareness, eventually utilizing the breath to direct nervous energy toward the spine and realize intuitive knowledge. Systematic regulation of the breath, they found, ultimately allows humans to intuit a more expansive self. In fact, the terms for breath, wind, spirit, and soul are the same in many languages, reflecting their intimate connection.

From a broader perspective, pranayama becomes a scientific approach to life and truth seeking. Based on universal principles of electromagnetism rather than on local beliefs or mythic ideals, its practice and beliefs require no particular affiliation, tithing, or intercession. It considers the human body the only temple of God, or spiritual laboratory, and the infinite substance of self the only source of absolute knowledge. Unlike religions, pranayama has no founder or recognized authority to validate its power; nor does it promote divisiveness, exclusivity, or factional political and economic interests. As with other material sciences, only sincere experimentation can prove its efficacy.

Pranayama empowers spiritual investigators by offering techniques that enhance receptivity to intuitive knowledge. Genuine yogis, aware of its experimental nature, give guidance in these techniques free of charge. They feel it is unethical to claim their theory can be verified only through practice and then charge for teaching it. Such ethical considerations, combined with the felt need to lessen material indulgences, probably gave rise to the Indian paragon of the wandering ascetic.

The goal of pranayama is liberation of the intuited sense of self from its bondage to sensory conditioning. This objective emerges directly from the theory of self's assertion that human beings lack the sensory apparatus to register the cosmos as infinite substance. Certainly the sense organs, no matter how strengthened or purified they are, can record only finite gross forms and overt forces, all of which are then interpreted by the mind. As a result, the idea of self derived from interactions with the phenomenal world is tailored to fit the parameters of incoming sensory data and the mind's conditioned interpretations of them.

Sense perceptions are further limiting because they suggest that the world is absolutely real, prompting understandings that narrow the likelihood of intuiting an expansive identity. The senses portray a world consisting of categories of phenomena, such as forests and oceans, friends and strangers, stars and planets, pleasure and pain, hours and years. The constant play between the individuated self and the senses, as mediated by the mind, stirs up endless installments of human drama, yielding an ever-flickering sense of self. However, while the world may appear real to the senses, the theory of self purports that nothing out there is solid other than the infinite substance of self registered by the narrow bandwidth of the human senses as a finite cosmos fragmented into bits of space-time. For the intuitive scientist, eternity emerges the moment the senses are withdrawn and the mind-made illusions of space, time, and individuation are eliminated. Along with eternity of substance comes the awareness of an ever-expanding sense of self.

A third difficulty of a worldview composed exclusively of sensory data is that it can lead to obsessions with survival instincts, material acquisitiveness, short-term gains, momentary pleasures, and exploitation of people and natural resources. On the other hand, knowledge gleaned through periodic disassociation from sensory input reveals that awareness is infinite and omnipresent regardless of the finite, circumscribed reality portrayed by the senses. Further, this superconscious knowledge, as opposed to conscious knowledge obtained from the senses, provides access to a broader perspective on the meaning of existence, which heightens spiritual sensitivities. Present world conditions, punctuated by war, extreme inequities, and sectarianism, indicate an urgent need to integrate into human ambitions a larger understanding of life born of superconscious knowledge.

Differences between sensory perceptions and superconscious knowledge can be illustrated by the following analogy. Suppose you move to a small mountain town and while driving around you spot the local church. Stepping inside, you acquaint yourself with members of the congregation. A few weeks later, you meet several couples who are indifferent to churches, living in the town only seasonally to enjoy its weather and views. Months later, you encounter people who are rebelling against the church's overzealous proselytizing campaigns that are disrupting the peace of the town. Guided by your sensory perceptions, you begin identifying with the group that most closely mirrors your beliefs and past sensory conditioning.

Now imagine you have moved to the same town as someone receptive to superconscious knowledge. While exploring, you notice a building adorned with traditional religious emblems and become acquainted with people who congregate in it, a seemingly select group bound together by a shared physiomagnetism manifesting in their appreciation of the symbols and beliefs they represent. A few weeks later, you meet several couples who are indifferent to such gatherings, turning instead to nature for its ability to release patterns of stress and offer a form of rejuvenation unconditionally available to everyone. Months later, you encounter townspeople whose ideas of self battle attempts to divide their fellow citizens into those who do or do not find nourishment in the religious symbols. Your superconscious knowledge allows you to identify with everyone in town since they are all a part of your expansive self. At the same time, you note that whereas the churchgoers have equated the eternal self with their finite religious sense of self, the rebels, professing expansiveness, mistake the churchgoers for their narrow religious sense of self. Meanwhile, the nature lovers have confused the eternal self with rejuvenation through nature. In all instances, including your personal situation, you acknowledge the same self seeking its infinite substance—demonstrating a certain degree of superconscious knowledge.

Pranayama seeks to liberate the narrowly intuited sense of self by converting thoughts, feelings, and actions into inner focal points of concentration leading to superconscious knowledge. Every form of meditation, worship, prayer, and breath regulation that directs nervous energy to a cerebrospinal plexus comes under the rubric of pranayama. Even sitting in prayer with palms pressed together at the chest is pranayama since it harnesses nervous energy, develops magnetism in the spine's dorsal plexus behind the heart, and shifts the awareness from finite sensory perceptions to intuitive understandings of the infinite self.

Even so, pranayama's efficacy varies from one technique to the next. Prayer is generally an extremely weak form of pranayama since sensory and memory preoccupations tend to thwart concentration, inhibiting the retirement of nervous energy into the spine to expand the sense of self. Meditation utilizing repetitive statements, such as mantras or unanswerable questions, can be somewhat stronger. Deep thinking, inward philosophical observation, and introspection on the parameters of the self usually offer more vigorous assistance in rising above body awareness. Concentration exercises like watching the breath are routinely taught to beginners, while techniques utilizing an outer object of concentration develop into more advanced methods of inward listening at a cerebrospinal plexus. Methods combining localized tension, concentration on the plexuses, breath regulation, and moderate breath retention are considerably more powerful. The most potent techniques are applied once the breath has been stilled, the senses switched off, and the awareness effortlessly centered in the cerebrospinal axis.

Pranayama's most important application is the enlivening of the brain's intuitive faculties so practitioners can identify with the infinite substance of self. Though the brain is largely dormant, the investment of more and more nervous energy awakens its intellectual and intuitive faculties, much as nervous energy directed toward muscles will flex and build them. Pranayama exercises the brain specifically through regulation of the nervous energy responsible for thoughts, emotions and desires, motor responses, sensory awareness, breathing, heartbeat and pulse—empowering practitioners to switch the senses on and off at will. With nervous energy routed into the spine and brain, the sense of self dependent on identification with the body becomes dislodged and cerebral intuitive awareness awakens.

Human beings unwittingly practice forms of pranayama while yawning, laughing, and sleeping. Yawning temporarily floods the body with energy. When the mouth opens wide, the throat expands, allowing more air to enter the lungs, and the muscles at the top of the neck surrounding the medulla oblongata tense as the yawner momentarily holds the breath before exhaling. Similarly, pranayama techniques involve the intake of air with expansion of the throat, maintenance of localized tension at the medulla oblongata, and retention of breath. The major difference between yawning and these techniques is their extreme invigoration of the spine and brain resulting from the regulation of far greater amounts of nervous energy. While yawning protects against drowsiness, pranayama techniques combat the sleep of spiritual ignorance.

Laughter's parallels with pranayama are equally striking. During laughter, the body instinctively begins to exhale in a choppy fashion, akin to pranayama techniques that employ multiple exhalations to expel bodily waste in the form of carbon dioxide, resulting in increased vitality and longevity. Smiles that accompany laughter produce tension in the scalp, ears, and skull, directing energy toward the brain and inducing a feeling of joy and well-being. Likewise, pranayama practices utilize tension to direct vast amounts of energy to the brain, activating its near-limitless intuitive potential and bestowing the infinite bliss of the substance of self.

Sleep shares still other characteristics with pranayama. While sleep relaxes the senses by submerging body awareness in subconsciousness, pranayama ensures a rest for the senses by dissolving body awareness in superconsciousness. In the first instance, nervous energy is directed to the lower spine, where the individual is subconsciously reminded of the infinite self free from diurnal duties and physical cravings; in the second, nervous energy is centered in the upper spine and brain, providing direct superconscious knowledge of the infinite self. During sleep the body also produces less carbon waste to be eliminated through inhalation of oxygen-rich air. Likewise, pranayama reduces carbon waste through immobility, then floods the body with the nervous energy released from sensory absorptions, electrifying the system and stilling the breath as carbon waste is further eliminated.

Even animals routinely practice forms of pranayama. Felines curl and extend their tongues to keep cool in summer, similar to a pranayama technique in which practitioners develop a cooling breath by inhaling through the "tube" created by a curled tongue. And whereas the eyes of sleepers droop downward, those of deceased creatures look upward, like the pranayama upward-gazing techniques used to induce states of stillness conducive to the reception of superconscious knowledge. Also, many animals hibernate by lowering their breathing and heart rates for extended periods of time without suffering brain damage or dying. Bears, for instance, simultaneously direct the movement of nervous energy in their bodies, much like pranayama techniques that accompany breath regulation designed to overcome sensory flooding. When pranayama practitioners achieve a comparable state of suspended animation, the breathing stills and superconscious awareness is maintained. Just as people do not worry about dying during sleep though they are breathing less, neither do practitioners of pranayama concern themselves with dying when the breath and heart are calmed.

A central principle distinguishing pranayama from the innate practices of humans and animals is deliberate magnetization. Currents of nervous energy passing through the spine and brain produce physiomagnetism. Techniques that increase oxygen saturation in the blood to nearly 100 percent convert excess oxygen into a powerful nerve current capable of regenerating and magnetizing the cerebrospinal plexuses. Beginning practitioners direct this current toward the spine through concentration, breath regulation, breath retention, postures that increase cranial pressure, and localized tension by way of energy seals, as described in Technique 9. At first, the current is faint, producing a weak spinal magnet, but with practice its intensity increases, leading ultimately to superconscious knowledge of an infinite self.

 ## TECHNIQUE 9

Forming Energy Seals

Energy seals lock the body's nervous energy to muscles along the cerebrospinal axis that, when tense, establish the potential for intuitive awareness. An infinite number of seals are theoretically possible, from the popular hand gestures of Eastern dance that produce a psychophysiological pattern of awareness to facial expressions causing a psychological pattern. Practitioners who use this technique to seal energy in the brain venture along a path straight to God via the intuitive faculties.

To begin working with energy seals, sit in a chair with your spine erect, chin parallel to the floor, hands on thighs, chest out, and eyes and mouth closed. While breathing normally, focus on the motion of your abdomen. After a few moments, with your eyes still closed you may notice your gaze shifting downward to follow your focus of attention. If so, direct the energy of attention into your spine and up to your brain by gently lifting your gaze and focusing on the point between your eyebrows. This spot, at the origin of the nose, has a polar connection to the medulla oblongata,[3] the part of the brain that regulates autonomic functions associated with breathing, heart rate, and sensory input (see "Anatomy of Intuition," on page 113). Now watch the breath as if you were inhaling and exhaling from this spot at the brow. Lifting the gaze helps in directing energy upward, sealing it in the brain, and gaining control over activities of the medulla oblongata. The ancients called this dam of awareness Siva's Seal, because the practitioner was said to look like the meditating Siva, the god representing Brahman, the infinite self, and symbol of the perfect yogi.

Another practice for forming an energy seal while watching the breath involves touching the tip of the tongue to the soft upper palate. With your tongue in this position, continue watching the breath from the vantage point of the brow. This seal creates tension at the base of the skull, again locking energy in the medulla oblongata.

A third seal employs the hands to prevent energy from leaving the brain and generating restlessness in the body. Because we use our hands frequently, they are capable of holding our attention even when relaxed. To form this seal, bring your palms together at the chest, with fingers extended upward, while maintaining concentration at the brow. This technique creates a dam of awareness at the dorsal plexus, impeding the flow of nervous energy on its way down the spine.

Once an energy seal is in place, the sounds of the outer world begin to recede and those of the interior activities of the body, and later of the body electric, become audible. At this point, you can shift your attention from watching the breath to listening as this mesmerizing inner hum increasingly drowns out the sounds of the sensory world. The humming, produced by the movement of nervous energy in the spine, liberates awareness from the fluctuations of a mind busy interpreting in space and time to an engrossment in the soothing sound of river water. In fact, stories of ascetics listening to the sounds of a river may symbolically represent intuitive scientists listening to the currents of energy in the spine.

To form an energy seal capable of amplifying these electrical sounds in the spine, bring your shoulder blades together as if endeavoring to hold a comb between them. Maintain this tension for about ten seconds, listening for sounds in the spine and the medulla oblongata. Release, then re-form the energy seal again and again while also maintaining the energy seals described earlier. In time, the internal sounds will become loud, galvanizing more and more of your attention. Concentrating on this internal roar will eventually cause the nervous energy feeding your breath, heart, and senses to retire into the spine and place your body in suspended animation. This state of dis-association rests and recharges the body, promoting good health.

It is possible to again change the center of concentration—this time to the very substance of self—by realizing that the expanding sense of self is intuited from motions of energy in the spine and brain. The states from disassociation to infinite expansion mark increasing degrees of effortlessly controlling the energies that normally feed this motion. The more control you manifest, the greater the intuitive capacity of your spine and brain will be, and the more solid your identification with the substance of self that has become the cosmos. With ongoing practice, your sense of self can stretch beyond the intuited motions of energy in your spine and brain to unite with the broadcast itself, encompassing an awareness of all prana, total self-knowledge, and the bliss of the infinite substance of self.

The path straight to God through pranayama practices can be described as follows. When energy feeding the senses is freed to retire inward, the spine accumulates enormous amounts of nervous energy, electrifying every cell. In response, the cells stop producing carbon waste; breathing slows; the heart rests, no longer needing to pump so much blood; and in turn, the senses switch off even more, pulling additional nervous energy to the spine. Eventually, the nervous energy that previously fed the breath, heart, and senses shoots up the spine to the brain. Once that energy is sealed in the brain, eventually uniting with infinite substance, intuitive knowledge obliterates the world of space-time, the narrow sense of self vanishes, and superconsciousness ushers in an experience of eternal bliss, or direct awareness of God.

From a psychological perspective, pranayama practices foster a healthier ego, reinforcing the theory of self's basic principle that the substance of finite ego is the same as the infinite substance of self. Initially, the small ego is beset by worries, fears, and insecurities; it is easily offended and apprehensive of challenges; narrowly identified, it defends itself without introspection, avoids entertaining different views, and often displays cultic behavior. Its happiness is contingent on sensory and emotional gratification. However, through pranayama methods designed to induce catharsis, such as eye exercises, deep breathing, and tension-relaxation methods (see Technique 11, on page 174), the small ego dislodges trauma, guilt, loneliness, anger, low self-esteem, and other electrophysiological patterns that have been hindering intuitive awareness.

In response to more advanced practices, including those that require one-pointed concentration, the ego becomes healthier. It identifies with larger groups of people, gains confidence, and acquires an interest in questioning, exploring the unknown, and self-discovery. As nerve currents recede increasingly from the senses, through inward concentration and the philosophical investigation of human nature, the ego begins to balance gratification of sensory appetites with the needs of others, and outer ambitions with inner happiness.

Sophisticated methods of pranayama then awaken intuitive faculties, encouraging the ego to engage in service to humanity, positive affirmations, and self-study. Extending itself further, it fearlessly looks upon life and death as similarly unconditioning circumstances, identifies with many more portions of humanity, willingly questions everything, accepts no sacred truths based on authority, and relies on fewer material commodities. In developing an intuitive awareness of the eternal bliss of the infinite, the enlarged ego attains happiness primarily from internal accomplishments and realizations.

A more highly developed ego is the superego of an accomplished ascetic with expansive knowledge and energy control. The superego, free from most conditioning, relies primarily on superconscious realizations to determine the parameters of the self. Still lacking absolute knowledge of the substance of self and subject to interpretations of a mind, however, it views the cosmos through a space-time lens.

The most highly evolved ego, the cosmic ego emerging from awareness of the entire cosmos, is possessed by individuals with infinite self-knowledge and therefore direct intuitive knowledge of God. It is an ego so colossal that it not only identifies with all things but sees only itself everywhere and has no idea of mind or of divisions of space and time.

From the standpoint of the theory of self, the ego, or I-ness, poses no obstruction along the spiritual path. Rather, it is the direct conduit to the infinite self. As such, a large ego is preferable to a small one as long as it is truly large and inclusive, and not simply acting overblown to compensate for inadequacies. When the finite ego then departs, the cosmic ego of God enters. A cosmic "I Am"—a direct outcome of going straight to God through energy control—is the immortal apotheosis of everyone's self.

The Self in Society

To know men is to be wise.
To know one's self is to be illuminated.

—Lao-tzu

East and West, some of the greatest thinkers have attempted to assemble the formative aspects of human existence—morality, the psyche, and social behavior—under the canopy of a single system of thought. Hegel, for example, believed the highest development of the human race would be to acquire an understanding of conditioning and use of that knowledge to reduce human history to a science. The theory of self, for its part, asserts that these three aspects of the self in society can be understood within the context of physiology. Accordingly, the science of intuition's impact on ethics, psychology, and sociology, once explored, could help in replacing religions that have assumed positions of authority in these domains.

The relationship between ethics and organized religions is precarious. On the one hand, organized religions are often considered the root of moral behavior, while on the other hand they distort morality. For example, it was at one time moral for Americans to enslave Africans; uprooting and killing "savage" Native Americans was divinely sanctioned, according to many European colonials; during the Holocaust, church authorities considered it unnecessary to speak out against the genocide taking place across Europe; and extremists of all faiths routinely order the death of nonbelievers who appear to threaten their religious or socioeconomic security. Perversions of right and wrong occur almost any time centralized religions project moral codes onto society for their own social and political welfare.

A second problem with centralized religions' moral systems is that they atrophy the capacity of adherents to intuit a larger identity. Such degeneration occurs because the systems impose artificial boundaries on the sense of self that breed a fear of embodying greater expansiveness. In the process, followers become indoctrinated with moral codes that represent not an inclusive ethical system but rather the ambitions of religious authorities who draw their power from a divided, sense-bound humanity.

Another ramification of centralized religious morality is that it propagates behavioral edicts in the form of unchanging, irrevocable truths. While an unchanging God or substance may be considered an eternal basis for right and wrong, temporal verdicts can only be determined moment to moment for they are contingent on context, outcome, and cultural consensus. For example, while birth control is decried by religions, calling it forever immoral or "ungodly" could lead to great suffering at a time when overpopulation is an acknowledged source of violence, scarcity, war, and ignorance. Designating anything as eternally good or bad in this world of relativity overlooks the changing nature of human circumstances and the many dangers in predefining "right conduct" for all people throughout their lifetime.

Ironically, in attempting to eradicate evil by imposing fixed perspectives consonant with antiquated worldviews, fear of divine retribution, and strict as well as polarized limitations on conduct, religion's moral systems force followers to adopt untenable extremes in behavior. Most believers attempt to conform to artificial standards of goodness; and in reaching for the good while rejecting the bad, they erroneously separate the two, slide into unwanted conduct, and perpetuate the dreaded evil, when instead they might have set their sights on moderation. In disallowing people the freedom to experiment and learn from their mistakes, religious authorities may be making the greatest mistake of all.

In contrast to the codifications of divinely forbidden acts espoused by organized religions, the science of intuition recommends adopting a physiological system of ethics that is directed inward. Ancient mystics discovered that ethical and unethical behavior is registered in the body, enabling individuals turning inward to intuitively weigh right from wrong. Instead of imposing moral edicts on themselves and others to avoid evoking the wrath of a god, intuitive scientists therefore focus their efforts on looking within to unravel the idea of self. Ancient societies that practiced this method concluded that murder, for instance, is unethical because it arouses feelings of revenge and despair, potentially more murder, and a community too infiltrated with patterns of reprisal and despondency to function harmoniously or, more importantly, nourish an expansive sense of self. Mystics took this conclusion a step further, claiming that such physiomagnetic patterns are unwanted because they narrow the intuitional bandwidth of reception to the infinite substance of self.

With the expansive sense of self established as a model for ethical conduct, it becomes each individual's responsibility to act in ways that further this expansiveness and thus to investigate the inner effects of their behavior—especially on the magnetic shifts of awareness that generate an idea of self. In terms of outer consequences, the theory of self proposes that the more energy a person focuses in the cerebrospinal axis, expanding her sense of identity, the more naturally ethical she will be. The inverse is also true: the more a person's attention is pulled away from the intuitive centers in the spine and brain, narrowing her sense of self, the more unethical she is apt to be. Unethical behavior would be seen as an outcome of physiological patterns caused by fear, worry, guilt, self-loathing, or other reactive emotions; restless habits of living; lack of receptivity to the inclusive ideas of others; or general disregard for societal interests. Hence, these patterns would be termed unethical not because of a divine decree delivered to only a select few but because they physiomagnetically limit the intuitive capacity in a person whose awareness has been distanced from the cerebrospinal axis, further narrowing the individual's sense of identity and causing more unethical behavior the more they are engaged. Additionally, since an individual's physiomagnetism is interwoven with the sur-rounding society's, violent patterns would be seen as both a social disruption and a societal symptom, occurring when the compelling patterns and influences are present simultaneous-ly in the individual and society.

This "feedback" interpretation of criminal behavior ignites new insights into crime prevention, based on the observation that it is the patterns, not the people flooded with them, that require removal from society. One inference is that the physio-magnetic patterns narrowing the sense of self may not be extinguished through prison sentences since, symptomatic of society's ill health, these patterns prevail inside as well as outside penitentiary walls. Similarly, laws enforced through punitive measures may fail to prevent crime because they, like religion's threats of divine retribution, instill a pattern of fear about being caught, paradoxically increasing the like-lihood of discreet and systemic criminal activity. But if peo-ple learn to change their center of awareness through breath regulation, localized tension, and calm dialogue with others, especially when violent responses erupt, patterns that induce crime can gradually be dislodged from the body.

The criminal offense of lying takes on a particularly interesting meaning when viewed physiomagnetically. Lying, generally regarded as a falsification of facts, is thought to be unethical because it engenders distrust and destroys the confidence needed for societies to function properly. But when lying is approached physiomagnetically, it's unethical because of its departure from an expansive identity's mode of expression. To an intuitive scientist, words spoken from the perspective of this larger identity represent the only truth there is—the infinite substance of self.

Consider the classic example of a Nazi at the door asking if the occupants know of any Jews in hiding and in fact they do. If the occupants' responses are influenced by patterns of fear, bigotry, or apathy, the facts they impart will reflect the untruth of a narrowly intuited sense of self. But if their responses emerge from a fearless identification large enough to encompass the Jews in hiding, then even if the occupants falsify facts they will be expressing the truth of the larger self.

From this perspective, suppressing the truth of the expansive self constitutes unethical behavior, whereas falsifying, fictionalizing, or mythologizing may actually deliver a truth that unites all people by magnetically fostering an expansive sense of self. The distinction between truth and fact is generally overlooked, probably because of the tendency to falsify facts in service to the narrow self and the expectation that facts would not be falsified for other purposes. But since it is sometimes necessary to tell a falsehood in order to speak truthfully, especially to those living the lie of the narrow self, falsehoods cannot be simplistically equated with untruth.

Just as falsehoods do not always represent untruth and facts do not always represent truth, ethical conduct cannot be codified for all time, recorded in a book, and then dictated to humanity. In fact, rigid adherence to some biblical commandments, such as not to bear false witness, may end up corroborating a narrowing of the sense of self and associated outbreaks of violence. Physiological patterns of bigotry and other manifestations of spiritual myopia that are not immediately expressed in violence tend to impel unethical thoughts and habits that eventually do culminate in violence.

Aware of this danger, intuitive scientists do their best to ensure their thoughts and actions emanate from an expansive sense of self regardless of good intentions. Good intentions, they note, promote limiting physiological patterns that may eclipse intuitive knowledge—a phenomenon that reveals itself each time someone is found to have unwittingly hidden unethical conduct behind good intentions. Even a noble intention, such as the resolve to save lives, can be perverted by a narrow sense of self, leading to the saving of lives only with which the person identifies or only in the name of a provisional ideal. Good intentions prompted by a narrow sense of self often lead to the same violent outcomes as planned misconduct, a dynamic seen in organized religions that have historically hidden behind morality while conducting missionary or combative activities.

In the end, ethical considerations hinge on whether or not one's activity is limited by sensory conditioning. The theory of self maintains that attention squandered exclusively on the senses, with no regard for the subtler centers of intuition in the spine and brain, narrows the sense of identity and leads to unethical behavior. By contrast, the prevention of misconduct is attributed to energy control, indicating why the ancient theory of self made no distinction between ethics and asceticism. Ethical injunctions calling for nonviolence and truth telling function as virtues not in and of themselves but rather because they *articulate inner regulations of energy and awareness,* helping adherents avoid digressive physiomagnetic patterns and turn their attention to intuiting the larger self, the real source of virtue.

The science of intuition's contributions to ethical concerns portray an ancient system of ethics that, based on the theory of self, has profound applications, underscoring not only the idea that morality is physiological but that the practice of intuition is itself an ethical imperative. For instance, if, as the theory of self asserts, the essence of the cosmos is the infinite substance of self, then right and wrong would have to be determined in relation to this substance, for the cosmos offers us no other unconditioned basis on which to guide conduct. Expansion of the sense of self, then, would be the only absolute good and the only ideal that eradicates moral absolutism from human experience. In the words of Einstein, "The true value of a human being is determined by the measure and the sense in which he has attained liberation from the [individuated] self."[4]

This ethical system also maintains that one's behavior in adult society ultimately affects nothing but one's own sense of self. When one adult harms another, the pattern of violence persists within the offender, narrowing her intuitional capacity. The target of violence, by contrast, is free to decide how to respond, and it is the response, not the bodily harm, that determines both the sense of self and any resulting physiological patterns of trauma. On the other hand, an adult who abuses a child is said to have committed a terrible crime because children, whose intuitional and intellectual capacities are still developing, react to violence by internalizing the destructive patterns.

Further reinforcing the significance of the world within is the system's notion that the consequences of every thought and action are configured in the spine and brain's centers of intuitive awareness. Here thoughts, actions, and reactions form a boomerang effect by setting up a physiomagnetic attraction for similar thoughts, actions, and reactions. Expressions like "An eye for an eye" and "As you sow so shall you reap," reminiscent of the ancient doctrine of karma, remind us of these physiomagnetic behavioral consequences. The principles they illuminate suggest that though the infinite substance of the cosmos guides all life through physiomagnetic cause and effect to expand the sense of self, we as human beings, by virtue of our enormous spiritual potential, are further obligated to consciously expand our intuitive self-knowledge.

By turning our attention inward to the dynamics of the self, this decentralized system of ethics puts us in tune with the "voice" of conscience, which echoes intuited knowledge of right and wrong. Depending on the degree of magnetization of the spine and brain, the voice of conscience may be distorted, drowned out, misinterpreted, ignored then modulated into guilt, or mistaken for conditioned reflexes, but it can never be utterly silenced. And even in whispers, its articulations testify to the individuated self's endless opportunities for expansion. Gradually, more pronounced utterances—heard when the breath slows, the sensory world recedes, the mind stills, and time frames collapse—succeed in overpowering the chorus of centralized authorities that too often propagate unethical behavior.

Through these and other means, the system of ethics arising out of the theory of self diminishes a person's capacity to judge the actions of others fairly since moral interpretations of others' behaviors are colored by the self's identification with them. For instance, while tempted to morally denounce violence in strangers, we can easily overlook it in friends. Lacking absolute standards of measure, we may suddenly realize that there is no isolation of physiomagnetic patterns, and consequently everything is connected to everything else. Judging others is then seen as an example of the narrow sense of self rejecting its own potential for growth, forgetting about itself in others, and ignoring the responsibility we all must take for ourselves and society, an accountability that can be experienced inwardly through the practice of Technique 10.

 **TECHNIQUE 10**

Supporting Ethical Conduct

The causal connections between mental and emotional patterns, physiological conditions, and the potential for expanding the sense of self make pranayama practices uniquely advantageous in supporting ethical conduct. To better understand how this works, recognize that every pattern of energy has an accompanying respiratory rhythm that manifests physiologically and either expands or contracts the sense of self. This means not only that mental and emotional patterns affect breathing rhythms but that changing your respiration is one of the quickest and easiest ways to influence all other physiomagnetic patterns in the body. Breathe like an angry, sad, happy, or pensive individual and you will become angry, sad, happy, or pensive. Alternatively, if you are angry and about to behave unethically, the most efficient way to stop yourself is by taking slow, calm, full breaths. It is no wonder that the word *huff* refers to both a breathing rhythm and an emotion.

Though no single method can ensure ethical conduct since it is a product of the expansive self, breathing rhythms conducive to expansion are beneficial. According to the ancient philosopher-yogis, manifestation of the infinite self is characterized by a cessation of breath, stillness of the heart, and withdrawal of awareness from the senses. Fortunately, the breathing rhythms of an expansive sense of self are more easily achieved. By practicing the following technique two to four times a day you may feel your attention gradually pulled away from patterns associated with restless desires of the body and a narrowly identified personality.

Sitting in the meditative posture—with spine straight, chin parallel to the floor, and palms upturned and resting on the thighs—close your eyes, lift your gaze, and concentrate intently on the point between your eyebrows. Breathe out through your mouth with a multiple exhalation sounding like "huh, huh, huuuuuh." Next, close your mouth and breathe in very slowly through your nostrils, gradually allowing your abdomen to expand while mentally counting the seconds that go by. As you continue inhaling, expand your chest, but stop before your shoulders lift. Hold your breath for 1 to 3 seconds while deeply concentrating on your brow, then exhale through your mouth for the same duration as the inhalation. Repeat the technique for 10 to 15 minutes, then sit quietly in contemplation and focus on the magnetized point between the eyebrows as your spine and brain intuit a sense of self to the best of their capacity. In that stillness, you may talk with your personal image of God, practice positive affirmation, or listen inwardly, all the while locking your attention to the medulla oblongata's expansive center of awareness.

This technique fosters ethical behavior because of three pronounced physiological features. One is that in waking consciousness exhalations last longer than inhalations, resulting in uneven breathing that keeps attention on the finite world by directing nervous energy toward the senses and autonomic bodily functions. By slowing the breath and equalizing inhalations and exhalations, it is possible to conserve nervous energy and direct it toward the spine and brain, increasing your intuitive awareness of the infinite self.

A second physiological benefit comes with the breath retention, which helps to still the otherwise incessant fluctuations of awareness. Until sensory relaxation is achieved, the patterns of energy and awareness flowing in the body produce restless thoughts and emotions. Gently holding the breath partially arrests such motion by building magnetism in the spine and brain. In advanced stages of practice, it is possible to instantly quiet the breathing by lifting the gaze and directing sensory and respiratory nervous energy to the spine and brain.[5]

Third, there is a hidden physiological advantage to the stillness achieved while practicing this technique. Simply by breathing slowly or focusing on the magnetized point between the eyebrows you can reproduce this stillness in the midst of everyday life, inspiring you to seek happiness in the expansive sense of self instead of in the sensorial world, to serve all others, and moment by moment to intuit conduct that sustains an ever-new expansive identity.

Investigations into how the science of intuition impacts on psychology might usher in a replacement for organized religions in this arena as well. Sigmund Freud, the founder of psychoanalysis, believed that psychiatrists would relieve priests of their jobs. However, despite their many contributions, Freud's advanced studies of the psyche led to equally narrow views of human potential. Influenced by Freud, popular psychology has propagated its own idea of the well-adjusted self and spawned a self-help industry advocating ways to treat the self and others. Ironically, this well-adjusted self, said to embody a balance of material and spiritual aspirations, simultaneously tethers nervous energy to sensory awareness, limiting the person's intuitional capacity and potential for spiritual success. The resulting model of the societal sense of self is simply too commercialized to benefit a global society.

This narrow model of self has become further entrenched in Western society by the treatment of symptoms rather than physiomagnetic patterns which, according to the theory of self, are the causes of psychological imbalance. When treating a client's symptoms, psychologists cannot help but use their own sense of self as the standard of measurement. Thus treatment by a psychologist whose sense of self is circumscribed by societal expectations will reflect those limitations. If psychologists do not vigorously challenge the model of self endorsed by society and instead address solely the inner turmoil it provokes, then even the most progressive methods will reinforce symptomatology. By contrast, the theory of self asserts that since symptoms of poor psychological health have their roots in patterns informing an intuited self, then even though a treatment may bring short-term relief the physiological patterns of nervous energy that inhibit the intuition of a wider self must eventually be sublimated for more permanent healing.

Specifically, behaviors considered psychologically damaging from a physiological perspective are those that monopolize the senses. Engaging in substance abuse or other forms of addiction, unabashed displays of wealth, or similar sense-absorbing activities is commonly considered unsound because these behaviors are construed as personally impairing and capable of decreasing society's productive output. Physiologically, however, patterns focused on sensory gratification impel unwanted behavior because they narrow the intuitional bandwidth of the cerebrospinal radio. Any repetitive activity geared toward excessive sensory input—whether it's pornography and masturbation, hours upon hours of television viewing, or fast-paced living devoid of inner reflection—contributes to an apathetic sense of self preoccupied with limited and limiting pleasures. The identity of the larger self comes with the tempering of sensory awareness by turning inward for intuitive awareness, the precursor to psychological well-being.

Aware of the limitations of old-school psychology, some progressive Western psychologists have been introducing their clients to variations on pranayama, including gazing techniques, breath regulation, and tension-relaxation methods to promote the cathartic release of patterns associated with psychological disturbances. Their work confirms the underlying importance of physiology, and they are finding that a few sessions of regulated breathing can uproot patterns that might otherwise require months or years of conventional psychoanalysis.

Shifting treatment from psychoanalysis to breathing presupposes that neuroses and psychoses can be approached as unhealthy electromagnetic energy patterns rather than psychological or biochemical imbalances, both of which, according to the theory of self, are caused by yet finer patterns of nervous energy introduced by reactions to trauma, or by habits or heredity. For example, trauma in the body is reflected in an agitated breathing pattern. During the practice of breath regulation, shifts in the sense of self may be accompanied by pain and irregular breathing, caused by the movement of attention away from a well-worn pattern and toward the establishment of a new one. Pain in such instances tends to signal the release of a tenacious habit that has contributed to the very sense of self attempting to undermine its release. Viewing habits as patterns of energy connected with particular thoughts and actions, the theory of self posits that even the finite idea of self is little more than a glorified habit. And because a socially conditioned self is so highly venerated in society, questioning it is extremely difficult. As a result, very few people experience radical shifts in the sense of self unless they are provoked by a powerful crisis.

A shift to tension-relaxation methods is also on the rise, especially in the treatment of reactions to trauma, counterproductive habits, or inherited conditioning. Tension-relaxation methods operate on the principle that where there is energy in the body there is awareness. Nervous energy, guided through tension to various parts of the body, directs awareness to these places, awakening the practitioner to the presence or absence of "grooves" caused by recurring or long-held energy patterns that impede intuitive awareness; an experience of conscious tension pulling nervous energy away from these grooves; and the healing taking place through their eventual unseating. The quickest and easiest way to direct awareness to areas of the body in need of healing is through the application of Technique 11.

 **TECHNIQUE 11**

Tension-Relaxation Methods

During a crisis or any time afterward, one can train the body and mind to direct awareness internally through tension and to withdraw it through relaxation, resulting in increased calmness and freedom from limiting trauma-reactions, habits, and hereditary influences. The following twenty-two methods may be practiced in either a sitting or standing position, keeping the back straight and the eyes closed and focused upward. Unless stated otherwise, tense and relax very slowly, holding each position for 3 to 6 seconds while sending healing energy to the tensed body part or simply noting how it has galvanized your attention. Practice each method up to three times consecutively before moving on to the next. The sequencing that follows was devised to stimulate and relax particular polarities in the body. For best results in your personal practice of this technique, select methods that most meet your needs, sequence them to energize the desired muscle-group polarities, memorize your routine, then practice it daily, modifying it as necessary.

- Tense the head and medulla oblongata area, at the base of the skull, with a slight vibration. Hold and then relax.

- Tense the entire body, making sure to clench the fists, curl the toes, tighten the buttocks, and squeeze the entire face to the tip of the nose. Hold and then relax.

- Tense the throat, neck, and medulla oblongata area. Hold and then relax.

- Tense the ears by grimacing sharply with the face and eyes. Hold for as long as is comfortable, and then relax.

- Clench both fists tightly. Hold and then relax.

- Tense all parts of the neck for 1 to 3 seconds. Then quickly drop the chin to the chest with a bounce while withdrawing the energy.

- Tense the entire spine and head, from coccyx to cerebrum, pulling the shoulders back and tensing the abdomen as well. Hold for as long as is comfortable and then relax.

- Tense the feet, legs, and buttocks. Hold and then relax.

- Tighten the perineum by squeezing the anal sphincter muscles. Hold and then relax.

- Knit the brow at the point between the eyebrows, close the eyes, and tighten the eyelids, gently scrunching them. Hold and then relax.

- Tense the arms from the fists to the shoulders. Hold and then relax.

- Puffing out the chest, press palms together there as in prayer and tense shoulders, chest, and upper spine. Hold and then relax.

- Tense the entire abdomen and feel the tautness in the spinal area opposite the belly. Hold and then relax.

- Tense the buttocks and lower spine. Hold and then relax.

- Scrunch the face tightly as if bringing it all to the tip of the nose. Hold and then relax.

- Gently tense the eyes, moving the eyeballs in a circular motion to the right then to the left. After 6 rotations in each direction, relax.

- With the mouth closed, pull the tongue back to touch the uvula—the nipplelike organ that hangs at the back of the mouth—or the point as close to it as you can reach. Hold for as long as is comfortable, and then relax.

- Exhale, place chin to chest, and bend over, lowering the head between the knees. Hold for as long as is comfortable, then relax and inhale.

- With mouth closed, drop the head to the chest, tense the neck, and with added tension, pull the head back until the forehead faces the ceiling. Next, relax the neck, open the mouth, and hold for up to 12 seconds. Then lift the head, repeat the practice, and relax entirely.

- Lock chin to chest and, exerting a pull on the back of the neck, press chin firmly into the chest for several seconds, then press chest against the chin for several seconds. Relax.

- Open the mouth then close it with slight tension, gently clenching the teeth. Hold for 1 to 3 seconds, and then relax.

- Make a triple exhalation through the mouth, vocalizing, "Huh, huh, huuuuuuuh." Closing the mouth, allow the body to inhale on its own. Perform this multiple exhalation several times, resting silently in between.

Such effective modalities as eye exercises, breath regulation, and tension-relaxation appear to be challenging the relevancy of conventional treatments in psychology. There is little reason to go to a mental health specialist when these cathartic procedures can be learned at no cost and practiced at home.

Another challenge to standard mental health practices comes from science fiction writer L. Ron Hubbard, founder of the Church of Scientology. A longtime opponent of psychiatry, Hubbard proposes an alternative treatment: psychological "auditing" sessions for relief from haunting aliens. Scientologists believe that seventy-five million years ago a galactic ruler named Xenu deployed H-bombs and murdered billions of drugged beings whose souls now inhabit our bodies, necessitating our shelling out thousands of dollars to auditors until we are "clear" of the aliens—a scenario reminiscent of the belief that by purchasing indulgences from the Catholic Church we extricate ourselves from the consequences of sin. Scientology's beliefs, like those of the Catholic Church, while giving lucrative names to the human condition, explain nothing about the psyche and how it operates in society.

Hubbard's Xenu hypothesis, departing radically from psychological theory, lends itself to pranayama treatment modalities since the alien souls, even if they existed, would have no recourse but to manifest in our bodies as nervous energy patterns. But a Scientology auditor, characteristically employing a lie detector during treatment, would be unable to tell the difference between patterns influenced by upbringing, environment, reaction to trauma, or Xenu's aliens, suggesting the Xenu story is superfluous to the sublimation of harmful habits. Far from representing a breakthrough in mental health, the financial success of Scientology's methods, say cult experts, is symptomatic of a social disease spread by a bait-and-switch ploy that takes advantage of the believer's low self-esteem and turns over the psychiatrist's job not to the individual, where it has always belonged, but to unlicensed mental health practitioners insulated by laws protecting freedom of religion.

Equally challenging, the science of intuition's impact on sociology can assist in replacing religious institutions that have assumed authority in this sector of society. The theory of self asserts that people who interact frequently with one another begin to share physiomagnetic patterns, giving rise to the admonition that company is stronger than willpower. Identification with others on a global scale, or in a nation as large and diverse as the United States, is unlikely in the presence of divisive social institutions. To assist citizens in relating to at least the widest group possible, federal governments can oversee only those things to which everyone in the nation identifies. For example, due to the lack of a monolithic social sense of self in America, a small federal government, preferable to the present large one, could be in charge only of defending the country, protecting its citizens, and supporting community life. Individual communities, in recognition of the fact that the societal sense of self varies from place to place, might then be entrusted with overseeing their own systems of education, services for the elderly, health care, distribution of tax revenues, as well as moral and socially lawful jurisdiction.

Political parties, especially those based on extreme ideologies, also function much like religious institutions, making it difficult for members to question candidates since loyalty to a party supersedes the commitment to truth seeking. Further, each of the two major political parties in America and elsewhere reflects only half of the theory of self's view of a government's objective. On the right, people want small government and instinctively know that big government can be wasteful and tyrannical; on the left, people want social solidarity and instinctively know that without it individuals will suffer at the hands of political and economic opportunists. Both parties are correct; but the community, not the federal government, is the best distributor of tax revenues because community members can more easily identify with one another. Communities, practicing self-rule, would also expect citizens to take a more responsible role in their own governance; sap power from the centralized government and the favoritism it bestows on the wealthy; and respect differing perspectives and lifestyles, learn from one another's mistakes, and exchange ideas along with goods and services.

An additional social institution that can be reevaluated from the vantage point of the science of intuition is marriage. Churches exert considerable influence over marriage, beholding it as a divine institution. Defending the sacredness of marriage, however, often translates into sanctification of a fixed and biased view of marriage, affecting the societal sense of self by generating narrowing patterns of guilt and self-righteousness. Once the term "marriage" is understood as an arrangement requiring periodic reassessment to suit an evolving culture, societal attitudes toward it will begin evolving as well. Finally, when the ideal of the larger self is in place, dictating who can contract with whom will be unnecessary.

For example, monogamy is sometimes viewed as a sociological attempt to regulate the instinct of sexual aggressiveness that would otherwise perpetuate matings outside the pair bond. Philosophers like Arthur Schopenhauer, however, considered it inevitable for most men to seek multiple sex partners; likewise, certain cultures, especially along the coast of the Alaskan archipelago and in portions of the Himalayas, practice polyandry. In the final analysis, the form a marriage takes is irrelevant to the emerging societal sense of self as long as the configuration does not cause personal turmoil for the adults or their progeny. At best, marriage as an institution assists in expanding the sense of self from an individual to a partnership identity.

Religious opposition to same-sex marriage places yet another burden on the societal sense of self, for it fails to account for naturally occurring homosexual impulses. Physiologically, every human body has both male and female poles, with personality and sexual orientation reflecting a blend of both and sexual repertoires stimulating the respective erotic zones. Examples of male (positive) and female (negative) poles include the left and right hemispheres of the brain, the right and left sides of the body, the penis/anus and clitoris/vagina/anus, the medullar and coccygeal plexuses, and the front and back of the body. As a result of this bipolarity, the motions of energy and awareness during sexual activity are generally the same regardless of a partner's gender. And magnetically, bodies exhibiting sexual attraction are heterosexual regardless of their genitalia. Thus, while the theory of self advises against excess sexual stimulation because of its tendency to expend considerable energy, the theory does not caution against stimulation from a particular gender. By contrast, today's societal prejudice known as homophobia mirrors a religiously induced fear of expressing our inherent male and female attributes. So strong is this fear worldwide that millions of African women every year suffer through religiously prescribed genital mutilation because of a superstition that deems a woman's male parts, like the clitoris, an impurity to her femininity.

Social practices, like social institutions, impact strongly on the sense of self. The practice of eating red meat, for example, produces an aggressive pattern in the body by stimulating the sympathetic nervous system.[6] Among human beings having no other viable source of protein, this pattern is advantageous for it ensures the arousal necessary to secure enough food for their survival. But among human beings who do not need to hunt for their food, the result is an aggressive drive manifesting as anxiety, ill health, protein poisoning, and physical violence toward others—as in war, domestic violence, or cutthroat business practices—and ultimately toward oneself. Many eventually embrace a vegetarian diet because of the inhumane killing, health problems, and aggressive tendencies associated with meat eating, while others become vegetarian because of the strain on the environment and the annexation of enormous tracts of land incurred by the widespread ingestion of meat. The motivation in each instance may be guided by an expansive sense of self. Narrower ambitions, such as adopting vegetarianism to secure membership in a particular group, would actually establish a physiological magnet that obstructs intuitive awareness. In fact, intuitive scientists see themselves less as vegetarians and more as "propertarians," people who merely eat what is proper for their bodies. To them, this dietary choice is both a physiological and sociological consideration arising from intuitive knowledge of an expansive self.

A social practice more associated with religious mandates and currently attracting heated debate is the opposition to abortion. Pro-life religionists oppose the practice because of the sacredness they project onto a fetus's hypothetical soul, causing them to equate abortion with murder. But murder implies the presence of violent thoughts and reactive emotions that narrow the sense of self, hence abortion cannot be called murder unless the mother acts on violent patterns in aborting her unborn and the unborn actually has a soul. Other pro-life enthusiasts who subscribe to the idea of a fetal soul equate abortion with killing since it entails discarding the organic matter associated with fetal life. But these individuals see nothing wrong with removing a tumor or discarding cow parts, vegetables, or other forms of life.

Ultimately, the accuracy of calling abortion killing or murder depends on the underlying theological assertion about whether or not fetuses are human beings with human souls. The concept of innumerable human souls appearing seemingly out of nowhere at conception is superfluous to the theory of self, which postulates that everything intuits a sense of the one infinite self, or God, in accordance with its capacity. Nor does the theory of self consider the fetus a human being, because it is not yet capable of intuiting an individuated sense of self—the hallmark of being responsible for one's actions in a world of cause and effect. Just as seeds cannot be called trees until they burgeon forth with trunks, branches, and leaves, the ability to intuit an individuated sense of self depends on the presence of breath regulated by an autonomous nervous system, something a fetus lacks. A newborn, though, attains a degree of individuation with its first breath, simultaneously shouldering the responsibilities that come with individuation—the first being to continue to breathe. Indeed, past traditions, including Judeo-Christianity, link inception of the human soul with the breath. In Genesis 2:7, God breathes the breath of life into Adam's nostrils, imparting to Adam a "living soul," something he presumably did not have before. Also, *neshamah,* Hebrew for the human soul, comes from the verb *leenshom,* to breathe; and the Hebrew word *ruach* means both spirit and wind. The word *spirit,* from the Latin *spiritus,* is cognate with inspiration. And the Sanskrit *prana,* meaning energy, is used throughout ancient Indian texts to connote breath and spirit, whose intuited presence in the cerebrospinal plexuses is made outwardly apparent by its investment of nervous energy in respiration.

The theory of self sheds further light on the social practice of opposing abortion by maintaining that when the lives of different beings are equally at risk, favoring the one with more intuitive capacity invites the potential for more self-expansion. From this point of view, the life of a pregnant woman would be valued more highly than the life of her fetus. And both points make it clear that the theory of self places abortion considerations solely at the feet of women, who for purposes of self-expansion must retain power over their bodies. Women alone, it seems, are responsible for determining all things pertaining to their bodies, including when and whether to have children, because such determinations influence their sense of self. Moreover, forcing on any woman the shift in awareness that comes with childbearing is not only socially destabilizing but some-times deadly.

From the perspective of the science of intuition, any social institution or practice can potentially function to nar-row the self by triggering physiological patterns laden with limitations imposed by history or culture, a dynamic charac-teristic of every juncture where the self meets society. Suppose, for instance, a friend in academia tries to convince you to earn a degree. Your receptivity to this physiological trigger would validate your friend's identification with and glorification of academic credentials. However, despite the promise of a future blessed with more knowledge and happi-ness if you enroll in the degree program, you would be required to accept the authority of an institution that demands your respect, outranks you as an individual, and harnesses your awareness to particular studies. After earning your degree, you might continue narrowing your energy pat-terns by speaking highly about your new credentials and attempting to persuade other people to get accredited, even if it's likely to drive them into debt.

The self meets society not only in academia, which trig-gers the intellect, but in cults triggering the emotions, social clubs triggering the senses, as well as political parties and military conscription triggering the will forces. In all these potentially addictive arenas, societal forces act on the sense of self by way of a powerful magnetism—a "sociomag-netism"—that can easily cause a person to be more like a product of her social milieu than an active participant in it. Sociomagnetic patterns, like physiomagnetic ones, take up residence in the body, where they produce magnets of awareness that define the sense of self.

Individuals can break free of this sociomagnetic conditioning by generating physiomagnetic forces of their own. Liberation from the societal sense of self not only expands one's identity but introduces the possibility of becoming a formidable force for social change. Ultimately, spiritual aspirants who counter pervasive sociomagnetism in this way may become freethinking social revolutionaries, through progress easily tracked using Technique 12.

 **TECHNIQUE 12**

From Sociomagnetism to Social Activism

Sociomagnetic environments barrage the body with a constant stream of information about how to "fit in"—how to keep thoughts, feelings, and behavior aligned with the necessary expectations and therefore in support of the status quo. These types of environments, whether educational, medical, corporate, political, economic, or religious, are all centralized, their power and authority arising from physiological patterns harbored by millions of individuals. Entry into any one of them, invariably fraught with adjustment difficulties, contributes to the development of a societal sense of self, a perverse narrowing of personal identity.

If you are strongly influenced by sociomagnetic forces, you are likely to become disempowered and eventually conditioned, feeling distanced from the natural world. Through the practice of intuition, however, you can replace this sociomagnetism with a refined personal magnetism by centralizing power in your spine. Once you have built up this power, the influence of centralized institutions crumbles and is at last seen for what it is: cerebrospinal energy borrowed from individuals on a massive scale. Better yet, you become an active participant in your world, perhaps even a freethinking advocate for revolutionary change. To gauge your progress in evolving from sociomagnetism to social activism, trace your current level of awareness according to the following nine steps.

1. You feel vulnerable to other people's expectations, spiritually defenseless, and too helpless to change your situations with other people. Your sense of self has been narrowed by social conditioning.

2. With increased intuitive awareness, you find that the underlying exchange between human beings is not intellectual, emotional, materialistic, or other societally endorsed conduits, but rather magnetic.

3. Through the practice of energy control, asceticism, and sensory introversion, you discover an inherent potential to expand your sense of self.

4. You start exercising your personal power by extending the idea of self that was distorted by social conditioning. Toward this end, instead of directing forces outward toward a ruling minority you direct them inward toward your spine.

5. You notice that intuitively expanding your sense of self minimizes the magnetic influence of societal forces on you and simultaneously heightens your physiomagnetic capacity to assist others in their expansion of identity.

6. You view centralized institutions, intent on promoting a narrow self, as obstacles in the journey toward an ever-widening spiritual identity for yourself and others in society.

7. You consciously stop distancing yourself from your spirituality, observe your interests broadening, and perceive your self as the self of humanity.

8. You choose a new role in society, freed by the knowledge that you are no longer stamped with the magnetic birthmark of sociological concerns and that what you are exchanging with others is the magnetism necessary to intuit the infinite substance of self.

9. You recognize that your freedom from sociomagnetic conditioning has removed any remaining vestige of perceived antagonism between nature and humanity and revealed their underlying unity of purpose: expansion.

The claim of the ancients that intuition frees human beings from conditioned existence is comprehensible when conditioning is perceived in terms of electrophysiological patterns of limiting awareness that were recorded in response to sensory stimuli. Intuitive methods disrupt these patterns and reroute them to the more sophisticated cerebral plexus, further developing intuition and liberating the practitioner from the dominance of historical and cultural influences, value biases, and other effects of finite conditioning that pervade society like radiation. Finally, impulses of social activism arise with the awareness that it is possible to encourage others in society to embrace methods for expanding the sense of self— an understanding of self in society that can unfold only with a focus on spirituality apart from centralized religion.

A New Myth to Spark Social Reform

Wherever we go, whatever we do,
self is the sole subject we study and learn.

—Ralph Waldo Emerson

Just as a stream of myths seeded social change throughout human history, so can a new myth invigorate social reform in our times. To succeed, attempts to formulate and introduce a new myth require an understanding of how social reform occurs and how mythologies operate. Many myths of the past persist, shaping overly simplistic ways of thinking in today's exceedingly complex world. In replacing them, care must be taken to avoid proposing lofty solutions that would be equally impossible to implement.

The pragmatic applications of the theory of self suggest it might play several roles in the delivery of a new myth. For one, the theory of self asserts that physiological patterns of the majority of people in any group dominate its general landscape. In totalitarian states, where dictators or extremist political parties impose their agendas through feigned patriotism, nationalistic sentiments, and warnings of social chaos, the masses' societal sense of self is generally riddled with patterns of fear, bigotry, or greed. Due to their sheer abundance, these patterns rule, at times overpowering the determination of the few people actively resisting the fascistic agendas. For social reform to take place, individuals with strong creative magnetism would need to gradually shift the magnetism of the majority toward patterns of fearlessness, inclusiveness, and sacrifice for humanity—patterns that ignite decentralization of political, economic, intellectual, and spiritual power. Since progress depends on the combined magnetism of the masses, all types of social change are obliged to take a bottom-up approach.

The theory of self further proposes that when pattern shifts reach a critical mass, social reform is inevitable. This means social reform ultimately reflects changed patterns of thinking, interpreting, and responding to circumstances, along with a more expansive societal sense of self. For example, where a poorly educated majority is consistently oppressed and the resulting physiological patterns of deprivation and desperation reach a critical mass, they unleash violent reformations in the societal sense of self, which may come to expression in political executions, looting, and the destruction of cultural antiquities, as occurred during revolutions in France, Russia, and China during the last few centuries. If instead reform is to come about through nonviolent means, the critical mass would have to mount gradually within the majority, guided by the expansive magnetism of individuals who, rather than reacting blindly to the oppression, respond to it creatively by embodying expansive spiritual ideals such as forgiveness, patience, and equanimity.

Sociospiritual reformers employing the theory of self might first assess the opposing forces of expansion and contraction on individuals, paying particular attention to religion's mythic forces that directly affect the majority. In the last book he completed in his lifetime, *Inner Reaches of Outer Space*, religious scholar Joseph Campbell writes, "One of the first concerns of the elders, prophets, and established priesthoods of tribal or institutionally oriented mythological systems has always been to limit and define the permitted field of expression of [the] expansive faculty of the heart, holding it to a fixed focus within the field exclusively of the ethnic monad, while deliberately directing outward every impulse to violence."[7] Reflecting the expansiveness of the substance of self, the natural tendency of the hearts of all creatures is to broaden. But, as Campbell points out, instead of encouraging followers to expand the sense of identity beyond ethnic confines, the spokespeople of organized religions often warn against it.

Avowing that the old myths advocating exclusivity be replaced by a new vision of the cosmos reflecting the expansive tendency of the heart, Campbell inquires: "The old gods are dead or dying and people everywhere are searching, asking: What is the new mythology to be, the mythology of this unified earth as of one harmonious being?"[8] In the course of considering such a vision, Campbell devotes significant discussion to pranayama's scientific approach and cross-cultural practice. He theorizes that human spirituality universally revolves around an inner battle against the narrow self, won through retiring the energy of the body, mind, and senses into the spine and up to the brain, and that outer wars result when the narrow self rules, inhibiting expansion of the heart.

Interpretations of religious myths underscore this idea. For example, progressive Muslim scholars claim that jihad represents an internal battle against the little self, yet others explain jihad as warfare against nonbelievers. A Sufi mystic battling the small ego will cease to identify with divisive teachings because they cause contraction inwardly. Likewise, a spiritual investigator would reject the unquestioned authority of the Qur'an and other scriptural writings, recognizing that only intuition, not printed books, can reveal the expansive nature of the infinite substance of self. Campbell echoes the theory of self in his sentiment that humanitarian and therefore universal interpretations of religious myths, along with an understanding of pranayama, would play an important role in the new mythology encouraging global social reform. Unfortunately, he does not say how pranayama might be introduced to the masses.

Before attempting to formulate a myth capable of inspiring social reform, it is important to comprehend how myths function. They are not accounts of past events but rather notions of God, self, and the cosmos. As such, myths function as metaphors for humanity's primal urges toward infinite life, awareness, knowledge, and happiness. Myths are complex, but many people today give them reductionist interpretations, perhaps because they are too contracted to perceive how even rival myths reveal cross-cultural similarities among human beings.

Religious scholars use the term "supertrue" to denote the universal merit of certain myths. Calling a myth supertrue, however, can divert attention away from the super falsehoods and violent attitudes it embodies. For instance, the Jesus myth's portrayal of Christ is upheld as a supertruth because it serves as a model of humanity's universal quest for eternal life. Yet concealed beneath this branding is the myth's divisive insistence that failure to employ the image of Jesus as a focal point of devotion will consign nonbelievers to an eternal hell. When this exclusive aspect of the myth remains hidden, so too does the accompanying narrowness of the societal sense of self that invests in the myth in order to acquire a secure identity in a largely precarious world.

Rival myths, when allowed to coexist, easily retain the metaphoric power of their divine images. That is, if two people adopt contradictory histories of Jesus both images can still serve as focal points of concentration. Competing historical details fail to dilute the power of a mythic image because they are immaterial to it. Saint Francis and others had no need even to know the details of Jesus's life in order to worship God in the form of Jesus. Neither historical details nor lack of them necessarily diminishes the mythic stature of figures like Christ.

Myths function not only as metaphors for humanity's innermost aspirations but as mirrors reflecting the idea of self. For example, Mary Magdalene was at times portrayed as an upright woman close to Jesus; at other times she was depicted as a whore, a mythic model of impurity made pure by the grace of Jesus. Today she is interpreted as an upright woman whose image was tainted by misogynistic church leaders. It was not Mary who changed but rather people's tendency to venerate or revile her shifting mythic image—that is, their ways of thinking about themselves.

Another myth nearly transparent in its reflective capacity is that of the Buddha and his Four Noble Truths. The first truth states that human existence is one of suffering; a spiritual investigator working with the theory of self might interpret this suffering as a direct result of the narrow self with its shallow pleasures and short-lived joys that limit human awareness to sensory impressions of the body. The second truth, that suffering is caused by desires, might be explained as follows: since eating and bathing require desires, the only way out of all desires would be to kill ourselves, which itself requires a desire that would then lead to suffering. The third truth asserts that there is a way out of suffering; the spiritual investigator might decipher this to mean that since it is the desires of a narrow sense of self that cause suffering, distinguishing between these desires and those of an expansive sense of self will resolve the second truth's contradiction of desiring to be free of desire. The fourth truth, the Buddha's Eight-Fold Path, might be interpreted as signifying the spiritual desire to uproot narrow-ing desires and identities and expand the sense of self. However we decipher the myth of the Buddha and his Four Noble Truths, our interpretation depends on the idea of self we are entertaining at the time. Even our attraction or aver-sion to it hinges on how we think of ourselves.

The fact that the three major monotheistic faiths—Judaism, Christianity, and Islam—worship the same God scripturally yet interpret God so differently suggests that mythic images of God likewise reflect diverse ideas of self. This would explain why despite the belief in a common God, a worshipper narrowly associated with one faith is unable to identify with someone of another faith. For instance, use of the mythic image of Abraham to unite Muslims and Jews has failed because the two groups cannot agree on the details of Abraham's life; and the conflicting details, authored by differ-ent ideas of self, parallel the very animosity expressed in the groups' current life situations. Jews say that Muslims distorted their original stories of Abraham, not realizing that their Abraham myth arose out of an ancient narrow sense of iden-tity to which they still cling. Any of religion's mythic images, whether of Abraham, the Buddha, Mary Magdalene, Jesus, or God, can only be interpreted to suit the self of the interpreters, who simultaneously project their ideas of self onto it and everything else.

Mythmaking as a form of projection is a pervasive activi-ty: human beings, motivated by their ideas of self, continual-ly convert artifacts of the past into facts used to establish historicity. And while some facts may be universally agreed upon, the line between converting and subverting artifacts remains forever fuzzy. Ironically, theologians who engage in such conversions pay little attention to the inevitability that many artifacts they fashion into myths are themselves myths generated by earlier theologians.

Certainly history, defined as a chronicle of actual events, is a misnomer. Interestingly, the concept of recording events as they transpired was not fully considered until the fourteenth century, when the famous Arab historical philosopher Ibn Khaldun wrote *Kitab al-Ibar*. Before that, events were routinely transfigured by the storyteller's sense of self. Today, even assiduous historians admit that historical documentation is a kind of fiction since no written rendering can possibly encompass every perspective on every detail of every event.

This process of conversion, or mythologizing, occurs not only while reading the Bible or analyzing an ancient relic, but with each memory we recall. And it is these mythic images of ourselves that form our worldview and our beliefs. These, in turn, shape our recollection of events that transpired in the past, short-circuiting any awareness of our expansive identity and the ever-shifting nature of the narrow sense of self. The seemingly stable sense of self presiding over memories actually emerges from the narrow sense of self that is by nature capable of remembering only itself.

It follows that images of God thought to benefit one group of people over another are simply projected images of the self, and nothing more authoritative. When some individuals claim to have conversations with God, meaning everyone's God as opposed to merely their personal image of divinity, they are referring to a mythic God, built from the artifacts informing an experience of self. In effect, they have been talking to themselves—an occupation that may be harmless, or even instructional if their intent is to focus the mind. But if their minds tell them they are the next prophet or war leader, they will invariably prophesy or wage war against a reflection of their identity and desire to defend it, inundating the minds of their followers with the same mythic ideas.

If everything we understand to be true, including God, is a mythological creation of the sense of self, then today's new myth to hasten social reform would have to be the forerunner of them all: *the individuated sense of self.* This mother of all myths and images of God, rooted in the theory of self, can be understood as our own self-image based on the artifacts of memories and sensory data that, assembled and shaped through repeated interpretation, provide us with an apparently stable sense of identity. Paradoxically, the more we engage with this myth, the more self-absorbed we become, eventually breaking free from narrow identities in the discovery that the individuated sense of self we have been intuiting is stable only within the finite reality we have constructed whereas the cosmos, composed of the infinite substance of self, offers only an illimitable self stable in an eternally expansive reality. As our intuitive capacity itself increases, our sense of self gradually transcends the seeming divisions on which the cosmos is based. This new myth for our times thus responds to the historical necessity for shared rights and resources in an age of unprecedented globalization.

Historically, cultures were unaware of the individuated sense of self informing their projections and consequently used myths to express local truths as supertruths in an effort to sanctify their past and divinize their society. Rejecting the essential unity of the human race, these mythmakers did not consider that the cosmos, plainly viewed, was sufficient to reveal the indivisibility of the world. Or perhaps the infinite substance of the cosmos was inaccessible to them. Today's cosmic supertruth, in keeping with the new myth, is that God is everywhere, playing the role of innumerable selves in this divided space-time reality to which the senses are privy. Stated differently, ours is a world where countless individuated selves, human and nonhuman, of the one infinite self perceive and project in accordance solely with their sense of self. Here, the narrow idea of self is the only source of ignorance; the expansive idea, the only wellspring of knowledge.

From this perspective, it follows that no one truly worships Christ or any other image of God. Rather, we all worship the same infinite self called God, in the form of our own selves. Though this infinite self cannot be proved to exist, the finite intellect can propose that a substance of self constitutes the basis of existence—a proposition that may be repeatedly tested. In doing so, one finds that while a sense of self escapes the five senses, individuals unfailingly realize various degrees of self-knowledge. It also becomes apparent that everyone intuitively knows a fragment of the infinite substance of self and nothing more, since awareness is entirely self-awareness, a form of knowledge that seeks to increase by building upon itself.

Education is therefore self-education, with humanity as the primary instructional source. And supertrue applies only to myths that are universal and unifying. Individuals who agree on these principles will no longer be swayed by organized religions' efforts to sanctify divisive myths lacking a foundation in reason, science, and social justice.

If Campbell and the ancients are right and pranayama leads to self-education, its new unifying myth is still difficult to realize since myths by their nature are not understood universally but are predominantly created and interpreted to unify one group in opposition to others. Curiously, the Christian European colonists, while considering themselves the chosen people in relation to Native Americans, did not generally identify with Jews, the originators of that self-divinizing myth. Because of the projection involved in myth-making, the endemic challenge in introducing humanity to the new myth is to offer meaning about the cosmos without appealing to the instinct to believe. It may need to be woven into more mainstream mythic cloth, yet it is precisely when theories become precepts to clothe the masses that divisive materials and deceptive ceremonials may be sewn in. In the end, we are left with a choice of either watering down the new myth, as has been done with New Age myths recently converted from self-knowledge quests to self-help allegories, offering little advantage to humanity, or uplifting humanity to the degree that the science of intuition becomes popular so that the new myth may take hold amongst the masses.

⊛ Uplifting humanity to increase receptivity to the unifying myth of the individuated sense of self requires teaching people about intuition's compatibility with critical thinking. Nearly every human being is born with the potential to think critically, but too often this faculty remains dormant, despite a multitude of bright ideas passing through the mind. These have as much to do with thinking as jotting down words on paper has to do with writing. Surely the greatest deterrent to thinking is societal conditioning. Historically, thought was feared in religious circles because it provoked an undermining of authority and questioning of traditions. In New Age movements, it is erroneously believed to stop individuals from being "in the moment." Equally misleading, we are taught to regard intuition and thought as mutually exclusive faculties.

The anti-intellectual trends spawned by organized religions centuries ago are now mainstream. Ethnic and nationalistic fearmongers claim that proficiency with words is designed only to fool and that the purported ability of philosophers to identify with humanity through introspection is mere sophistry. Corporatism also stunts intellectual growth, encouraging people to think primarily about the benefits of making money rather than more universal concepts. And public education, too exam-driven to support the development of thinking skills, renders society beholden to thoughtlessness at the highest levels of policymaking.

Faced with the compromised state of humanity's intellectual capacity, historians like Arnold Toynbee would counter that a thinking majority has never occurred in human history and therefore the best we can hope for is a majority that imitates the thinking of the creative minority and in so doing overrides patterns imposed by agendas breeding fear, bigotry, or greed. He might be right, but he did not know about the Internet and other space-annihilating resources to come, or about the earth-shaking crises humanity faces today, all of which call upon intellectual inquiry, making use of this faculty more imperative now than perhaps ever before.

In addition to promoting intellectual competence, another means of uplifting humanity to increase receptivity to the science of intuition and its unifying myth is education in the expansive properties of the heart. The theory of self emphasizes, as does Campbell, that every human being is endowed with an expansive heart—a premise that can be confirmed by watching children, who are as yet unspoiled by anti-intellectualism, materialism, and divisive myths. Most infants and toddlers who have been given an abundance of love and warm physical contact will open their hearts to people and animals they have never before met. And when we invest in an education for our children that instills critical thinking skills in tandem with a fully functioning expansive heart, we till the ground for the new myth inspiring social reform.

Toward that end, the techniques of pranayama can be taught in schools to help foster expansiveness of the heart. And whereas separation of church and state is threatened by school prayers that call upon a separatist ideal of God, it will not be challenged by the nonsectarian and purely psycho-physical methods of self-expansion through pranayama, the science behind prayer, any more than by biology, mathematics, or physical education. The pranayama practice described in Technique 13 helps children learn from a young age how to fight against patterns that shut down the natural expansiveness of the heart so they might introduce social reforms capable of accelerating scientific progress and ensuring world peace. Perhaps the war heroes of future myths will be those who conquered the narrow sense of self.

 **TECHNIQUE 13**

Magnetizing the Expansive Heart

The human emotive heart naturally yields an expansive feeling if sufficient awareness is directed toward it. The best way to experience this phenomenon is by magnetizing the heart—directing nervous energy toward the spine's dorsal plexus behind the heart—rather than glorifying the self by pretending to love humanity. Awareness then shifts to intuitive understandings decreasingly bound by sensory ambitions associated with the lower plexuses. As a result, the societal sense of self becomes defined less by reactive impulses and more by transpersonal values. Whereas prayer uses an image of God to move one's attention up the spine to the heart, this technique produces the same effect more powerfully by engaging the breath.

Most children, through imitating their parents, can successfully begin employing this technique at age three, provided they practice it daily before eating.

Sit in a chair of comfortable height in a quiet room, with your spine straight, shoulders back and shoulder blades drawn slightly together, palms together at the chest as if in prayer, eyes closed and focused slightly upward, mouth closed, and chin pressed gently against your chest. This position, because it directs nervous energy away from the senses and toward the spine, will turn your attention more inward.

Next, tense your abdomen and exhale fully through your mouth, then close your mouth again and slowly inhale through your nostrils with a slight sobbing sound, caused by the partial closing of your epiglottis. While inhaling, allow your abdomen and lower back to expand; as you bring the breath up to your dorsal plexus, let your rib cage expand as well. Placing your attention on your hands, extend your fingers outward like antennae and let your expanding chest push them forward. Keeping chin to chest and fingers stretched outward, focus on the sensation of expansiveness in your heart. Hold your breath for 6 seconds, allowing your abdomen to sink in below your rib cage. Then exhale slowly with your epiglottis still slightly closed, making a soft aspiration sound, and finally reverse the motion of inhalation by allowing your chest to deflate, gently tightening your abdomen and squeezing out the remaining air. The exhalation should be of the same duration as the inhalation, thus sending considerable nervous energy to the dorsal plexus and magnetizing the heart.

Begin by practicing this technique 12 times per sitting, with 1 or 2 sittings a day. As time passes, advance to 4 sittings a day and then gradually, over several months, to 18, 24, and finally 36 rounds of practice per sitting. With progress, your inhalations and exhalations will get longer, and as they do be sure they remain of equal duration. Start with 6-second inhalations and exhalations, building very gradually to inhalations and exhalations lasting 12 or more seconds. If pain occurs in the lungs or chest, discontinue practice for several days.

After working with this psychophysiological technique for about six months, you may find your attention gravitating toward your expansive heart at other times during the day. To make this a conscious practice, pull energy toward your heart any time you are standing in a crowded room, walking across a busy intersection, or performing other select tasks. That is, instead of artificially self-divinizing by pretending to act out of an expansive feeling, which can lead right back to a narrowing of the self and bouts of affectation, change your center of awareness and allow the expansive feeling of the heart to be intuited naturally. To aid your shift in attention, concentrate on receiving through the antennae at your chest the infinite expanse of the substance of self seated in the hearts of all things.

A humanity uplifted through intellectual generativity and expansion of the heart becomes fertile ground for the bottom-up dissemination of the theory of self's new myth sparking social reform by invigorating a shift in the societal sense of self and ideal of God. Many gods of Dark Age myths are dying because the narrowness out of which they were created and later interpreted has caused suffering and unhappiness. Collectively, the ideal of God projected by any organized religion in competition with that of other faiths has caused divisiveness and stratification among societies, undermining world peace. James Baldwin, sensing this predicament, wrote, "If the concept of God has any validity or any use, it can only be to make us larger, freer, and more loving. If God cannot do this, then it is time we got rid of Him."[9] To achieve peace and happiness, however, seekers need not get rid of God but rather, through worshipping by wondering, arrive every day at a new ideal of the mythic God image.

Redefining God through the new myth of an individuated sense of self invites us to embrace more unifying interpretations of God images. For example, the Hebrew myth that says God created Adam in his own image and from the dust of the ground can be newly interpreted as follows. If humans are created in the image of God, then humans would be creators, too—but humans have no power to create something from nothing, only the ability to move gross and fine substances around. If God does not have the power to create something from nothing either, but only to move the primordial dust around to bring stars and worlds into being, then who needs a creator God to shape stars, worlds, and life from stellar gasses, especially in today's scientific age when the laws of nature already account for such a feat? Interpreting the part of the old myth that says God created Adam from the dust of the ground, one might say that if humans are made of dust and in God's image then perhaps God is the cosmos and everything has been made in the image of God, from the animals to the atoms, all with varying degrees of likeness and all procreating in their own image.

According to this new profile of divinity, God is everything, manifesting a fragment of infinitude in gross atoms and stars, plants and insects whose awareness of self is barely awakened, crude finite animal forms that subconsciously strive for infinity, and refined human forms capable of consciously looking within for the expansive self of the cosmos. Turning outward to look at another human being or even a rock, we subsequently realize we are seeing a part of God.

Seeing more of God, as in a large boulder or grand vista, can inspire awe. The euphoria many astronauts feel upon viewing the entire planet from outer space most likely results from a felt sense of having seen an enormous piece of God.

Whereas to humans the earth appears large, it is but a speck of dust in comparison to the infinitude of the cosmos. The individuated sense of self likewise seems colossal though it is but a small part of humanity. Human faculties register only minuscule portions of infinitude because of the narrow band of space-time accessible to the senses. It is this predicament that drove ascetics, who wanted to see all of God all at once, to turn inward for direct knowledge of the infinite self of God.

Children and adults who directly intuit increasingly more of the self of God by nurturing their expansive faculties will have a natural defense against the narrowing influences of anti-intellectualism, materialism, and divisive myths. They will be the pioneers of major social reform, introducing, among other improvements, environmentally friendly technologies that decentralize the generation of electrical power, promoting loyalty to humanity instead of nations, strengthening the United Nations or some similar multinational entity to fight any necessary wars, and removing sectarianism from spirituality. Change cannot happen overnight, but a noticeable shift in the societal sense of self could conceivably be accomplished within a generation.

CHAPTER FOUR

Testing Today's Choices

Can We Know God?

*We make our world significant
by the courage of our questions and by the
depth of our answers.*
                                        —Carl Sagan

For thousands of years the question of whether humans can know God—that is, gain knowledge of infinity—has preoccupied spiritual seekers and followers of organized religion alike. Belief in an eternal heaven assumes that humans attain such knowledge after death, but despite the comfort derived from viewing death as a door to eternity, it may not be possible for a finite being to realize infinitude. The theory of self, which proposes the possibility of an infinite intuitive knowledge, may provide insight into this age-old question.

The theory of self offers a method to test for infinite knowledge just as physicists test for finite knowledge. In physics, the cosmos consists of four forces: gravity, electromagnetism, weak nuclear interactions, and strong ones. These forces of nature represent the workings of increasingly finer aspects of matter, from planets and stars to electrons, atoms, and subatomic particles. The power to technologically utilize them comes with knowledge of them, implying that a person harnessing such a power possesses knowledge of the corresponding finite forces. Likewise, a person with infinite power would have infinite knowledge.

A standard for testing infinite power is therefore necessary to determine whether humans can know God. To arrive at such a standard, it is essential to understand that according to the theory of self, the cosmos consists of four substances: the infinite substance of self and, from it, the increasingly gross manifestations known as causal ideas, prana, and atoms. As nervous energy and awareness ascend from the coccygeal plexus at the base of the spine to the cerebral plexus in the skull, a person intuits finer and finer substances. The more a person's awareness transcends the interpretive function of the mind, the greater that person's power to intuit the infinite substance of self.

Infinite power, then, requires ever-increasing freedom from the sluggish, scattered, and sense-bound mind intuited as an attribute of an individuated self. Whereas the mind fragments the substance of self into its hierarchy of cosmic substances, liberation from the mind eventually reveals the substance of self's essential indivisibility. Mind is but a causal idea, an elementary aspect of all substances other than the eternal self. As such, to the mind the eternal self's division is real, while the power arising through freedom from the mind promotes triumph over physical limitations, based on the awareness that every part of the cosmos reflects the substance of self. To better understand the indivisibility of the one self, it is helpful to contemplate modern physics' comparisons between the cosmos and a hologram, where every part reflects the whole in accordance with its intuitive capacity.

Having infinite power would make it possible, for example, to overcome space and time. Based on the theory of self, the earth's space and time dimensions are functions of the substance of self in its manifestation as atoms in motion, and when atoms revert to prana their space-time values give way to the wider parameters of a prana-based existence; by contrast, the division of causal ideas results in prana and atoms. Because ideational, pranic, and atomic existences all participate in the panorama of cosmic nature, the overcoming of space and time would awaken an awareness of the laws of nature as they extend beyond the boundaries of atomic matter. If the causal idea of mind also were to be overcome, the cosmos would consist merely of the indivisible infinite substance of self playing with finite ideas. Fully identifying with this infinite substance of self would ultimately endow a person with whatever power might come from intuitively reducing all of the cosmos to a unified substance.

More specifically, the theory of self indicates that a person's infinite knowledge becomes evident through the power to dematerialize and rematerialize the body at will. The feat of dematerializing as a means for demonstrating the acquisition of infinite knowledge makes sense in this context since the body is considered an atomic manifestation of the individuated self; an infinite self prior to individuation would not be conditioned by the presence of a body. And the power to dematerialize arises from intuition. A person who intuits prana and causal ideas, said the ancient yogis, would be able to convert the atoms of the body to prana and prana to causal ideas.

Because the ancients asserted that the power to dematerialize and rematerialize was within the scope of human capability, one might wonder what sort of world they thought they inhabited. We now know it was probably composed of waves of light and energy, the world modern physicists describe. Actually, the theory of self and the theory of relativity meet in the enigma of light, which has properties in both domains. In the former, bodily atoms are considered congealed light finally realized to be light through the breathless state, and the way to the infinite is to unite one's awareness with the substance of self and thus see the cosmos as infinite light without divisions of space and time. In the realm of relativity physics, the velocity of light, *c,* can never be reached by a material object because at velocities approaching *c,* mass and energy increase to infinity, time slows down and ultimately stops, and space collapses. It is as if the cosmos is saying, "You cannot overcome space and time and become infinite light through attempts to materially reach the speed of light. But if you mimic moving at the speed of light by accelerating the mind's vibratory rate through inward concentration and stilling the breath, my secrets will be revealed and I will make you light." Perhaps the mystic Jesus was explaining this practice when he said, "The eye is the light of the body. So, if your eye is single, your whole body will be full of light" (Matthew 6:22). As for the ancient Indian yogis, they may have selected the superhuman power of dematerialization as proof of knowledge to prevent practitioners from succumbing to delusionary claims of infinitude while bound to a finite body.

Whatever the actual reason for its origin, the dematerialization method of testing for infinite knowledge undercuts the human tendency to presume possession of absolute truth. For example, asserting that human souls go to an eternal abode after the body dies is tantamount to claiming infinite knowledge. Challenging preachers and imams who profess eternal heaven to test their infinite knowledge of it through infinite power, perhaps by converting their bodies into pranic light, would reveal they lack such knowledge. In pragmatic terms, if they in fact had infinite knowledge of an eternal heaven awaiting them after death, that knowledge would prevent mourning the death of a heaven-bound family member or friend, eliminate fear of mortality, and propel renunciation of narrow self-interests in this ephemeral world—none of which typically characterizes the lives of exclusionary religious authorities. From both perspectives, it appears that sectarian heavens are just theories, and divisive ones at that. Religious authorities and sincere truth-seekers who instead acknowledge ignorance of the infinite will naturally refrain from foisting these and other beliefs on others as if they are absolute truths.

The theory of self further reveals that testing for knowledge through manifestations of power requires certain conditions. First, *the realization of knowledge can be tested only by those striving for it.* The outward display of power proves nothing to individuals lacking the knowledge it confirms. For example, a bushman may observe the capabilities of a cell phone, but they will remain inexplicable and fail to prove the inventor's knowledge of electromagnetic radiation unless the bushman investigates electromagnetism. Similarly, if the power of dematerialization were displayed before a crowd, the theory of self would remain hypothetical for everyone present until they personally intuit knowledge of the infinite self.

A second condition required in testing for knowledge through the exercise of power is that *the determination must be made utilizing the same avenue taken to acquire the knowledge.* Pathways to material knowledge cannot be utilized to confirm intuitive self-knowledge because the self is not within their purview. In fact, intuitive self-knowledge cannot be proved through material methods any more than material theories can be proved through theology. For instance, the use of science to prove that a meditation technique might induce a more expansive sense of self would not only subvert science and distort spirituality, but be utterly ineffective. The intellect and senses cannot even confirm that an expansive sense of self inspired the actions of saintly individuals like the late Mother Teresa, since she could have been motivated by any number of factors.

Self-knowledge can be confirmed only through intuition. This means knowledge of the expanding self cannot possibly be validated or refuted by way of sensory data, thoughts, beliefs, feelings, or material sciences. Because the individuated self interprets such information by its own finite standards and through its own finite faculties, to know itself it must look within.

The mind-boggling test for knowledge of the infinite self, while potentially disheartening, frees the intuitive scientist from external contradictions by propelling the understanding that all knowledge is self-knowledge; that the ability to acquire infinite self-knowledge translates into the potential to realize infinite knowledge, or God; and that the individuated sense of self is the only conduit to the indivisible self of God. In terms of the theory of self, the self is one and, as individuated atom-based manifestations of it, we all naturally seek to know the indivisible infinite self that may be called God. This quest endures despite fragmented images of the self, such as those portrayed by the three major monotheistic faiths, where Moses's God might instead say, "I am that self"; Jesus would say, "I and the self are one"; and Muhammad might say, "There is no self but the self, and the individuated sense of self is the final messenger of the self." Though the self, whether individuated or indivisible, can never be proved by way of the senses or intellect, it is always known intuitively, at least to some extent, and is therefore primed for looking within so it can come to know God.

Applying these testing standards gleaned from the theory of self, truth seekers may scientifically investigate the question "As selves, can we know a self larger than one limited by our senses?"—in other words, "Can we know God?" For many people, such an inquiry clarifies their life choices as they wonder: *Am I willing to test my knowledge base? What tools do I need? How might my efforts be worthy of this goal? What if I find I'm steeped in information but lack abilities (have "knowledge" but no power)? How might I move beyond the sham of empty knowledge and take the next step in my spiritual unfolding?* Testing for knowledge of God rejects the "anything goes" approach to spirituality that is prevalent in today's world, undercutting the tendency toward pride and self-deception, especially in spheres that purport to increase our knowledge of God, such as organized religion, traditional mysticism, and pranayama, the theory of self's chosen technique.

At the core of organized religion is each faith's particular idea of God as a being approachable through rituals prescribed by religious authorities. Such rituals might include praying, wearing phylacteries, chanting, listening to sermons, donating money, confessing, receiving the Eucharist, kissing the Bible, attending healing ceremonies, dancing, or marking passage from one station in life to another. Though participants in these activities often build social bonds and a more clearly defined sense of self, their awareness remains chained to the sensory world, where indoctrination into the corresponding belief system supersedes the acquisition of knowledge. Most would therefore fail the test for possessing not only infinite knowledge but also finite knowledge of the expansive self.

Religious authorities also advise congregants seeking knowledge of God to faithfully attend worship services. In these settings, their awareness is drawn outward toward the congregation, ceremonial events, and the art and architecture of the house of worship. But when the self's avenue to intuitive knowledge is directed outward, dividing into currents that feed the five senses, the individual ends up worshipping the narrow, individuated self as defined by sensory information. By contrast, when the avenue to knowledge is directed inward the person is able to worship indivisible being. The first instance leads to all manner of idolatry, or worship of atom-based realities circumscribed by space and time, while the second leads to what the ancients called isolation, union with the infinite substance of self as one's own self beyond all causal ideas of division. Worship services, by virtue of their emphasis on cognitive faculties, fall short of expectations because in directing attention to finite sensory objects one cannot acquire knowledge of an infinite God as one's self.

The most a person can do during "outer worship" is engage in a disguised form of self-worship. People often worship themselves by worshipping individuals with whom they identify. Revering Muhammad, for example, amounts to revering oneself identified with a Muhammad that reflects the self's parameters. Identifying with a book and calling it holy is another means of canonizing oneself and one's opinions.

To move beyond worship of the narrow self, it is important to realize that human awareness is constantly being divided and scattered by the sensory apparatus. *Maya,* the Sanskrit word the ancients used to describe illusion, or ignorance of the infinite self, literally means "divider." It is through "inner worship" that we overcome this state, uniting the streams of our fragmented awareness and directing them to the ocean within, where the individuated self flows back into the infinite self. Stated differently, just as our two eyes register duality, the "single eye" of intuition variously referred to by Jesus and other mystics knows the indivisibility of God. The implication is that through intuition we progress from worship of the narrow self to identification with the infinite self, which alone can know and worship itself as God.

It is no wonder that in the realm of testable knowledge,

outer worship remains unsubstantiated as a means for accruing knowledge of God, and the same can be said of faith. Confidence in religious messengers, for instance, cannot deliver knowledge of infinite substance because such knowledge comes not through others but through the only self one can know, which is one's own. The faith a worshipper claims to have in Abraham, Jesus, or Muhammad is actually blind faith, or wishful thinking, or at best, a form of positive affirmation. Intuition, on the other hand, is an avenue to direct knowledge that bypasses the narrow self protecting itself from expansion via the roadblocks of faith and belief. From the perspective that intuition is our only avenue to knowledge of God, knowing God is entirely up to each individual, and everyone and everything in the sensory world either inspires that inward investigation by offering support or, like religion, discourages it by further dividing human awareness.

Compared with organized religion, traditional mysticism promises a more intimate knowledge of God. Most modern-day mystical movements in the West, while in the spirit of monotheism still describe God as a separate being, advocate worshipping God in "God's presence" rather than in a house of worship where a go-between such as a cleric conducts services. To facilitate this more direct experience of God, neophytes enrolled in mystical movements are presented with supposedly secret, powerful, and even deadly texts. In addition to studying their contents, the students are expected to participate in ascetic programs and in occult rituals ranging from chanting, dancing, and specified sexual regulations to herb or alcohol intake, incantations, acts symbolic of self-sacrifice, prayer, and meditation.

Traditional mysticism, like other mystical movements throughout history, derives from scientific practices of the ancients that in numerous instances degenerated during the Dark Ages. Originally mysticism, which spawned the theory of self, revolved around sense introversion and ascetic practices intended to free energy for intuitive purposes. In its corrupted version, mysticism became more extroverted, ecstatic, and often revelatory, unleashing catharses and psychotic episodes. Today's pseudomystical approach to God glorifies a divine mystery that some religious scholars, such as twentieth-century German theologian Rudolph Otto, claim is infused with numinous knowledge.

Traditional mystical literature guides students along an inner journey to the divine presence, often complete with way stations and signposts to help mark their progress. In some instances the mystic sees God sitting on an inner throne, exuding unfathomable power, while in others the spirit of God visits and imparts a sense of awe or terror. Signs of "contact" with God range from crying and laughing to trembling, visions of one's deity, moaning and other vocalizations, and comatose states.

Traditional mysticism's penchant for reveling in these practices gives the impression not of helping to realize nonfinite knowledge but almost the opposite—of obscuring it. Objective experiences that provoke awe or terror do not invite identification with the infinite self, the conduit for intuitive awareness of infinitude. Nor do experiences of ecstatic catharsis on their own impart infinite power.

As for the numinous knowledge that Otto and other academics claim is revealed to the mystic, it appears to be "empty knowledge." Modern New Age writers and transpersonal psychologists, referencing yoga and other Eastern philosophies, attempt to validate Otto's views by arguing that the euphoria constitutes a genuine avenue to knowledge;[1] but ancient yogis, like Francis Bacon, Bertrand Russell, and other Western philosophers who criticized claims to knowledge devoid of power, denounced these experiences for their incapacity to transmit testable knowledge. While the ecstatic experience of unity with the universe is considered intuitive, during these episodes the senses are still limiting the awareness, contributing to a *feeling* of unity but not unity itself. It therefore appears that the cosmic unity of ecstatic mysticism is figurative; the idea of an expansive self is transient and shaped by historical conditioning; and the manifestations of nonfinite power adulterated by sensory activity are limited to clairvoyance, precognition, out-of-body perceptions, and other commonplace intuitive abilities that arise when awareness is externalized from the physical body. Otto and other scholars, in representing numinous knowledge as a mysterious experience inundated with examples of contact with God,[2] fail to distinguish between mysticism and mystification reflecting cultural conditioning, religious expectation, and uncritical tests for knowledge.

Ecstatic catharsis often has potent physical and psychological healing attributes yet does not fulfill the requirements of an avenue to infinite self-knowledge, or knowledge of God. Many Dark Age mystics, such as Omar Khayyám, Adi Sankara, Milarepa, and Saint Francis, are said to have practiced sense-introverting and ascetic techniques with both cathartic and knowledge-based outcomes. More contemporary variations on these techniques, however, bear little physiological resemblance to the process of retiring sensory nervous energy inward. Throughout the world, dancing and singing, which naturally induce cathartic states, promote physical and psychological healing by disrupting the habitual physiological patterns established by social conventions. Chanting also has been found to have great therapeutic value. But the chanting, dancing, and singing of contemporary mystics do not activate superconscious intuition for they fail to withdraw sensory nervous energy into the spine. And the Sufi's whirling dance is no more an intuitive practice than the ecstatic motions common to rave parties.

In addition to mistaking ecstatic catharsis for infinite self-knowledge, pseudomystical traditions confuse esoterica with nonfinite knowledge. Information derived from glorified occult texts detailing theological systems merely imitates nonfinite knowledge. Traditions like Qabalah, for example, are cloaked in mystery, yet very little of Qabalah practice involves the control of sensory nervous energy. Its focal points—devising cosmological models for existence, defining keys to life, retelling rabbinical anecdotes, and crafting unconventional interpretations of the Hebrew Bible—appear unrelated to intuition and are more reminiscent of fringe theological and hagiographic activities. Information transmitted in a coded or otherwise secretive language is often mistaken for mystical knowledge because it is not immediately accessible to the intellect.

If the only infinite knowledge that traditional mysticism conveys is of an ineffable God ideal devoid of any commensurate power, then this pathway to God fails the test for knowledge established by the theory of self. In fact, unless it is approached for its healing properties, traditional mysticism can degenerate into escapism, and its knowledge into a patent euphoria attainable through a host of psychophysical and psychotropic methods.

Unlike mystical and religious traditions, pranayama—also known as energy control in the service of sense introversion, or the science of intuition—substitutes theories for beliefs. In doing so, it rechannels the complacent surety forged by beliefs into an active urge toward discipline and effort. Similarly, pranayama rejects methods that tangentially direct human awareness and nervous energy inward, devoting itself solely to techniques that accomplish this task to the exclusion of all others.

Because of pranayama's dedication to scientific rigor, the theory of self calls it the sine qua non for knowing God as an infinite self. Like any science, which first determines its unit of investigation, pranayama, in lieu of venturing into the world of causal ideas, reduces everything in the cosmos to the subatomic, intelligently guided energy called prana. Defined as a product of the causal idea of division, prana is responsible for all manifestations of nature and the mathematically precise laws governing them, including everything that bears witness to what Einstein called "the grandeur of reason incarnate in existence."[3] In the body, superfine prana grossly manifests as nervous energy, breath, mind, and sensory awareness. And it is through mastering the bodily fluctuations of prana, by directing its various currents to the brain, that intuitive scientists realize knowledge of God.

For optimal effectiveness, advanced techniques of pranayama call for an ascetic lifestyle, as well as several hours a day of concentrated practice. Since they are energetically demanding, maintaining vibrant physical, mental, and emotional health through ecstatic catharsis and balanced living is of great benefit. And since injury is possible, along with glorification of the narrow sense of self, personal guidance is indispensable. Because of these requisites, sincere instructors do not teach advanced techniques publicly.

But perhaps pranayama's greatest shortcoming is this: where God is defined as the infinite self, as in the theory of self, intuition is advanced as the only avenue to knowledge of God, causing pranayama as a universal technique for knowing God to sound fundamentalist. This perception is largely dependent on use of the word God. If the word God is eliminated from the description and pranayama is instead plainly defined as a universal procedure for consciously retiring sensory nervous energy to the brain and thereby expanding one's identity beyond the confines of sensory impressions, all traces of fundamentalism vanish. In fact, one could legitimately argue that pranayama has nothing to do with God, provided that God is defined as something other than the infinite self. Certainly, pranayama stakes no claim to being a way to know God Jehovah or God Allah or God personified as any other being, but only God as an infinite self, for which one goes within to intuit the expanding sense of self.

Defining God as a potentially knowable infinite self, however, challenges the intellect, for it seems unlikely that human beings can access such knowledge. Even the theory of self asserts that the finite cannot know the infinite any more than a spaceship can reach the speed of light. Acquiring infinite knowledge must therefore remain speculative, a theory proposed most likely to free human beings from delusions of grandeur or an easy knowledge of infinitude. Always, the quest for knowledge of the infinite self is a matter left to individuals and their desire for spiritual adventure. Those prepared to step forth will find pranayama capable of bringing about results because it operates on the premise that the narrow self is already of the infinite self and that removing constrictions on self-awareness leads to knowledge of its inherent nature. To satisfy the intellect, then, trapped as it is within testable limits of the theory of self, pranayama might be considered a finite method utilizing electromagnetic principles to lift finite constrictions so that the self can intuit itself as infinite and thus acquire knowledge of God.

Another shortcoming of pranayama is the manner in which a sense of self is generated in the body. During practice, measurable changes take place in the body, such as increased alpha brain-wave patterns signifying withdrawal of the sensory nerve currents and slowing of the breath and heart, which raises the possibility that the experience of self-expansion is merely the effect of biochemical and neurological alterations. Though medical instruments record data about states into which a practitioner enters, the information fails to elicit an understanding of these states. Still, based on findings that do exist the possibility remains that the expansive self is physiologically grounded.

In answer to the question "Can we know God?" material science and the theory of self alike are at a stalemate, and for good reason. The ancient Upanisadic dictum *"Isvara asiddhe"* asserts that God can never be proven. Isvara, God as ruler of the cosmos, refers to the infinite self, implying the self (God) can never be proven, nor can knowledge of the self (God). A better question might therefore be "What is the difference between biochemical and neurological reactions registered in the body and an intuitive awareness of God realized through the body?" In response, some people might conclude that there is no difference and therefore they have no need for a knowledge of God that is physiologically induced; however, they would also have to admit that knowledge of the sense-bound self too is physiologically induced, implying their conclusion may be an incongruous excuse for sensory overwhelm. Others, more receptive to a sense of self dependent on patterns of energy in the body, may determine that these patterns assist them, but only to a degree, in striving to know a God defined as something other than the awareness behind human self-awareness. Spiritual adventurers seeking to know God as the expansive self beyond sensory perceptions would acknowledge the importance of a switched-on intuitive faculty, an outgrowth of working with Technique 14.

 **TECHNIQUE 14**

The Single Eye of Intuition

The intuitive eye is an organ not of sight but of knowledge surpassing anything furnished by the two sensory eyes—a knowledge that spiritual scientists rely on to realize an expansive existence. If a man were to suffer amnesia and forget his name, family and friends, and personal history, he would still have intuitive capacities and thus know a sense of being. The seat of intuition in the human body is the spine and brain, in particular the cerebrum and the medulla oblongata. It is in these crowning portions of the cerebrospinal axis that the "I am" of an individuated sense of self converts into the "I Am" of the indivisible self of God. Once you know you are infinite, you will know the "isolation" of God, a self that knows nothing apart from itself.

This technique assists the practitioner in "opening" the single eye of intuition, an activity that automatically shuts down the sensory apparatus by retiring nervous energy from it. In switching off the senses and switching on intuition, it relies on pranayama's emblematic slow and even breathing, which the ancients called the breathing ritual of the gods. While days went by for the gods, they observed, entire ages went by for human beings. Indeed, through slow and even breathing yogis were said to approach godly time frames, eventually stopping the breath, stilling the heart, and halting time. And it is with the collapse of narrow time-frames that the sense of self expands— in much the same way that time, the heartbeat, and breathing gradually stop as one travels at a speed approaching the velocity of light.

To begin opening the single eye of intuition and thereby awakening your full intuitive capacity, sit in an armless chair with your eyes and mouth closed, spine straight, chin parallel to the floor, and hands resting on thighs. Lifting your gaze behind your closed eyelids, concentrate on the point between your eyebrows. Place the tip of your tongue on your palate and, keeping your mouth closed, press upward toward the point between your eyebrows.

Next, perform 3 sequences of multiple exhalations, then slowly inhale through your nostrils for approximately 12 seconds. Hold your breath for about 6 seconds while continuing to maintain your focal point and press upward with your tongue. Exhale through your nostrils for about 12 seconds. Repeat the inhalation, retention, and exhalation 11 more times in immediate succession.

Now, inhale again through your nostrils, with the tip of your tongue pressed against your palate. While retaining your breath, knit your brow and tighten your eyelids, still pressing upward with the tip of your tongue—forming a localized tension the ancients called Seal of Light. Practice the entire routine of 12 rounds of breathing and 1 Seal of Light 3 times at night before retiring. As prana, in the form of optical nervous energy, is being "squeezed" out of your eyes with each seal, you may see light behind your closed eyelids. This light can illuminate your intuitive eye, an orifice shaped like a five-pointed star in the medulla oblongata through which prana is pouring into your body.

In gaining a vision of the single medullar eye, you have an opportunity to reverse your flow of awareness from the dualistic temporal world viewed frontally through two eyes to the gate of the medulla oblongata, the single eye of intuition at the top of the spinal column, essentially making your eye "single" to know the body is "full of light." While exiting this gate by projecting your awareness through it, you open your intuitive eye and unite your awareness with the light of the cosmos, much as seawater in a bottle floating on the ocean mixes with the ocean water when the cork is removed. You will then know you exist apart from your senses, body, name, personal biography, race, religion, nationality, and ethnicity, and that you extend all the way to the cosmic self of God.

As God, you will know that the individuated sense of self is but a shadow play choreographed within the contours of the finite idea of division. And you will realize that frontal eyes are called windows to the soul because the prana of the infinite self that enters the medulla oblongata splits into the currents directly feeding the eyes. When looking into someone's eyes, you glimpse the light of the infinite self, albeit divided and diffused by intervening patterns of energy and awareness. Interpreting these patterns, we instinctually "read" individuals in terms of their current capacity to intuit the light of the infinite self.

Testing for knowledge of God brings the intellect to the brink of sensory awareness of power, beyond which there may or may not lie a vast realm of possibility. If there is no possibility that a human being can attain infinite power in life or death, then the otherworldly promises of religion and mysticism are invalid. Yoga without yogic power, for instance, would become at best a preventive healthcare system and at worst a sham.

For a person uninvested in the possibility of infinite power and yet hoping to acquire nonfinite knowledge, asceticism is perhaps good for health but otherwise an unjustifiable waste of human potential. Similarly, sitting for hours a day practicing a method of meditation that does not effectively redirect the sensory nervous energy would be like using binoculars to study the terrain of a planet in a distant galaxy. Instead, such time could be better spent accumulating material knowledge and then placing oneself in service to humanity, as do scientists, freethinking philosophers, humanitarians, and social activists. Service to others enlarges one's sense of identity and demonstrates the spiritual striving for an expansive sense of self, as opposed to some spiritually normalized ideal of self on the one hand or infinite self-knowledge on the other.

A person adventurous enough to entertain the possibility of infinite power, however, will see as justified the asceticism and dedication to intuition that Jesus, the Buddha, and other bona fide mystics embodied. To such an individual, yoga masters like the twentieth century's Swami Vivekananda, world-renowned disciple of Ramakrishna, and Paramahansa Yogananda, author of *Autobiography of a Yogi,* would represent the pinnacle of intuitive possibility. According to the prevalent myths, these yogis manifested infinite knowledge by dematerializing the body and also sacrificed finite appetites and ambitions of the narrow self on an altar of service to humanity. Sacrificing the narrow self to humanity, while a lifestyle choice to individuals striving for a more expansive sense of self, is a basic technique to those reaching for an infinite self. To spiritual adventurers, not only is infinite knowledge possible but its measure, infinite power, is all that can satisfy their need for inner proof, which is why they turn within and seek its source.

Despite the various perspectives on the possibility of infinitude, spirituality is ultimately about expansion of the sense of self. And developing an increasingly expansive sense of self does not require the formal practice of asceticism and pranayama since it can also be accomplished by actively identifying with more and more of humanity. The informal renunciations and the sense-introverting concentration of scientists and philosophers, as well as humanitarians and activists, are apparently able to direct sufficient energy toward the spine and brain to switch on intuition and yield a larger sense of identity. For scientists, this occurs through consistently renouncing attachments to particular theories, temptations to sell their credentials to the highest bidder, and research for the sole sake of technology. Philosophers frequently renounce a comfort zone of thought, physical pleasures, and entertainment. Large-hearted humanitarians and activists, for their part, often deny themselves luxuries, personal safety, and exclusively material ambitions. Success for all these groups, especially scientists and philosophers, is dependent on the heralding of great powers of concentration that other vocations may not require. The expansive sense of self that manifests as a result of these endeavors reflects, through its power of sacrifice, a unifying knowledge of humanity—the flesh-and-blood God of which we are all a part.

Modern Spiritual Movements

Our age is the age of criticism, to which every-thing must be subjected. The sacredness of religion [is] by many regarded as grounds for exemption from the examination by this tribunal. But [if it is exempted, it becomes the subject] of just suspicion, and cannot lay claim to sincere respect, which reason accords only to that which has stood the test of a free and public examination.

—Immanuel Kant

Today's numerous spiritual movements offer options for expansion of the sense of self, but some also entail significant limitations while others pose risks to psychological health. Then too, since over the last few decades New Age spirituality, inspired by Eastern religions and Western mysticism, has become a multibillion-dollar industry in the West, with some movements utilizing the principles of pranayama, though their power and usefulness are at times compromised due to the emphasis on commercialism and concomitant oversights. A discussion of the strengths and weaknesses of major movements can help guide an informed understanding of the choices.

Progressive spiritual movements can be tested for their expansion potential against criteria set forth in the theory of self. Progressive religious movements attempting to further their members' spiritual development have, from a physiological standpoint, little effect on expansion of the sense of self because the attention placed on sensory stimulation gives worshippers' nervous energy little opportunity to retire inward. The physical aspects of such rituals as attending a house of worship, wearing a yarmulke, kissing a book deemed sacred, joining in congregational prayer, singing hymns, chanting, burning candles and incense, and bowing before altars are too externalized to dislodge familiar patterns of a narrow sense of self.

On the contrary, psychological attitudes ensuing from these and other group rituals can have major effects, including a tendency to forsake personal identity for a collective identity, confuse one's finite image of God with a universal God, mistake one's individuated sense of self for the only God, and misinterpret the rituals as universal methods of worship. Many such outcomes are directly proportionate to the person's depth of belief. Attitudes about rituals reflecting exclusionary dogmas reinforce a narrow sense of self with every performance of them. In the extreme, they establish patterns of divisive fundamentalism.

Private worship offers an opportunity to more strongly affirm parameters of the self and generally encourages nervous energy to retire inward. The positive effects, however, can be limited if the worship instills or reinforces myopia. Psychological attitudes about personal devotion help expand the sense of self, but only if one's God ideal is universal. Praying to a God defined as justifying violence directs energy to physiological patterns that may cause violence. For example, if God is believed to detest abortion, then praying to such a God may activate the death of obstetricians, or if God is thought to curse fornicators and adulterers, believers who engage in premarital or extramarital sex may feel guilty even if their actions involved honesty and consent between participants.

Because nervous energy freed by solitude can reinforce patterns of both myopia and broadmindedness, the development of intuition depends on one's ability to constantly challenge the narrow sense of self. Toward this end, individuals immersed in private worship are advised to balance instruction in energy control with an engaging colloquium. Members of a colloquium who critically assess central questions can simultaneously help deter the delusions of grandeur that sometimes result from meditative solitude and be more spiritually uplifting.

Similarly, forms of yoga and meditation now taught in the West have a variety of advantages and disadvantages. Yoga— which means realization of the union of the finite sense of self and the infinite substance of self—prescribes ethical and ascetic injunctions, proper meditative posture, pranayama, and a devotional, service-oriented lifestyle. Hatha yogis, misinterpreting the spiritual import of the ancient yoga tradition, focus more on achieving physical immutability and less on the changelessness of the substance of self. Likewise, popular methods of meditation, especially those emerging from modern movements in Zen, Shambhala, and Vipassana, attempt to "empty the mind." The coveted void, however, is the opposite of thought-free awareness of the expansive self arising from effortless superconscious concentration centered in the spine and brain.

In lieu of this superconscious intensity, meditation methods in the West tend to encourage passivity and quietude. According to the theory of self, however, the cerebrum is like any muscle and benefits from being exercised. Passive meditation, unable to enliven the spine and cerebrum, prohibits the practitioner from intuiting direct knowledge of the self. Worse, some practitioners confuse passive meditation with freedom from the mind. Swami Vivekananda, upon observing this general phenomenon, remarked, "When persons without training and preparation try to make their minds vacant, they are likely to succeed only in covering themselves with *tamas,* the material of ignorance, which makes the mind dull and stupid, and leads them to think they are making a vacuum of the mind."[4]

In addition, open-eyed meditation is practiced to induce acceptance of the sensory world as a manifestation of the infinite. Though the finite is the infinite inasmuch as there is only the infinite, the theory of self would assert that the infinite cannot be realized through the finite instruments of the senses. And while it is possible to detachedly contemplate a dualistic view of the world through the eyes, it is nearly impossible to entirely liberate one's awareness of it through this method. Consequently, open-eyed meditation cannot allow sensory nervous energy to retire inward as profoundly as closed-eyed or half open–eyed meditation where the gaze is focused on the border between light and darkness.

Meditation with an unfocused gaze is also popular, because it can lead to a state of mental absorption. Yet since the gaze is intimately connected to mental states, an unfocused gaze reflects a diffused mind. Though such practices can lead to a state free of thoughts, it does not result in superconscious concentration and practitioners should therefore not confuse it with freedom from the mind. According to the theory of self, states of mental absorption have no intuitive value in realizing the infinite substance of self. Basically, modern methods of passive meditation that use an unfocused gaze are effectively aiming for a coma-like void of the mind.

Nor do downward-gazing methods, which mimic the gaze of sleepers, develop superconscious awareness. On the contrary, recent studies of this form of passive meditation reveal that it causes a shift from the beta waves of sensory awareness to the theta waves of semiconscious drowsy states and sleep. Proponents of downward-gazing meditation regard such findings as evidence that these methods help practitioners center themselves, calm the mind, observe personal tendencies, develop intuition, foster self-trust, appreciate aspects of life more fully, and enhance their well-being by disturbing reactive patterns of fear, anger, and hatred that infest the mind. But it is also true that millions of people achieve these benefits by way of upbringing, culture, prayer, philosophical thought, or even cycles of REM sleep.

Despite the benefits of passive meditation claimed by some practitioners, more than half admit to experiencing relaxation-induced anxiety, panic, tension, decreased motivation, confusion, depression, negative disposition, judgmental behavior, guilt, symptoms of psychosis, delusions of grandeur, or suicidal tendencies. By contrast, practitioners of intuition avoid the negative side-effects of an "empty mind" by taking control of the mind, often through regulating the breath or directing the gaze upward with concentration. Intuitive practices also heighten the alpha waves of conscious sensory relaxation. And while passive meditation methods lead to partial sensory disassociation through subconsciousness, intuitive methods usher in complete sensory relaxation through superconsciousness.

Though efforts to prove the value of meditation abound, many studies glorifying passive meditation techniques are unreliable because they were conducted by students of these methods under the financial auspices of organizations that promote them. Their assertions are not necessarily false, but independent researchers come to very different conclusions. Further, studies that attempt to validate or disprove any meditation method in relation to the self are fundamentally flawed by material science's inability to measure the self. Indeed, while pranayama may increase alpha waves whereas a passive meditation method increases theta waves, neither datum directly proves anything about the sense of self. The theory of self repeatedly affirms that the sense of self can be known only through the avenue of intuition.

The theory of self is also useful in uncovering erroneous assumptions implicit in contemporary meditation techniques, especially those purporting to be derived from pranayama. For example, the East Asian meditation method of "just sitting," with no preconceived agenda, is defined as a psychophysiological means for attaining enlightenment. However, it is possible for an individual to "just sit" for decades and still not achieve enlightenment because while sitting the senses remain active, the breath and heart promote outward-flowing attention, and the awareness gravitates toward memories, feelings, and intellectual pursuits. According to the theory of self, the limited agendas of the narrow sense of self cannot be expanded upon unless the center of magnetism shifts from the senses to the cerebrospinal axis. Until such a shift is accomplished, the psychophysiological patterns that inform personal agendas will continue to influence every sensory impression. Only individuals who have mastered sense introversion through energy control can effectively just sit.

Similarly, mindfulness meditation is said to promote tranquility by establishing a detached observation of events and the mind, encouraging practitioners to live from the center of their being. But doing so without locking awareness in the intuitive center of the spine and brain can exacerbate one's patterns of conditioning, triggering a variety of spiritual affectations. In the extreme, it can exaggerate sensory disturbances and erupt in catharses. The theory of self states that mindfulness instead arises naturally and effortlessly as an expression of the expansive self once nervous energy has been locked in the cerebrospinal axis, thus releasing the practitioner from patterns of conditioning and enabling him to identify more and more with the infinite self.

The flawed teaching of mindfulness fuels today's popular belief that the universal practice of this passive meditation will usher in world peace. But passive methods of mindfulness meditation, when practiced by someone who exhibits violence, cannot on their own alter this propensity because the mindful observation of it is being conducted by a sense of self that may only justify violence. Thus, it requires more than mindfulness, as it is taught today, to dislodge narrow ideas of self. If a meditator instead endeavors to impose the ethical standards of a teacher or religion, the observation of tendencies designated as unspiritual can engender feelings of guilt and thus actually provoke undesirable conduct, while the observation of those deemed spiritual may be either ignored or seeded with divisiveness. Indeed, indoctrination in mindful actions leading to violent consequences is the training of choice for religious fanatics because it can silence the voice of reasonable doubt. Agents of peace, on the other hand, critically assess their perspectives and, as a result, expand their identity.

In contrast to passive methods of meditation, the theory of self presents meditation as a means for actively increasing the practitioner's concentration—in which case the practitioner, without sincerely endeavoring to challenge narrow interests, can likewise end up serving a brutal ideology, as is illustrated in the lives and teachings of many proponents of modern Buddhism. For example, Eugene Herrigel, author of the widely read *Zen and the Art of Archery,* later became a Nazi. This outcome suggests that practicing nonviolence while wielding a bow or sword cannot stop us from practicing Zen and the art of cross burning or suicide bombing. It is perhaps because martial arts, like musical arts, are performed without the intrusion of critical thinking that they were confused with spiritual pursuits transcending the mind, despite their inability to retire energy inward for self-expansion or to help challenge personal biases. Indeed, there is evidence that the spiritual and martial arts training known in Japan as Bushido contributed significantly to kamikaze piloting in the Pacific during World War II. Similarly D. T. Suzuki, one of Japan's foremost proponents of Zen in the last century, seemed to have no philosophical difficulty combining it with fascism. All these examples shatter the hope that meditation leads automatically to an expanded sense of self. Indeed, people who are calm and focused yet unpracticed in self-expansion and critical thinking will calmly and concentratedly act on their limited perspectives. Napoleon Bonaparte epitomizes the extreme to which calmness and coolheaded concentration can serve a person's narrow self-interests.

Another misleading assumption underlying modern meditation techniques is that nonviolence ensues from teachings combining Buddhism with the path of the warrior, especially as practiced in East Asia. Buddhism began in India when the Buddha—a yogi and ascetic—incorporated the ancient precept of nonviolence into his descending Iron Age teachings about the illusoriness of individuated awareness and about its potential for expansion to infinity. The much older theory of self defines nonviolence as peace-promoting action guided by the ambitions of an expansive sense of self that is concerned with the effects of actions and inactions. But this ethical injunction became distorted as the Buddha's precept moved into East Asia during the Dark Ages until, eventually wed to the way of the warrior, it was used to afford violence a place in spiritual life. In the process, humanity lost both the kernel of wisdom linking nonviolence to identification with all things and the recommended tools for self-expansion.

A further connection between present-day meditation methods and violence is the tradition of applying inflictive measures in the name of enlightenment, as is sometimes practiced in Asian Buddhism. Stories of meditation masters cutting off their students' fingers, knocking their devotees down flights of stairs, reveling in sex with them, or beating them for falling asleep—all of which conflate mystical and martial arts training—glorify violence by calling it spirituality. Such glorification still prevails in Buddhism, partially because the stories are retold without questioning their ramifications, perhaps to champion a master's perceived moral superiority or to empower believers who, supposedly willing to withstand abuse for the sake of illumination, suffer from low self-esteem.

According to the theory of self, development of the non-violent expansive sense of self requires uniting into a single intuitive current the many psychophysical patterns that bind awareness to sensory input. Though pranayama and asceticism can theoretically accomplish this if they are effectively mastered through superconscious concentration, they do not have the power to remove all psychological risks and limitations of the individuated sense of self when unchallenged conditioning hampers practice, or to achieve world peace when so many social and personal factors contribute to war. These objectives can be accomplished by pursuing a lifestyle that encompasses the many practices contributing to a sentient expansion of the self, as delineated in Technique 15.

౷ TECHNIQUE 15

Invigorating Self-Expansion

Expansion of the sense of self, the summum bonum of human life, unfolds naturally in response to going within guided by a willingness to think critically and open the heart. As such, it is activated less by doing than by not doing, requiring the practitioner to periodically pull back from worldly engagements. Even the proactive practice of pranayama amounts simply to conscious sensorimotor relaxation. Asceticism, too, entails consciously disengaging from activities in order to deliberately give the senses a period of rest. In minimizing excessive sensory input, a mystically centered life frees up energy for inner exploration and for infusing outer actions with the spirit of service.

Because no single technique is capable of enlivening self-expanding patterns of energy and awareness, the routine that follows draws from several spiritual disciplines that introduce major aspects of these patterns. You may use it as a to-do roster consulted in the morning to remind you of the day's self-expansion needs or as a checklist to review during your evening introspection, or both. In any case, bear in mind that the more you engage in these activities the more likely you are to continue engaging in them. Remember, too, that the only way to monitor expansion of the self is through testing your power to renounce materialism, narrow self-interests, and restless sensory activities in favor of simple living, service to others, and innate bliss.

౷ ***Participation in a colloquium*** (see Technique 1). Spirituality is an ongoing educational adventure deepened through weekly participation in a colloquium. Setting aside a few minutes each morning to contemplate ideas shared at a recent colloquium gathering contributes to increased freedom of thought and expression. By challenging assumptions of the narrow sense of self in the company of fearless critical thinkers, you clear a path for self-expansion.

⁊ ***Devotion to your personal image of God*** (see Technique 2). Once you have decided on an image of God that secures your attention, recall this image throughout the day and use it during meditation to focus your mind and open your heart. To counteract flights of intellectual or emotional imbalance, pull your tongue back and place its tip on your palate intermittently throughout the day, thereby locking nervous energy and awareness in the medulla oblongata. To ward off unwanted thoughts that might arise during or after interactions with others, silently repeat a mantra—such as "Aum" (rhymes with "Home"), "Omne," (rhymes with "Calm-nay"), or "Amen"—all the while focusing on your image of God, or on your heart or the point between your eyebrows. A combination of these methods is also possible. This practice expands the sense of self by directing nervous energy toward the cerebrospinal plexuses, banishing mental fluctuations through an increased devotional capacity of the heart, and establishing an inner center for rendering service-oriented and ethical actions.

⁊ ***Visualizing and mentally intoning affirmations*** (see Technique 3). To improve your odds of performing affirmations consistently, begin by using them to overcome obstacles to success as you presently define it. For example, if you want to surmount fears of finding a partner or acquiring a material object, utilize visual and verbal affirmations that focus on the realization of your desired outcome. Once practice becomes regular, advance freely to affirming spiritual progress, the uprooting of unwanted habits, enhanced health, and positive thoughts about others. The ideal time to practice affirmations is during the calm morning hours. Affirmations help catalyze self-expansion by satisfying nagging desires or removing restless habits that impede inward concentration.

ᢧ *Introspective reading and writing* (see Technique 4). Take a moment each morning to read a few words that might assist you in facing a particular challenge or keep you centered throughout the day. Read for longer periods at night, jotting down notes and questions to take to your colloquium, or analyzing the day and crafting affirmations to counter negative attitudes and reinforce positive ones. For reading material, choose anything from an academic textbook on world religions that might help to expand your sense of identity to the life-altering works of great philosophers from East and West, such as Nagarjuna or Baruch Spinoza, Adi Sankara or Friedrich Nietzsche. To better assimilate the content, write for at least as long as you have read, examining your motives and desires, challenging your inherited belief system, and penetrating your individuated sense of self with better and better questions.

ᢧ *Tension-relaxation methods* (see Technique 11). Tension-relaxation methods are best practiced in the morning when the body is already relaxed. You can even try them in bed. Also practice them to regain a sense of balance after slipping into a reactive state. When energizing muscles, it is best to build tension slowly, maintain it for 3 seconds, then gradually relax. When striving to relax muscles, practice quick tension, hold it for 1 or 2 seconds, then quickly relax.

This psychophysical method assists in broadening the parameters of the self by training muscles to energize and relax at will and thus helping to eradicate unwanted habits recorded in stifling physiological patterns.

✍ *Balanced asceticism* (see Technique 8). At the start of each day, decide on a set of guidelines to follow for moderating behaviors involving food, speech, and sex. Periods of fasting, silence, and celibacy conserve energy for intuitive practices. To devote more time and energy to sensory introversion, gradually decrease your sleep and social activities as well. Ascetic injunctions free considerable amounts of nervous energy to gravitate toward the higher plexuses in the spine for intuiting self-expansion.

✍ *Minimizing the ingestion of animal products.* Concentration and sensory introversion are generally impacted by congestion due to the overconsumption of protein. From the perspective of physical health, countless studies emphasize that a diet natural to human beings consists of fruits, vegetables, nuts and seeds, and grains and legumes.[5] Diets rich in eggs, dairy, and meat products, said to be too high in fat and protein to be ingested on a regular basis, are shown to increase the risk of heart disease, osteoporosis, obesity, and various types of cancer. A diet largely free of animal products, especially flesh, leads not only to better health but to enhanced concentration, decreased aggression, and a lighter experience of the body—all of which can help to broaden the boundaries of the self.

✍ *Magnetization through pranayama and energy seals* (see Techniques 7, 9, 10, 13, and 14). Sitting for sensory introversion, as you magnetize your spine and brain through pranayama and energy seals, is most effective if practiced

early in the morning, when the majority of people and animals in your hemisphere are still sleeping, and again in the
evening, after others have retired. With your day sand-
wiched between practice sessions in pranayama and energy
seals, you may intermittently feel the magnetization of the
medulla oblongata as a throb midway between the eyebrows. Daily practice of these powerful methods of energy
control vastly amplifies the intuitive capacity.

℘ ***The Great Seal.*** This method, combining pranayama and
an energy seal, was highly praised by ancient Indian and
Hebrew ascetics for its ability to magnetize the spine, building pressure in the skull and directing awareness of self-
expansion to the brain. To practice the Great Seal, sit on
the floor with your feet flat on the surface, knees raised,
thighs pressed against your chest, arms wrapped around
your legs, and fingers interlinked. Keeping your spine
straight, use your arms to pull your legs closer to your chest,
supporting your lower spine; then close your eyes and
focus on the point midway between your eyebrows.

Now, with your mouth closed and the tip of your
tongue touching your palate, slowly inhale through your
nostrils for about 6 seconds. As you continue to hold your
breath, let your tongue relax to its natural position, drop
chin to chest, stretch your legs out in front of you, and
bend your head toward your knees. Keeping most of your
fingers interlinked, grasp your lower legs or feet and gently
pull your torso forward and down. Still holding your breath,
maintain this position for 3 to 6 seconds, feeling pressure in
your skull, before reversing the motions, raising your torso,
bringing knees to chest, using your arms to pull them
close, and lifting your chin so it is once again parallel to the

floor. Placing your tongue against your palate, slowly exhale through your nostrils for about 6 seconds. Repeat this exercise 5 more times.

Lying chest-down on the floor with your legs straight out behind you, interlink your fingers slightly in front of you and, sliding your forearms under your upper torso, gradually lift your head and chest. Breathing normally, reverse the forward stretch of the Great Seal by keeping your head and chest raised and your head tilted slightly upward, resting your upper torso on your bent arms for about 2 minutes, with your lower spine, buttocks, and legs relaxed. Keeping your chin up, close your eyes, focus on the magnetization midway between your eyebrows, and mentally scan your lower body for tension, relaxing where necessary.

Beyond an indelible sense of the self incorporating more and more of life comes a blissful knowledge of the infinite substance of self—an aspiration of most modern spiritual movements that trace their origins to an accomplished mystic. Few seekers find success, however, because when the avenue to knowledge is tapered by the senses the experience of the self's innate bliss is interpreted not as a quality of the self but as an ephemeral physical, emotional, mental, or ecstatic joy. As the sense of self expands a bit, the bliss may be experienced as the joy inherent in unconditional love, friendship, and giving—or to the larger self of the humanist, the happiness and well-being of all of humanity. And with the further development of intuitive knowledge through the steadfast practice of pranayama and repeated entry into the breathless state, bliss permeates one's life. This occurs because as soon as an awareness of it is locked in the spine and brain, the intuition of bliss becomes physiologically stabilized, at which point the self searching for its infinitude meets with success, discovering that all along it was seeking itself.

The terminology associated with infinite bliss sometimes differs. The substance of self, for instance, is occasionally referred to as the true nirvana and the true void, empty of atoms, prana, and causal ideas, including time and space, and even life and death. Practitioners intent on realizing "the supreme nirvana" or "no self" are simply describing efforts to intuit the substance of self.

Methods for realizing the substance of self, whatever its designation, often lead back to seekers' earlier experiences involving their ideas of self. Diced by space and time, such experiences tend to reinforce discriminatory perspectives, enhancing an attraction to teachings that provoke guilt or rationalize violence, a propensity to revel in divisiveness, or an urge to pine for an otherworldly Shambhala or Shangri-la. But the final test of any life method is lasting and unqualified happiness here and now. Those derived from Dark Age practices and intentionally or unintentionally exploiting the principles of pranayama for commercial purposes, end up functioning much like monotheistic religions by imposing their ideals on unquestioning followers. Paths of spirituality anchored in the theory of self, on the other hand, illuminate the infinite substance of self as the Pure Land humanity seeks, and finds right here on earth.

Vulnerability of the Self

Every great advance in natural knowledge
has involved the absolute rejection of authority.

—Thomas Huxley

The self's vulnerability causes billions of people worldwide to adopt detrimental modes of thought and behavior while seeking to expand. Such vulnerability is a direct result of the psychological insecurity and social uncertainty aroused by the degeneration of institutions our society and others have long held dear. Inundated by the sociomagnetism of these deteriorating religious, cultural, political, economic, educational, legal, and even medical institutions, many individuals prefer not to face their vulnerability and to instead pursue forms of escape. Testing these forms and others, by way of the theory of self, might elucidate ways to reverse the widespread vulnerability of the self.

There are several ways to escape the challenges of the day, some religious and some not. The mode of choice for many individuals is sensual abandon or puritanical morality, both reactionary signs of social disempowerment. Other people opt for archaism, an escape to the past where life was seemingly simpler or more meaningful, investing old sagas with new life because they consider the present deprived of opportunities for pious or heroic deeds. The popularity of literary archaism can be seen in the soaring sales of fantasy novels. Examples of religious archaism include Ayatollah Khomeini's fiery Islamic Revolution and black-clothed ultraorthodox Jews "returning to the answer." The more benign and festive Society for

Creative Anachronisms and the popular Southern pastime of reenacting American Civil War battles both commemorate past etiquettes, attitudes, and animosities between political and social factions.

Still other people escape into futurism, hoping humanity will live more happily and progressively in times to come. Attempts to counter futurists' depictions of a perfect tomorrow can be found in the harsh realism of dystopian novels by such authors as Eugene Zamiatin, Aldous Huxley, Margaret Atwood, and George Orwell. Members of millennial organizations look to the future, as well, causing today's skyrocketing sales of end-time novels. More radical than Star Trek or other sci-fi groupies, many contemporary millennialists think of themselves as part of a space-faring generation and create places of worship that may replicate the deck of the *Enterprise* or imagine aliens will rescue them from earthly existence, some even committing suicide, as did Heaven's Gate members in March 1997, in the belief that their freed souls would float up to a spaceship docked elsewhere in the solar system.

These and other forms of escapism prevent engrossed participants from confronting society's deterioration and directing their creativity toward improved conditions. Beset by feelings of helplessness, many become smug and incapable of entertaining challenges. The cost of escapism, it seems, is indifference to society's eroding institutions and an increased incidence of cloistered views.

Individuals who face the challenges of societal decay, on the other hand, remain vulnerable to its sociomagnetic patterns. For a person lacking intellectual and intuitional readiness to expand and find creative solutions, it becomes easy to spiral into patterns associated with destruction. Such gyrations widen the frontiers of violence, extending them from personal domains (drug or alcohol abuse, estrangement from parents or other close family members, delinquent behavior or poor grades resulting in inadequate education and feelings of inferiority, economic or emotional impoverishment, embittered relationships, failure to find fulfilling work, and general lack of perceived meaning in life) to collective realities (gun toting in high schools, sadism in the pornography industry, slavery in underdeveloped nations, the establishment of near-permanent military frontiers, and desolation of the rain forests). In other words, vulnerable individuals who do not engage in self-expansion inadvertently stifle their creative energies and, to diminish their psychological distress and secure a solid sense of identity, direct attention outward in violence toward predefined rivals, other ethnicities, and the natural world. In the process of harming others, they cannot help but inhibit their inner experience of resourcefulness.

Religionists, observing these violent changes in social patterns, erroneously conclude that humanity today needs more religion than ever. A few, however, eventually see that ministering to humanity through unfounded promises, fear, and guilt can no longer effectively regulate conduct. Promises of heaven, fear of hell, and theological systems based on reward and punishment only intensify the problem, rather help to eradicate it. These ecumenical measures actually endanger humanity's survival by advancing the virtues of a thwarted intellect, suppression of natural urges, and expressions of divisiveness. In the best of circumstances, they reveal the underlying defects, causing many adherents to drift away from their religious moorings.

People raised in every religious tradition are hungry for alternatives to the organized religions of their parents. This widespread search for a new spiritual identity leads multitudes each year to experiment with a variety of New Age spiritual movements or join devotional groups that advocate eclectic or extreme practices like fundamentalism. But while the search itself may reflect a healthy response, the state of mind people bring to it is not always conducive to finding a deeper meaning in life. Looking externally for a spiritual identity might be accompanied by discontent, unhappiness, or desperation. Searching while feeling empty can result in unhealthy discrimination, biased investigation, or identification with consumer spirituality. Especially vulnerable individuals often graft their sense of identity onto the personality or mission of a cult, forfeiting the development of their own expansive self.

The discovery of a new spiritual movement or devotional group is often fraught with peril for vulnerable individuals. The excitement of embracing a fresh idea of God or a new spiritual leader or religion can make some people suddenly feel a sense of belonging and power in response to their special access to spiritual dispensation. Often, this sense of belonging—whether to an orthodox Jewish yeshiva, a Buddhist colony, a Catholic seminary, a modern guru-led center, a meditation or prayer retreat, a fundamentalist sect, an apocalyptic cult, or a terrorist organization—swiftly spawns feelings of invulnerability. Many such movements and groups purposefully promote a compelling sense of community through cathartic activities that range from dancing and chanting to sharing religious experiences, breath work, use of herbs and crystals, exercise drills, service-oriented chores, counseling, artistic expression, holy rolling, group study reinforcing certain ideals, sexual regulations, isolation followed by togetherness, and animated speeches delivered by charismatic leaders. These endeavors align the physiomagnetism of newcomers, and hence their thoughts, with the organization's prevalent magnetic pattern while enhancing their health and temporarily bolstering their egos, previously weakened by insecurity and uncertainty. Signs of counterfeit ego fortification generally appear over time in displays of spiritual affectations, excessive use of insider terminology indicating narrowed psychological parameters, uninvited proselytizing, and other facades of piety.

The search for truth, a lifelong endeavor for most scientists and philosophers, generally ends for the narrow and no longer vulnerable sense of self that has found some modicum of comfort in belonging and believing. Besides, an organization's insistence on loyalty makes it difficult to question its foundational principles without experiencing guilt. Influenced both inwardly and outwardly, individuals who have been furnished with a well-defined spiritual identity along with their health-promoting ecstatic catharsis may therefore be unwilling to release this limiting identity.

Another problem for vulnerable individuals seeking spirituality is that New Age spiritual movements and devotional groups may not be equipped to assist members in expanding the idea of self, though they may advertise this capability. Most offer useful services, such as meditation retreats, vegetarian guidelines, classes in physical culture, and social events. They also provide instruction in understanding one's personality, accessing childhood memories through breathing or painting or writing, applying spiritual laws of success to family and workplace, finding truth in an exotic leader who may soon be visiting, and techniques of spiritual sex, all the while subtly affirming their particular ideology. In many cases, these teachings not only fail to challenge limited ideas of self but indirectly reinforce them.

Promotional methods of many New Age and devotional

organizations can be confusing or misleading, as well. Esoteric words like *infinite, supreme, divine, eternal, enlightenment, awakening, spirit, blessed, source, transcendent, truth, bliss,* and *God* are used to sell publications and instructional programs that purport to point the way to truth. But instead of clarifying the questions humanity faces, spiritually tantalizing terminology might further obscure today's social challenges. At best, such idioms may help adherents overcome the extreme divisiveness of organized religions and, through this wider lens, realize a healthier ego freed from trauma and issues of inferiority. More often, they are mixed into teachings calling for blind faith in prescribed dogma and subtly exclusionary beliefs that later fuel conceited attitudes.

When the self is pronouncedly vulnerable, it searches for its infinitude less in spiritual and devotional organizations and more in prefabricated cultic identities that quickly lend a sense of stability. Cults are characterized primarily by zealous glorification of a leader, economic or sexual exploitation of members, and physical or mental harm inflicted on them. Of these traits, personality worship is likely the most destructive since it entrains followers' minds to accept the exploitation and abuse. And unlike focusing on a nonliving object of devotion that embodies universal qualities, focusing devotionally on the image of a living person who has attained the status of a godlike savior can narrow one's perspective. Worse, identifying with such a charismatic individual can scar the psyche by stripping it of the self-esteem necessary for expansion.

Damage to the psyche became obvious during the counterculture decades of the 1960s and 1970s, when the Western world began deifying Eastern gurus and meditation masters. Obsessed with worshipping these personalities, Westerners started clinging to the individuals' identities rather than expanding their own. Also, uneducated in the complexities of Eastern thought, they naturally considered the teachings to be authentic, only to find in many instances that the person lacked ethical conduct. But rather than questioning a teacher's credibility, many followers opted for delusion, justifying the immoral behavior by claiming the individual was one with God, enlightened, no longer subject to everyday morality, or was using immorality as a teaching aid or to intentionally challenge social conventions. Next, they surrounded themselves with an impregnable wall of denial, demonizing anyone who challenged their leader's stature and all the while trapping themselves in feelings of codependence and helplessness. Before long, hundreds of thousands of Westerners mistakenly believed their self-worth was assured by the worthiness of their teacher.

Such psychological scarring became more pronounced in the decades since, accompanying a global upsurge in cultism. Beginning in the 1980s, the Hindu and Buddhist personality cults spread beyond the West and were joined everywhere by fundamentalist cults, in which charismatic preachers fanned flames of hatred, fear, and militancy; health cults in which doctors and self-styled specialists espoused formulaic approaches to disease, obesity, and unhappiness; and self-improvement cults championing "secrets" to financial success, career advancement, and the ability to win more friends. Again obsession, delusion, and denial came to the fore, eroding self-esteem. Consequently today, hundreds of millions of individuals worldwide lack the psychological strength to recognize their own exploitation and abuse at the hands of cult leaders.

Cult leaders, for their part, are only human and therefore as prone to vulnerability as their followers. In fact, it is out of excruciating vulnerability and lack of ethical grounding that they take advantage of their followers, encouraging the personality worship and reveling in the authority, money, and adulation streaming their way. Whereas genuine spiritual servants, inherently guided by moral principles, would have no interest in asking people to pay for meditation classes, cultic gurus are apt not only to commercialize spirituality but to incline minds indoctrinated by materialism into regarding the financial investment itself as a sign of spiritual growth. A cult leader teaching meditation, like a man inviting starving guests to dinner but only allowing them to eat vicariously through him, cannot mitigate the group's spiritual hunger. Devotees of all sorts would be wise to heed the advice of British author George Orwell, who said, "Saints should always be judged guilty until they are proven innocent."[6]

There are many ways in which cult leaders capitalize on the psychological dependencies they instill. Offering themselves as holders of "the final answer," cult leaders secure a loyal following that attend to their material needs. Those who enforce sexual hegemony are ensured of a variety of sex partners who consider intercourse with their leader a form of worship. Leaders who physically or psychologically mistreat their followers can expect supplicating requests for freedom from the pain they inflict.

Cult leaders also profit from the threat of war. After 9/11, several New Age gurus capitalized on promises of world peace if only their methods were given a chance. Others charge hundreds of dollars for simple mantras they declare are not just sounds but divine peacemaking and consciousness-expanding principles with "aspects" in each of the five senses. Actually, a common beginning meditation technique involves simply watching the breath and mentally chanting any sound that is free of undesirable associations, such as "Hong-Sau" repeated with the inhalation and exhalation, respectively, or "Aum," "Omne," "Amen," or even "Jesus Christ" with the inhalation, "Son of God" between breaths, and "Have mercy on my soul" with the exhalation. On their own these chants trigger a shift in brain activity and a slowing of the breath—at no cost.

Other lucrative offerings on behalf of world peace include one group's request of the international community for a billion dollars to build "peace palaces" in which meditators would send out "vibrations of cosmic consciousness to the world." The group also offers lessons in "yogic flying," tendered for a minimum of $3,000 per student. Of special appeal to vulnerable seekers, yogic flying calls for mentally chanting Sanskrit sutras, or aphorisms, and bouncing on cushions for hours in an effort to "lift off." Ancient texts that refer to flying mention nothing about bouncing or world peace, but rather cite a pranayama technique for controlling a particular nerve current in the body that can take decades to master; furthermore, Vedic and yogic writings were originally meant to be chanted for purposes of transmitting the information from one generation to the next, not for use as autosuggestive exercises. Subscribing to the fraudulent flying technique is akin to believing that the chanting of written material about architecture erects buildings. And unsurprisingly, the outcome most often associated with mastery of unusual yogic abilities is pride, not peace.

Too often, cultic solicitations in the interest of world peace are nothing more than thinly disguised attempts to capitalize on the fear of protracted global violence—a distinction indiscernible to most devotees. Secure in the narrow sense of identity conferred on them as "spiritually elite," many fail to see that a cult-generated technique heralding world peace might be preposterous. Nor do billion-dollar propositions to create peaceful vibrations seem farfetched. What matters more than anything else is the cushy invulnerability to the psychological and social stresses of our time. But this comes at great cost: once obsessed with possessing "special knowledge," captivated by delusions of grandeur, and driven by the power of denial, it takes almost superhuman effort to operate in the realm of free thought.

The greatest pitfall concerning today's many alternatives to organized religion—cultic, devotional, and spiritual—is their inability to promote self-determination. One difficulty is that their survival depends on uniformity of conviction. Unlike hospitals that patients leave upon healing, most of these groups model themselves after religions, insisting on obedience and centralization of spiritual powers while discouraging independent thought and challenges to authority. In addition, the temporary strengthening and consolidation of the self that occurs after identifying with a new body of seekers gives the mistaken impression that the self has found its true home. In fact, quite the opposite has occurred: the self has slipped steadily away from its course of expansion, dropping anchor in murky waters. The way back, as well as a good preventative against drifting off in the first place, can be found through the practice of Technique 16.

TECHNIQUE 16

Self-Reliance

Organized religions maintain that great beings of the past, such as Moses, Jesus, and Muhammad, communed with God for us and our task is to believe in those labors, attend worship services, drop money in the minister's till, be nice to people, and rely on religious authorities to infuse our lives with meaning. The teachings of Eastern mystics such as Krishna, the Buddha, Patanjali, and Kabir, however, advocate a very different prospect for finding more meaning in life: self-reliance. Their methods for accessing the truth reveal that the acquisition of nonfinite knowledge, power, and bliss is anything but facile and unable to be achieved by proxy.

Emulating the great mystics' lifelong reliance on the self as the avenue to knowledge, seekers establishing a well-balanced discipline can continually fortify their sense of self-reliance. As you come across a teacher's spiritual tenets or techniques that might serve this purpose, fine-tune your inner response to them by asking yourself these basic questions: *What aspect of the self does this discipline amplify? How might it influence my sense of identity? What will it require of me in terms of time, money, and self-esteem? Is it provocative enough to inspire effort on my part? What is the teacher's understanding of God? What is the goal of the practice? How does this discipline define daily success—in terms of a deepening dependency on the teacher as a conduit to God or, instead, a realization of my own connection to God? How is this success tested?*

In learning to use ideas of self as a sounding board, be suspicious of prepackaged answers to challenging questions. The self, especially when profoundly vulnerable, can easily be drawn to quick fixes, such as mastering yogic flying in a week, losing weight with minimal effort, becoming wealthy overnight, finding split-second romance, believing in a sure passage to heaven, and attaining instant enlightenment. In stark contrast, the teachings and the lives of ancient mystics make it abundantly clear there is no simple and painless trajectory to great accomplishments.

The self that resists confusing spirituality with a lack of critical thinking gradually overcomes its sense of helplessness, unfolding more and more of its infinitude as it clears a trail inward. In the process, one comes to regard the self as the repository of knowledge, power, and bliss, whereupon the infinite self—in lieu of an external authority—becomes the measure of all things. To be godlike, in this context, means to be utterly self-reliant.

Just as the path of reliance on spiritual authorities ends in a cult's artificial bolstering of the vulnerable self, the path of self-reliance terminates in its opposite: unity with the infinite self. As always, vigilance is required, for it is tempting to lapse into a ritual purporting to eradicate fear-provoking patterns of insecurity and disempowerment. The decision to opt instead for a well-tested inner discipline promises a form of reliance that seeks, rather than fears, the unknown.

Decades of experimentation with alternatives to organized religions have failed to produce a socially unifying spiritual ideal capable of remedying the self's excruciating vulnerability. What has emerged in its place is a new breed of narrow identification with self-styled gurus and meditation masters, or unabashedly egotistical marketeers. At the present juncture, amidst today's disempowerment of the self lost in the commercialization of spirituality and the death throes of outdated institutions, the recovery of its expansive capacity, more urgent than ever before, requires the decentralized vigor of intuitive science.

Celebrating Apostasy

Be patient toward all that is unsolved in your heart
and try to love the questions themselves. . . .
Live the questions now. Perhaps you will gradually,
without noticing it, live along some distant
day into the answer.
                                    —Rainer Maria Rilke

Institutionalized religions and their modern-day counterparts are not just belief systems but also social networks connecting followers to family and friends, imbuing their lives with familiar symbols, and giving them a sense of place and purpose. Consequently, long after the beliefs are found to lack usefulness and a viable context in today's world they can still serve social functions. Many people seeking to preserve family and holiday traditions or community harmony will therefore refrain from questioning their religion or spiritual affiliation. And for those who do raise questions, apostasy may be a solo event—stressful at first, perhaps, but following deepened understanding and communication with loved ones, a choice worthy of celebration.

A questioner's deepened understanding begins with a view of apostasy as freedom from exclusive group identities and of others' resistance as a fear-based psychological response to disturbing the foundations of these identities. Young children, who have no fixed group identities to defend, are unafraid of asking formative questions. Among children who are later instructed to adopt a group identity, the interest in questioning it quickly diminishes. By adulthood, few will have challenged their limiting identity unless it caused them severe intellectual or emotional difficulties. Among adults still identifying with group imperatives adopted decades before, the tendency is to occasionally explore select assumptions but more often shut out questions, and questioners, for fear of collapsing the only identity they know and finding no other to take its place.

Further understanding emerges with the realization that questioning the assumptions underlying exclusive group identities is not only an intellectual exercise or truth-seeking endeavor, but also a personal and social duty. It can feel like an obligation to one's self to embrace a larger self and thereby stop suppressing the natural expansion of the heart. At the same time, it becomes clear that a person who chooses to experience more of their humanity can foster expansion in others.

In times of stress especially, it is essential to reach for the pinnacles of understanding that propel forward momentum: a broad perspective and unwavering spiritual motivation. A questioner lacking in either of these attributes can easily get stuck judging a former group identity or even relax back into it. But when the perspective broadens, it becomes possible to stop devaluing an earlier identity and instead regard it as the catalyst that provoked a deeper examination of spiritual roots, revealing truths that underlie all religions and spiritual organizations. From this vantage point, future spiritual discoveries do not discredit beliefs accepted in the past but rather give them viable meaning and purpose. In terms of motivation, only by pressing beyond a former group identity can a questioner encounter vistas of experience that reduce divisiveness.

The stronger the individual's resolve is to privately question dogmatic beliefs while testing the theory of self, the more tempting it can be to communicate the resulting thoughts and feelings socially. But discussing progressive spiritual ideas with unsympathetic listeners, especially loved ones who still affiliate with the beliefs, can be harrowing and needlessly alienating. At this point the stress of apostasy is overcome in large measure by understanding the mechanics of group identification, one aspect of which is that a group identity attains validity in people's minds through social intercourse which, like sexual intercourse, entails a component of satisfaction. Suppose, for instance, that I want to be part of a group with you and you want to be part of a group with me. Though I may affirm that I belong to the group and you may affirm that you belong to the group, no group exists until we share our affirmations with each other. When I then tell you that I identify with our group and you tell me that you do as well, we recognize happily that our ideas of self encompass us both. *Mirroring the joy of the expanding sense of self within the confines of a group identity reinforces its exclusivity.*

The mechanics of group identification also reveal that the stronger a group identity becomes, the more its members tend to view it as their purpose in life and defend it at any cost. And since the group identity has no reality outside of their minds, they avoid this painful realization by projecting their idea of the identity onto others. *The strengthening of a group identity culminates in efforts to recast humanity in its image.*

A third aspect of group identification to bear in mind before engaging in discussion with loved ones is that a group determines its boundaries in response to real or imagined adversaries. In other words, if I see you as a contributor to the identity of a group to which we both belong I will be kind to you; considerate of you; recite unifying anthems, chants, and pledges with you; and affirm our shared identity by displaying group symbols for you to see or using group language in your presence. If instead you appear to be straying from the group, I might lie to you, blackmail you, or attempt to destroy your reputation for endangering what I perceive to be the group identity, all the while considering my reaction moral and just. *By inventing a threat, a group more clearly defines its boundaries and intensifies member cohesiveness.*

The mechanics of group identification are so intrinsically antagonistic that it would be prudent for a questioner early on to avoid introducing spiritual discoveries to affiliated loved ones. Rather than risk estrangement or reversion by engaging in potentially heated debates about the theory of self, one can simply apply its principles in day-to-day life. To personify the theory of self is to silently communicate its most powerful ideals—and perhaps the only way to dislodge patterns of narrow-mindedness in oneself and others. A biased mind will often entertain new thoughts in response to the physiomagnetism of a naturally expansive heart.

Pioneers setting forth on a path of spiritual investigation are advised to avoid conversations with loved ones until the spirit of inquiry has taken root, preferably through participation in colloquiums with people they may not know very well. After extensive investigation, an individual ready to renounce a former belief system and embark on the science of intuition might again feel challenged to express dissatisfaction to loved ones remaining in the fold. Communication at this juncture can be uniquely rewarding to both parties.

Learning that someone dear to them no longer accepts the tenets of their faith may at first cause loved ones to worry intensely about life-and-death issues. They may wonder, for example: *Will my child still go to heaven? Will my sibling be able to cope without the support of the congregation? Will God look upon*

my spouse as an infidel? Will my beloved friend be without spiritu-
al company for countless lifetimes? To set loved ones at ease and
perhaps win their support, it is a good idea to present discoveries within the context of their faith and then invite open
dialogue, as described in Technique 17.

 **TECHNIQUE 17**

Communicating Openly with Family and Friends

Once your loved ones realize that you are only questioning
religion or a modern-day counterpart, and not renouncing God
or leaving them, their anxiety about your well-being can trans-
form into respect for your spiritual journey. At the very least,
they are likely to let you carry on your investigation unimped-
ed. But you may first have to actively reach across to family and
friends, drawing courage from the fact that every belief system
began with someone who apostated from the spiritual options
of the time. Using a chosen revolutionary as an example,
explain your own thoughts and feelings in a language accept-
able to your loved ones.

This approach lends itself to any belief system you may have
been questioning. For example, if your family is Jewish you
could set your experience against the historical backdrop of
Judaism, describing how Moses, after rejecting the Egyptian
idolatry of his day, led the Israelites out of that spiritual wasteland in the name of the one God. You might add that the rep-
etitious liturgy of Judaism, along with the mindless standing up
and sitting down in unison at temple, have hurled you into a
wasteland of your own. You might further remind your loved
ones that the Jews of two thousand years ago saw prophetic

customs give way to the rabbinic tradition, and that you likewise need to renounce the worship of outer proprieties that has
seeped into modern Judaism to find the one God within you.

If you were raised in a Christian setting, you might ask family members to recall Jesus's desire to institute a new pact with
God, then convey ways in which you also are forging a new
pact with God. Explain, perhaps, that you intend to love God
free and clear of any expectation of reward in heaven. Assure
your loved ones that you no longer want atonement but rather
yearn for the knowledge that would prevent you from erring in
the first place. Let them know that you would prefer to make
heaven on earth for yourself and others, certain that the afterlife will then take care of itself.

If you were born into a Muslim family, you might refer to
Muhammad's desire to rid the Arab people of the maze of
supernatural beings and intertribal strife that had permeated
the Arab world of his day. Reassure your loved ones that your
objection is not to the infinite Allah but rather to the limiting of
his ability to send more messengers in his name. You could conclude by pointing out that, having taken the example of
Muhammad to heart, you realize that each person is their own
last prophet and spiritually responsible for themselves. As a
result, you now see Allah's final messenger in everyone and
everything.

If you come from a large family of Mormons who do not
understand your willingness to question the authority of The
Book of Mormon and to reject the Mormon Church, consider
presenting yourself as an admirer of founder Joseph Smith, who
felt he was commanded by God to reject all Christian denominations and establish his own Church of Christ. Explain that just
as God is ever expanding in perfection, according to Smith's
teachings, so are you expanding beyond your past understand-

ing of God. Since your loved ones most likely give credence to Smith's sincerity based on the testimony of others, it may not be too much to ask them to accept your sincerity as well.

If you are an ex-Hindu, you could explain that after studying the many philosophies and practices associated with your family's tradition, you have discovered the simple message of the *rishis.* Consequently, you no longer have a need for stifling caste systems or superstition-laden rituals. Like Adi Sankara, who wanted to reinvigorate Hinduism after it had suffered from centuries of Dark Age dormancy, you are determined to banish external distortions and attend an inner *satsanga.*

If your family is Buddhist, you could remind them of the Buddha's feelings upon seeing the glory of Vedanta crumble in the hands of priests. Then express your experience of Buddhism under the influence of modern-day lamas, rinpoches, and meditation masters who dilute the meanings of nirvana and enlightenment for their personal benefit. Perhaps add that you, like the Buddha, wish to reestablish the dharma in your life by invigorating from beneath this corrosion the essentials of yoga.

After establishing a familiar precedent for your renunciation of beliefs, you can point out that the memory of this celebrated individual is kept alive not only because they challenged the establishment but because of their determination to replace ideas that were no longer working for people. You may want to further remind your loved ones that interpreting this figure as a reflection of unification rather than divisiveness is scripturally valid and far more compelling emotionally. Few people who regard religion as a matter of the heart would dispute the possibility of feeling pain at the thought of a divisive God and rejoicing in images of God's infinitude and unconditional love.

More grist for discussions with loved ones consists of elucidating the experiences that led to your doubts and discoveries, then asking for their perspectives on the issues—essentially engaging them in a colloquium. This chance to challenge you conversationally may eventually ease tension that has surfaced for a family member or friend. But if after repeated efforts your colloquium proves to be difficult, stop and ask the person what would be required for your sincere resolve to be respected.

Mistaking your spiritual inquiry for a sign that you are failing a God-given test, a loved one might ask you to speak with a religious authority. If this occurs, welcome the encounter as an opportunity to further assess aspects of the religion and entertain possible solutions to your spiritual investigation. Before the meeting remind yourself that its purpose, like the goal of inquiry itself, is to accelerate expansiveness. With that in mind, prepare a list of observations and questions to bring with you and, free of expectations, approach the religious official with the same respect you give to colloquium members. If it turns out that he or she fails to guide you through your inquiry, you may come away from the meeting with even stronger convictions of apostasy.

I had one such encounter when, in my early twenties, I entered a yogic monastic order and my father, wanting me to be sure of my decision, asked me to consult the local rabbi. I agreed and listened carefully as the rabbi posed questions about the intuitive practices I was attracted to, my interest in whether Judaism taught similar methods of energy control, and the social and familial consequences of my apostasy. While answering each one to the best of my ability, I remained unflustered because I had already challenged myself with these questions, and many more besides. Evidently realizing he was unable to change my mind, the rabbi soon nodded his head and repeated several times, "I am very disappointed in you." This tactic did not work either, for my sense of identity was not dependent on his approval or disapproval. Despite his various attempts to inspire remorse, I did not feel guilty for rejecting my family's religion. Instead, I felt dissatisfied at being treated as less than a colloquial equal yet satisfied that his ratification of archaic rituals had failed to win me over.

To seek further understanding from family and friends directly, you could approach those who seem uncomfortable with your spiritual inquiry and ask them why it upsets them or generates concern for your well-being. In some instances, you may find increased acceptance; in others, you may learn important details about an individual's character, psychology, and personal history, or about their emotional investment in modifying your thoughts. At times you are sure to find individuals wanting you to be true to yourself, your powers of reasoning, and the spirit of inquiry. You may be less likely, however, to encounter people willing to join in your spiritual investigation, nor can you expect them to. The most we can realistically count on is family and friends who want the best for us and, toward that end, afford us the freedom to make our own choices.

Loved ones who support your spiritual investigations in this way may ultimately respect your freethinking approach and appreciate its effect on them. Once you know this to be true, you can stop withholding questions likely to upset the status quo and instead risk improving the status quo by asking them.

Of course, an apostate cannot always reconcile differences with loved ones—or worse, may be emotionally attacked or threatened by them. When subjected to violent words or actions, it is generally best to stay calm and note the perpetrator's assaults on his own sense of self, especially statements about narrow identifications and confessions of belief. Narrow identifications—such as "I am a white male American Jew" or

"I am a saved Christian and you are not"—disfigure the person's idea of self by binding it to a particular ethnicity, gender, nation, or religion. Confessions of belief, as in "I believe in Jesus, who died for my sins" or "There is no God but my God, and I believe in his revelations only," when crafted repeatedly, mutilate the sense of self beyond recognition of its expansive potential.

An apostate picking up on signs of a loved one's damaged potential for expansion can address their shared reality of living in a world rent asunder by divisiveness. In response, the loved one may acknowledge that the world is indeed "messed up" and there is nothing anyone can do about it. If so, the apostate under fire might suggest there is something everyone can choose to do about it: expand the self.

Martin Heidegger, a German philosopher of the last century, bluntly remarked that the "dreadful" already happened. Many people encountering this observation might think the dreadful thing was slavery, cultural demise, or genocide. But Heidegger's insight suggests that before human beings could possibly enslave others, enact laws that keep wealth and social power from the impoverished, strip women of power over their bodies and lives, or kill one another for resources or by divine edict, they had to have devoted centuries to debasing their ideas of self, desecrating their own intellectual capacity, and diminishing the value of their lives. In gaining distance from its potential for an expansive sense of being, humanity perpetrated endless cruelties doctrinally blessed as moral, patriotic, or God ordained, most recently taking itself to the brink of annihilation at its own hands by way of nuclear extinction.

Apostates in jeopardy of being violated bring spiritual awareness to this litany of horrors enacted to consecrate narrow group identities. Knowing that life at its core is spiritually seamless, they are unafraid of social stigma or censure. Still, threats of violence can be very stressful, motivating apostates to forge a circle of colloquium members into substitute families capable of activating the social networks once formed by a religion or spiritual movement, yet careful to retain their freedom from narrow identities. The next step for apostates is to choose a "group identity" that encourages self-expansion— preferably, the cosmos itself.

From the perspective of the cosmos, the dance of human existence is as integral to its rhythms as a stone rolling on a desolate planet, grapes sweetening on a swaying vine, or a billion worlds bounding with intelligent life. And the substratum of them all is the same infinite self choreographing its expansion in worlds viewed by humans as finite. Humanity can accumulate libraries of relative material knowledge, all of which might be annihilated by a bomb or meteor, with hardly a trace left in the scattered atoms or the recollections of intelligent beings. By contrast, a cosmos woven of infinite self-knowledge whirls in the winds of self-expansion, an aspiration that is consequently never smothered. Galileo observed that the sun could ripen a grape as if it had nothing else to do in the universe; it is in this sense that the cosmos also provides for the expansion of a single individualized self.

Such a state of affairs gives cause for rejoicing. Taken further, if the outer world reflects the inner self, then as an individual chooses a more expansive group identity the phenomenal world will faithfully mirror her apostasy from narrow group identities. Indeed, this process is already underway with more and more of humanity embracing inclusiveness, pluralism, and nonviolent resolutions to conflict. To further hasten its unfolding, we can be true to our expansive selves by endeavoring to respect everyone's personal relationship with their finite ideal of the infinite God, serve humanity and all of life at every opportunity, and regularly look within, thereby magnetizing the spine and brain. The outcome awaits our collective transformation. Apostasy, when viewed as a by-product of honestly testing spiritual options, just might be heaven sent, and every day a new day to celebrate the renunciation of a narrow sense of self in favor of the expansive self—the God—in all.

Conclusion

The single greatest power in the world today is the power to change. . . .
The most recklessly irresponsible thing we can do in the future would be to go on exactly as we have in the past ten or twenty years.

—Karl W. Deutsch

*T*he study of organized religion lays bare centuries of fiction passed along as reality from parent to child, missionary to convert, and friend to friend. Stories woven of heroes and villains tell of virgin births, resurrections, heavenward ascensions, and eternal paradises and hells. Believers, filtering their perceptions through these lenses, arrived at not only divisive but dangerously delusional conclusions. Consequently, personal identity and one's relationship to all of life now lies cocooned within a morass of inventions that can only be renounced after repeatedly asking the fundamental question of spiritual inquiry—namely, "What is real?"

One way to experiment with this question is by imagining a star deep inside the body that illuminates only real things as its light passes through the flesh and out into the surrounding world. Its luminosity would reveal no Jews, Buddhists, Christians, Muslims, or Hare Krishna devotees—just human beings. Synagogues, temples, churches, mosques, and spiritual centers would appear as ordinary buildings housing occupants who share a particular sociomagnetism. Religious attire would look like any other type of unusual clothing worn in public. Scriptural writings would be seen simply as people's thoughts about themselves and their outlooks recorded over a period of time. Traditions such as rituals, beliefs, and concentration on God ideals would appear as patterns of nervous energy and awareness in the body. And worshippers illuminated by the star's glow would be viewed as people conditioned by their patterns to intuit a unique sense of self—their real tradition.

As the shafts of light extend farther, distinctions between species would give way to the observable laws of nature. At this point the seeker might reason that just as the Judeo-Christian God is "no respecter of persons" (Acts 10:34), an infinite God is no respecter of the diverse life forms that inhabit this little planet whirling in the cosmos; in their stead, he would observe cosmic principles at work. The law of cause and effect, for instance, might appear as a prophet of the infinite self; the planet, its temple; the spine and brain, its altar; the electromagnetic forces, its unifying creed. In lighting up the overarching reality of human existence, the star might illuminate humanity's perpetual expansion to identify with one another, all of life, and all worlds.

A seeker oriented more toward intuitive investigation may prefer to probe the question What is real? by examining cognitive faculties, such as the senses and the intellect, that interface with the sensory world to produce a finite sense of self. Such a seeker would regard sensory perceptions as pixel configurations and would view ideas about religion, culture, and the sensory world as abstract concepts—both significantly removed from the anatomy of intuition. Reality for the intuitive investigator consists not of these remote phenomena but rather of energy patterns that awaken awareness of a self eager to expand infinitely, far beyond the circumscribed world.

Unlike religious dogmas that must be discarded when found resistant to adaptation, forays into reality—similar to investigations into the nature of God—are works in progress, constantly inviting curiosity, doubt, and more penetrating inquiries. Every answer is tentative because the questioner's response changes in keeping with his ever-shifting sense of self. The questioner, upon discovering the fleetingness of these answers, realizes that they all reflect a mythic sense of self and, later, that the infinite self is the only reality.

In the lifelong questioning of reality, seekers who avail themselves of the theory of self can penetrate the self and thus realize what the intellect can only ponder. But if they instead accept the intellect's interpretations of sensory input as real and project these finite parameters onto infinite substance, they become immediately vulnerable to illusions. In fact, this universal tendency to succumb to the illusions of intellect partially explains why humanity has remained seemingly content with so much unreality for such a long period of time. Indeed, in the more than two thousand years between Aristotle and Heidegger, the Western world neglected to produce a new hypothesis elucidating the nature of reality. Humanity's historic failure to probe its existence is evident in the gravity of the geopolitical, social, and environmental issues we now face.

The theory of self claims such issues emerge from four fundamental misperceptions of reality: space, time, phenomenal causation, and individuation. The perception of space induces mistaken inferences of provincialism, nationalism, and the existence of a localized self in a human body traveling across physical distances. The perception of time gives the erroneous impression of historicity; chronology; and the presence of a temporal self in a human body moving through past, present, and future dimensions. Perceptions of phenomenal causation breed faulty observations of change in the changeless infinite self and of cause and effect, prompting individuals to fear death and cling to promises of immortality. Perceptions of individuation spawn mistaken understandings of subjectivity, objectivity, and distinctions between self and other. Each of these perceptions narrows the sense of self and fuels divisiveness in the world.

This divisiveness is further sustained by the divisional misperception upon which the entire cosmos is predicated. Interestingly, as a narrow human self identifies more and more with the infinite self, it discovers the cosmos is merely a finite idea, after which the self, like a revolving door, negotiates an eternal paradox of finite and infinite. Maneuvering in the finite world while unraveling the four misperceptions of reality, it recognizes that a finite cosmos cannot possibly emerge from infinite being and that the notion of such a cosmos must therefore be born of ignorance, without which there would be no cosmos since the infinite self could not play with the idea of its own division. In its infinitude, by contrast, the self is unaware of the existence of a finite cosmos. Because of this perceptual incongruity, the theory of self cannot absolutely confirm whether or not there is a cosmos, and instead calls it "emptiness."

Just as the infinite self seemingly succumbs to the ignorance in division by sacrificing its infinite knowledge, so too can the narrow, finite self begin to reverse its ignorance by sacrificing its divisive provincialism, mythic identities, fear of death, and distinction between selves. When the finite self, suffering from a case of mistaken identity, then expands into the infinite self, the primordial sacrifice is reversed for that individuated self, for whom the cosmos subsequently vanishes. It is no wonder that classic literature in all cultures involves stories of self-sacrifice. Nor is it surprising that we feel great happiness while sacrificing willingly for others. Both direct and empathic experiences of self-sacrifice enkindle a spark of the bliss experienced by the self giving up its infinitude so that in a temporal state it might play with the idea of division and then consciously return to unity. Because self-sacrifice culminates in identifying with and loving others as oneself, it might be designated the consummate universal spirituality.

A spiritual path for people everywhere, self-sacrifice begins with the awareness that we humans, in identifying with anything less than our infinite selves, live as imposters impelled by physiological patterns of exclusionism and violence against enemies. En masse, as we take up the daily task of moving beyond apostasy by asking What is real? concerning every aspect of personal identity, we start sacrificing "unrealities"— in the process, expanding our sense of self and inching our way closer to unconditioned happiness in being. National citizenship gives way to world citizenship, and membership in a faith to membership in the human family. By example we can then teach our children, ambassadors of humanity's future, the importance of vanquishing narrowness, the real enemy, by placing expansiveness of the self above all other considerations.

Humanity now stands on the threshold of this new era, with centuries of accepted truths pulsing inside us as unquestioned patterns of limiting awareness. In exposing them one by one to the light of knowledge, we sacrifice everything that keeps us narrow, for the self cannot cling very long to anything found to be unreal. Day by day, we renounce something else—a long-buried belief, a consuming corporate or community alliance, a bite-size fragment of sensory input—until all that is left as real is our breath, as Rumi so eloquently illustrates in his poem "Only Breath":

> Not Christian or Jew or Muslim, not Hindu,
> Buddhist, sufi, or zen. Not any religion
>
> or cultural system. I am not from the East or the West,
> not out of the ocean or up
>
> from the ground, not natural or ethereal, not
> composed of elements at all. I do not exist,
>
> am not an entity in this world or the next
> did not descend from Adam and Eve or any
>
> origin story. My place is placeless, a trace
> of the traceless. Neither body or soul.
>
> I belong to the beloved, have seen the two
> worlds as one and that one call to and know,
>
> first, last, outer, inner, only that
> breath breathing human being.[1]

Breath, according to the theory of self, reflects the actualization of our awareness of God, Rumi's "beloved." Breath can be ignored, in which case it restlessly carries reactive emotions and divisional misperceptions into the world, erecting obstructions to our own and others' expansive knowledge of God. It can be extinguished, as occurs among mystics intent on uniting with the infinite identity of God. Or, universally, it can be sacrificed more moderately through regulation and gradual slowing, transporting the seeker from an awareness of God breathing individuation to an awareness of God breathing expansion to the realization of a breathlessly still God—known without religion.

Notes

Chapter One

1. Hebrew Bible citations throughout refer to the Jerusalem Bible (Koren Publishers, 1992).

2. New Testament citations throughout refer to the New Revised Standard Version (Oxford University Press, 1977).

3. Qur'anic citations throughout refer to *The Meaning of the Glorious Koran,* trans. Mohammed Marmaduke Pickthall (Penguin Books, undated).

4. The dorsal plexus, located behind the heart, corresponds to the thoracic sympathetic ganglia running laterally along both sides of the vertebral column.

Chapter Two

1. Carl Sagan, *Cosmos* (New York: Random House, 1980), 332–337.

2. For decades, historians believed that Vedic society dated back roughly 3,500 years, to the presumed Aryan invasion of the Indian subcontinent—a theory strongly supported in the late nineteenth century by the well-known indologist Max Müller. Today, based on subsequent archaeological and geological discoveries that discredit the Aryan invasion theory, the Vedas are generally said to have originated many thousands of years earlier. The Vedic sage Manu, author of *Manu Samhita,* is thought to have lived anywhere from 6,000 to 9,000 years ago.

3. This presentation of the Vedic cycle theory derives from Sri Yuktesvar's treatment of *Manu Samhita* in his book *Kaivalya Darsanam* (Los Angeles: Self-Realization Fellowship, 1984), 7–20.

4. Cited in Subhash Kak, *The Astronomical Code of the Rgveda* (New Delhi: Munshiram Manoharlal, 2000), 3–5.

5. Arnold J. Toynbee, *A Study of History* (New York: Dell, 1965), 106.

6. Ibid., 26.

7. Ibid., 663–664.

8. Timothy Ferris, *The World Treasury of Physics, Astronomy, and Mathematics* (Toronto: Little, Brown, 1991), 261–271.

9. Carl Sagan, *Cosmos* (New York: Random House, 1980), 330.

10. Toynbee, *A Study,* 57.

11. Joseph Jacobs, *The Fables of Aesop* (London: Macmillan, 1915), 85.

Chapter Three

1. Cited in Paramahansa Yogananda, *Autobiography of a Yogi* (New York: Philosophical Library, 1946), 74.

2. Jalal ud-din Rumi, *Selections from Rumi,* trans. Edward Rehatsek (Bombay: Education Society Press, 1875), 186.

3. The medulla oblongata extends from the lowermost portion of the pons to approximately the first pair of cervical nerves, where it becomes the spinal cord.

4. Albert Einstein, *Ideas and Opinions* (New York: Bonanza, 1954), 12.

5. Only a fast-moving electromagnetic force, as opposed to a slow-moving fluid or metabolic process, accounts for

the yogic ability to instantly stop the breath simply by lifting the gaze.

6. George Schwartz, *Food Power* (New York: McGraw-Hill, 1979), 63.

7. Joseph Campbell, *Inner Reaches of Outer Space* (New York: Alfred Van Der Marck, 1985), 16.

8. Ibid., 17.

9. James Baldwin, *The New Yorker* (17 November 1982), quoted in *The Great Thoughts,* comp. George Seldes (New York: Ballantine, 1985), 34.

Chapter Four

1. Stanislav Grof and Hal Zina Bennett, *The Holotropic Mind* (New York: Harper, 1993), 89–111.

2. Rudolph Otto, *The Idea of the Holy,* trans. John W. Harvey (Oxford: Oxford University Press, 1923).

3. Albert Einstein, *Out of My Later Years* (New York: Philosophical Library, 1950), 29.

4. Swami Vivekananda, *The Complete Works of Swami Vivekananda,* vol. 1 (Calcutta: Advaita Ashrama, 1998), 212.

5. John Robbins, *May All Be Fed: Diet for a New World* (New York: Avon, 1992), 92.

6. George Orwell, "Reflections on Gandhi," *Partisan Review* (January 1949): 1.

Conclusion

1. "Only Breath," *The Essential Rumi,* trans. Coleman Barks (San Francisco: Harper, 1995), 32. Reprinted, with grateful acknowledgment, by permission of the translator.

Index

W. Śaranam

About the Author

$\acute{S}$aṅkara Śaranam is founder of The Pranayama Institute, Inc. and head monk of the Nazir Order. Writer and teacher, world traveler and lecturer, he also plays classical guitar, composes music, and writes poetry. A disciple of Paramahansa Yogananda, he was initiated in advanced techniques of raja yoga pranayama in the Self-Realization Fellowship Swami Order of Kriya Yogis. He now devotes his life to making pranayama techniques available worldwide at no cost.

Born in 1968 to Iraqi Jewish parents who had fled their homeland years before, Śaṅkara was raised in the Midwest and New York City. He studied aerospace engineering at the University of Michigan and classical guitar at the Manhattan School of Music; received his bachelor of arts degree in Religion from Columbia University, where he graduated magna cum laude; and received his master's degree in Eastern Texts from St. John's College in Santa Fe, New Mexico. He currently resides in a log cabin in northern Georgia with his wife and their young son.

Śaṅkara writes a weekly online column that reaches students in over seventy countries worldwide. For information about his speaking engagements, teachings, and advanced pranayama techniques, please visit The Pranayama Institute's Web site: http://www.pranayama.org. To learn more about colloquiums and other activities associated with *God Without Religion,* visit http://www.godwithoutreligion.com.

Order Form

Quantity   *Amount*

____ *God Without Religion*–hardcover edition ($25.00) _____

Shipping & handling
($3.00 for first book; $2.00 for each additional book) _____

Total amount enclosed _____

Quantity discounts available.

Method of payment

☐ .Check or money order enclosed, made payable to The Pranayama Institute, Inc., in US currency

☐ MasterCard   ☐ VISA   ☐ Discover   ☐ American Express

Account number   *Expiration date*

Please contact your local bookstore or mail your order,
together with your name, address, and check, money order,
or charge-card information, to:

THE PRANAYAMA INSTITUTE
I N C O R P O R A T E D

PO Box 1360 • East Ellijay, GA 30539-1360
Phone: 877-NO RELIGION
http://www.pranayama.org • http://www.godwithoutreligion.com